Improving Multicultural Education

LESSONS FROM THE INTERGROUP EDUCATION MOVEMENT

Cherry A. McGee Banks

Teachers College
Columbia University
New York and London

KH

Published by Teachers College Press, 1234 Amsterdam Avenue, New York, NY 10027

Library of Congress Cataloging-in-Publication Data

Banks, Cherry A. McGee.
  Improving multicultural education : lessons from the intergroup education movement / Cherry A. McGee Banks.
    p. cm. — (Multicultural education series)
  Includes bibliographical references and index.
  ISBN 0-8077-4508-1 (cloth : alk. paper) — ISBN 0-8077-4507-3 (pbk. : alk. paper)
  1. Multicultural education—United States—History—20th century. 2. Intergroup relations—United States—History—20th century. 3. Educational equalization—United States—History—20th century. I. Title. II. Multicultural education series (New York, N.Y.)

  LC1099.3.B355 2004
  370.117—dc22   2004053669

ISBN 0-8077-4507-3 (paper)
ISBN 0-8077-4508-1 (cloth)

Printed on acid-free paper

Manufactured in the United States of America

12 11 10 09 08 07 06 05   8 7 6 5 4 3 2 1

9/15/05

MULTICULTURAL EDUCATION SERIES

James A. Banks, Series Editor

for
Myra Marie Nelson
Geneva Marie McGee
Angela Marie Banks
Patricia Ann Banks

Contents

Series Foreword

THE NATION'S deepening ethnic texture, interracial tension and conflict, and the increasing percentage of students who speak a first language other than English make multicultural education imperative in the 21st century. The U.S. Census Bureau (2000) estimated that people of color made up 28% of the nation's population in 2000 and predicted that they would make up 38% in 2025 and 47% in 2050. In March 2004, the Census Bureau revised its projections and predicted that by 2050 people of color and Whites would each make up 50% of the U. S. population (El Nasser, 2004).

American classrooms are experiencing the largest influx of immigrant students since the beginning of the 20th century. About a million immigrants are making the United States their home each year (Martin & Midgley, 1999). More than seven and one-half million legal immigrants settled in the United States between 1991 and 1998, most of whom came from nations in Latin America and Asia (Riche, 2000). A large but undetermined number of undocumented immigrants also enter the United States each year. The influence of an increasingly ethnically diverse population on the nation's schools, colleges, and universities is and will continue to be enormous.

Forty percent of the students enrolled in the nation's schools in 2001 were students of color. This percentage is increasing each year, primarily because of the growth in the percentage of Latino students (Martinez & Curry, 1999). In some of the nation's largest cities and metropolitan areas, such as Chicago, Los Angeles, Washington, D.C., New York, Seattle, and San Francisco, half or more of the public school students are students of color. During the 1998–1999 school year, students of color made up 63.1% of the student population in the public schools of California, the nation's largest state (California State Department of Education, 2000).

Language and religious diversity is also increasing among the nation's student population. In 2000, about 20% of the school-age population spoke a language at home other than English (U.S. Census Bureau, 2000). Harvard professor Diana L. Eck (2001) calls the United States the "most religiously diverse nation on earth" (p. 4). Most teachers now in the classroom and in teacher education programs are likely to have students from diverse ethnic, racial, language, and religious groups in their classrooms during their careers. This is true for both inner-city and suburban teachers.

An important goal of multicultural education is to improve race relations and to help all students acquire the knowledge, attitudes, and skills needed to participate in cross-cultural interactions and in personal, social, and civic action that will help make our nation more democratic and just. Multicultural education is consequently as important for middle-class White suburban students as it is for students of color who live in the inner city. Multicultural education fosters the public good and the overarching goals of the commonwealth.

The major purpose of the *Multicultural Education Series* is to provide preservice educators, practicing educators, graduate students, scholars, and policymakers with an interrelated and comprehensive set of books that summarizes and analyzes important research, theory, and practice related to the education of ethnic, racial, cultural, and language groups in the United States and the education of mainstream students about diversity. The books in the *Series* provide research, theoretical, and practical knowledge about the behaviors and learning characteristics of students of color, language minority students, and low-income students. They also provide knowledge about ways to improve academic achievement and race relations in educational settings.

The definition of multicultural education in the *Handbook of Research on Multicultural Education* (Banks & Banks, 2004) is used in the *Series*: Multicultural education is "a field of study designed to increase educational equity for all students that incorporates, for this purpose, content, concepts, principles, theories, and paradigms from history, the social and behavioral sciences, and particularly from ethnic studies and women's studies" (p. xii). In the *Series*, as in the *Handbook*, multicultural education is considered a "metadiscipline."

The dimensions of multicultural education, developed by Banks (2004) and described in the *Handbook of Research on Multicultural Education*, provide the conceptual framework for the development of the books in the *Series*. They are *content integration, the knowledge construction process, prejudice reduction, an equity pedagogy,* and *an empowering school culture and social structure.* To implement multicultural education effectively, teachers and administrators must attend to each of the five dimensions of multicultural education. They should use content from diverse groups when teaching concepts and skills, help students to understand how knowledge in the various disciplines is constructed, help students to develop positive intergroup attitudes and behaviors, and modify their teaching strategies so that students from different racial, cultural, language, and social-class groups will experience equal educational opportunities. The total environment and culture of the school must also be transformed so that students from diverse groups will experience equal status in the culture and life of the school.

Although the five dimensions of multicultural education are highly interrelated, each requires deliberate attention and focus. Each book in the *Series* focuses on one or more of the dimensions, although each book deals with all of them to some extent because of the highly interrelated characteristics of the dimensions.

The publication of this book marks a significant development in the field of multicultural education. In order for an emerging field such as multicultural education to attain legitimacy and to become institutionalized, it is essential that it constructs its history and describes the ways in which it is connected to the past. A field cannot sufficiently understand the present or envision its future unless it has a deep understanding of its past. This timely and skillfully written book also satisfies an important need: Until its publication, no book existed in the field which focused on the history of the intergroup education movement as a vehicle to inform and improve multicultural education today.

This book is the second volume in the *Studies in the Historical Foundations of Multicultural Education Series* (hereafter Historical Series) that was initiated in 1992 by the Center for Multicultural Education at the University of Washington. The first volume in the Historical Series is also the first volume in the Multicultural Education Series, *Multicultural Education, Transformative Knowledge, and Action: Historical and Contemporary Perspectives* (J. A. Banks, 1996). The purpose of the Historical Series is to uncover the roots of multicultural education, to identify the ways in which it is connected to its historical antecedents, and to gain insights from the past that can inform school reform efforts today related to race and ethnicity. Cherry has played a pivotal role in the conceptualization and implementation of the Historical Series since its inception. This book builds upon and deepens the work contained in her chapter in the first book in the Historical Series.

Cherry brings to this engaging, astute, and edifying book the experience, insights, and wisdom of more than three decades of work in education as a concerned parent, a junior high school teacher, a counselor, the president of an educational organization that she founded, a compassionate and acclaimed university professor, and a community leader. Her unique values, commitments, and journey in the world of education have compelled her to write a history—not just for the sake of informing readers about the past, but also to reveal to multicultural educators how to reform schools to make them just, caring, and humane communities. In conceptualizing and crafting this history of the intergroup education movement, Cherry focuses on ways that insights from the past can be used to improve schools.

I am very pleased—for both personal and professional reasons—to welcome this book to the Multicultural Education Series. Cherry and I have shared a project for more than three decades whose major goal is to work for social justice in schools, colleges, and universities. I have consistently found her voice caring, informed, and incisive. I am pleased that readers of this book will experience these qualities, which are evident on every page of this gracefully written and erudite book.

James A. Banks
Series Editor

REFERENCES

Banks, J. A. (Ed.). (1996). *Multicultural education, transformative knowledge, and action: Historical and contemporary perspectives.* New York: Teachers College Press.

Banks, J. A. (2004). Multicultural education: Historical development, dimensions, and practice. In J. A. Banks & C. A. M. Banks (Eds.), *Handbook of research on multicultural education* (2nd ed., pp. 3–29). San Francisco: Jossey-Bass.

Banks, J. A., & Banks, C. A. M. (Eds.) (2004). *Handbook of research on multicultural education* (2nd ed.). San Francisco: Jossey-Bass.

California State Department of Education. (2000). Retrieved from [http://data1.cde.ca.gov/dataquest]

Eck, D. L. (2001). *A new religious America: How a "Christian country" has become the world's most religiously diverse nation.* San Francisco: HarperSanFrancisco.

El Nasser, H. (2004, March 18). Census projects growing diversity: By 2050: Population burst, societal shifts. *USA Today*, p. 1A.

Martin, P., & Midgley, E. (1999). Immigration to the United States. *Population Bulletin, 54*(2), 1–44. Washington, D.C.: Population Reference Bureau.

Martinez, G. M., & Curry A. E. (1999, September). *Current population reports: School enrollment—social and economic characteristics of students* (update). Washington, D.C.: U.S. Census Bureau.

Riche, M. F. (2000). America's diversity and growth: Signposts for the 21st century. *Population Bulletin, 55*(2), 1–43. Washington, D.C.: Population Reference Bureau.

U.S. Census Bureau. (2000). *Statistical abstract of the United States* (120th edition). Washington, D.C.: U.S. Government Printing Office.

Preface

INTERGROUP CONFLICT has been a perennial problem in U.S. life from colonial times to the present. This book describes how a group of educators, social activists, and scholars tried to reduce intergroup tensions and create educational environments in which the histories, contributions, and cultural characteristics of ethnic, racial, and religious groups could be understood and appreciated. Most importantly, these men and women, who were called *intercultural educators*, tried to change schools so that they would be places where people of all groups could learn from and with each other.

The intercultural educational movement began in the early 1930s and continued into the 1950s as intergroup education. Intercultural educators were particularly concerned with the social context that surrounded European immigrants at the turn of the 20th century. Social commentators in the early 1900s frequently associated European immigration with class conflict, poverty, crime, and social disorder (Fairchild, 1926; Higham, 1972; Olneck, 1995). A major goal of the intercultural education movement was to reduce the fears and misconceptions of mainstream Americans about the new immigrants and improve intergroup relations (DuBois, 1928; Kilpatrick & Van Til, 1947). A related and equally important goal was to increase the social status of immigrant children (DuBois, 1930). Readers will learn about the ways that intercultural educators tried to infuse ethnic content into the school curriculum, reduce ethnic tensions, and develop and implement teacher in-service programs. They will also learn about their efforts to link schools and communities.

Intergroup tensions similar to those that gave birth to the intercultural education movement continue to exist today. Multicultural educators, like intergroup educators, are working to address those tensions and also to increase the academic achievement of all students. In several sections throughout the book, and in the final chapter in particular, parallels are drawn between intergroup education and multicultural education. The discussion of these parallels serve as lessons from the past in which contemporary educators can learn from the successes and failures of intergroup educators.

Educators will find this book helpful and informative in at least three ways. First, it provides information on the history and foundations of multicultural education by documenting intercultural education, one of multicultural education's important antecedents. Teacher educators will be able to locate contemporary discussions about diversity in schools within a historical context. Many teacher educators are unaware of the efforts made by their predecessors to provide classroom teachers with information about ethnic, religious, and cultural groups or the ways in which that information was used in classrooms. Teacher educators will be positioned to gain insights from past efforts to reduce intergroup tensions as they address contemporary problems related to diversity.

Second, this book provides a basis for better understanding the current debate over the curriculum canon. The contested nature of the school curriculum has deep historical roots (Kliebard, 1995). The intergroup education movement is, in many ways, a case study of contested curricula. Contested curricula and resistance to curriculum change, which were centered in the work of intergroup educators, are also reflected in the current battle over the curriculum canon (Apple & Christian-Smith, 1991; J. A. Banks, 1996; Evans, 2003). As readers learn about the conflicting values and perspectives that fueled the debate over Americanization in the 1920s and 1930s, they will be able to put the current canon debate in historical perspective. That perspective can help readers better understand the complexities of curriculum reform in a pluralistic democratic society.

Finally, this book can extend readers' knowledge about educating students in a culturally diverse society by uncovering past efforts to respond to ethnic, racial, and religious diversity in schools. The book includes descriptions of projects, approaches, processes, techniques, and materials used by intergroup educators such as John Granrud, Leonard Covello, and Hilda Taba. Their work provides an important departure point for teachers to rethink why students voluntarily segregate themselves at school functions and the role of the curriculum in addressing within-school segregation. Taba's work, along with that of the other intergroup educators discussed throughout the book, can help readers better understand the role that educators can play in reducing intergroup tensions, reforming school curricula, and helping students embrace democratic values.

OVERVIEW OF THE BOOK

The seven chapters in this book are divided into three parts. Part one focuses on the development of intercultural education. An important theme woven throughout this section is the centrality of intellectual leadership to the development of intercultural education. Burns (1978) defines intellectual leadership as galvanizing ideas, knowledge, and values. He notes that intellectual leadership is transforming leadership because it is not detached from society, but rather responds to society's needs. The three chapters that make up Part 1 of this book describe the intellectual leadership demonstrated by intercultural educators and the role that social science scholars played in providing an intellectual rationale for the intercultural education movement. Chapter 1 describes the historical and sociopolitical context in which intercultural education developed. Chapter 2 identifies and describes the school knowledge created by intercultural educators, and provides an overview of the leaders who helped create and sustain the movement. Chapter 3 gives readers a view of intercultural education in action during the 1930s at Benjamin Franklin High School, a school located in East Harlem.

Part 2 describes the extent to which the activities and knowledge created by intercultural educators had an effect on school knowledge and policy-level discourse on schools. There is some evidence that intercultural educators influenced thousands of teachers throughout the United States. For example, hundreds of educators regularly received *Intercultural Education News*, a newsletter published by the Bureau for Intercultural Education. Hilda Taba provided in-service training to hundreds of teachers through the Intergroup Education in Cooperating Schools Project. In 1938 the New York City Board of Education mandated intercultural assemblies and workshops in all of its schools. Yet intercultural education failed to become institutionalized in U.S. schools. The two chapters in this part of the book identify and discuss the achievements of intercultural education and factors that limited its ability to become institutionalized. Chapter 4 highlights the extent to which larger societal forces—surrounding World War II and the Japanese internment—overshadowed the democratic-social justice message of intergroup educators. The effect of internal and external tensions on the achievements and failures of intergroup educators is discussed in Chapter 5.

Part 3 includes two chapters. Both chapters focus on challenges that arise when efforts are made to transform school knowledge. They provide perspectives for multicultural educators to consider as they continue to institutionalize their movement. The challenges that intercultural educators faced as they tried to intervene in the ongoing cycle of negative attitudes directed toward immigrants are not unlike those that confront multicultural educators. The work in which multicultural educators are currently engaged to reduce intergroup tensions and to help students develop the skills, attitudes, and values necessary to become active participants in a pluralistic-democratic society are placed in historical perspective in these two chapters. Chapter 6 discusses the sociopolitical context that surrounded intergroup education during the 1950s and 1960s and the extent to which the movement addressed the needs of people of color. The final chapter in the book, Chapter 7, examines the legacy of intergroup education for multicultural education today.

Acknowledgments

A BOOK is a major undertaking and cannot be accomplished without the help and support of many individuals. I am fortunate that during the course of researching and writing this book, many colleagues and friends have sustained me. My work has also been supported institutionally with grants from the Royalty Research Fund at the University of Washington, Seattle; the Worthington Professorship at the University of Washington, Bothell; and with a fellowship from the Balch Institute of Philadelphia. The grants from the University of Washington provided support for a professional leave in which I completed the research for this book and began writing it. The Balch fellowship provided support for research in residence in Philadelphia and access to Leonard Covello's papers.

It is with deep thanks that I acknowledge Kathleen Martin at the University of Washington, Bothell, who served as my program director during the time that this project was under development. As a friend and colleague she consistently supported my work. I also wish to thank my colleague Carole Kubota who graciously shared her family stories and artifacts with me. Her materials helped me to put a human face on Chapter 4. Appreciation is extended to David Ment of the Milbank Library at Teachers College, Columbia University for his assistance in locating and obtaining materials during the course of my research.

I began the line of research that resulted in this book as part of a research project initiated by James A. Banks at the University of Washington–Seattle. Jim organized a research team to investigate the historical roots of multicultural education. His efforts resulted in research papers being presented at American Educational Research Association annual meetings over a 5-year period and culminated in the book *Multicultural Education: Transformative Knowledge and Action: Historical and Contemporary Perspectives*. My initial work on intergroup education was published in that volume. It is with admiration, appreciation, and deep thanks that I acknowledge Jim's support and encouragement in this project.

Introduction

THE EDUCATIONAL AND SOCIAL gains made by immigrants from southern and eastern Europe, who came to the United States at the turn of the 20th century, were supported by the dedicated work of teachers, scholars, and social activists who became known as intercultural educators. The term *intercultural educator* is used broadly in this book to refer to individuals such as Rachel Davis DuBois and William VanTil, who described themselves as intercultural educators, as well as individuals such as Ruth Benedict and William Heard Kilpatrick, who were actively involved in intercultural education but didn't use the term to describe their work. Both groups of individuals made important contributions to the field and played a role in its development.

Intercultural educators were committed to American Creed[1] values such as freedom, justice, and equality and to making schools more responsive to students from diverse ethnic, religious, and cultural groups. They saw education as a means to address social, economic, and political disparities in American society. This book tells their story. Readers will learn about the activities and philosophies of intercultural educators and the curricula, programs, and social changes initiated by them. While concerned with history, this book is not intended to be a comprehensive history of the intercultural education movement. Instead it focuses on what we can learn from intercultural educators as educators continue to grapple with reoccurring themes in American history involving prejudice and discrimination.

Intercultural education was actively a part of its time. Its story is written against the backdrop of the major historical events of the first half of the 20th century. During its day, intercultural education was often at the center of educational debates about whether and how diversity should be presented in the curriculum. Today multicultural education is often at the center of such debates. Multicultural educators, like intercultural educators in the past, are working to reduce intergroup tensions and to increase the academic achievement of all students. This book draws parallels between intercultural education and multicultural education and allows readers to situate contemporary discussions about diversity and education within a historical context.

The contested nature of the school curriculum has deep historical roots (Kliebard, 1995). Insights on contested curriculum can be gained by examining the conflicting values and perspectives that fueled past educational debates on curriculum. During the 1920s there was concern over the role of the school in Americanizing the second generation. The *second generation* was a term used to describe the children of immigrants who came to the United States in the early 20th century. In some cases the term was used pejoratively to convey the image of young people who were truants, juvenile delinquents, and essentially out of control. Advocates for Americanization argued that immigrants and the second generation should be assimilated into mainstream American society as soon as possible (Carlson, 1987). Cultural pluralists warned that assimilation was a long-term process and should not be rushed (Montalto, 1982). Moreover, they believed American society could be enriched by the diverse cultures of immigrants. Both cultural pluralists and advocates for Americanization turned to the schools for help in responding to immigrants and the second generation. Both saw the schools as an essential element in their ability to influence and communicate their message to the public (Zimmerman, 2002).

The debate between hard-line assimilationists and pluralists is similar to the current battle over the canon (Apple & Christian-Smith, 1991; Banks, J. A., 1996; Evans, 2003). However, as Carl Kaestle (1978) reminds us, "Despite the similarities between reform movements, the context is never quite the same, the tools of reform are never quite the same, and neither the clients nor their problems are ever quite the same" (p. X). Indeed, the context, clients, and problems that were a part of intercultural education are somewhat different from those of today's multicultural educators. Nevertheless, there are patterns of consistency with respect to immigration, the response to it, and expectations for schools that underlie both periods. Today, anxieties similar to those that emerged during the time of intercultural education have reemerged, and educators are looking for answers to perennial questions about how to respond to diversity. In that sense, intercultural education can serve as a theoretical template against which readers can reflect on contemporary educational issues. Insights drawn from curriculum battles in the past can help readers uncover important political, economic, and social issues that are buried in the subtext of contemporary curriculum debates. Such insights are more difficult to grasp without a historical vantage point for reflection, because highly charged educational issues are often too emotional and personally situated for a dispassionate analysis. By understanding how such debates were shaped and sustained in the past and the conflicting points of view associated with them, readers will be better positioned to analyze the complexities of contested curricula today.

INTERCULTURAL EDUCATION AND INTERGROUP EDUCATION: SIMILARITIES AND DIFFERENCES

Intercultural education and *intergroup education* were two terms that were used to describe organized efforts of educators and social activists to improve human relations in schools. There were similarities as well as differences in the usage and meanings of the terms. Intercultural educators focused primarily on the cultures of racial, ethnic, and religious groups (Stendler & Martin, 1953). European immigrants were a pivotal group for intercultural educators, although attention was also given to people of color (DuBois, 1939). Helping new immigrants and their children maintain ties with their ancestral cultures, feel good about themselves, and make positive adjustments to their new homeland were important goals for many intercultural educators (Department of Supervisors, 1942). Much of their work involved the creation and dissemination of assembly programs and the development of materials on the cultures and contributions of various ethnic groups (DuBois, 1942). It is difficult to date the beginning of the intercultural education movement. However, efforts to increase students' understanding of and appreciation for ethnic and racial diversity were implemented in secondary schools in the late 1920s (DuBois, 1928). However, the term *intercultural education* did not officially come into being until 1935 when the Progressive Education Association (PEA) established the Committee on Intercultural Education (DuBois with Okorodudu, 1984).

Pinpointing the beginning of the intergroup education movement is also difficult. The movement developed after intercultural education was already underway. The term *intergroup education* was commonly used to describe projects and programs that were implemented after race riots erupted in Detroit, Michigan; Beaumont, Texas; St. Louis, Missouri; and other cities across the nation during the 1940s. The riots increased intergroup tensions and created a sense of national urgency (Cook & Cook, 1954; Taba, Brady, & Robinson, 1952; Taba, Brady, Robinson, & Vickery, 1951; Trager & Yarrow, 1952). There was concern, particularly during World War II, that divisions within U.S. society could fracture the nation. Prejudice reduction programs, which were a key component of intergroup education, became a focal point for efforts to mend divisions between groups. Intergroup programs called attention to democratic and American Creed values and highlighted similarities among all Americans. Concepts such as tolerance and brotherhood, which were widely used by intergroup educators, played a dual role in intergroup programs. They were used to help reduce prejudice as well as to call students' attention to differences between U.S. society and totalitarian societies such as Nazi Germany.

Although intergroup and intercultural education had subtle differences, the terms were often used interchangeably (Cook & Cook, 1954; Kilpatrick & VanTil, 1947). Schools were the primary site of intervention for both movements. Intercultural and intergroup educators conceptualized and implemented projects, programs, and materials for schools, colleges, and universities. Both intercultural and intergroup educators were instrumental in developing school knowledge that challenged the status quo (Banks, J. A., 1993; Cook & Cook, 1954; Montalto, 1982). Intercultural and intergroup education leaders both used democratic principles to justify their work, and both addressed issues related to cultural diversity and prejudice reduction. Finally, they both focused to varying degrees on European ethnic groups and racial and ethnic minorities.

The primary difference between intercultural and intergroup education was the social context in which they occurred and consequently the emphasis each put on the groups they worked with and the issues they explored. Intercultural education developed during a time when immigration was a divisive national issue. Consequently, southern and eastern European immigrants and their children were important groups in intercultural education. Intercultural educators worked, through educational institutions, to help them gain full inclusion into U.S. society (Covello, 1937). The term *intergroup education* became popular during a time of racial unrest following the migration of large numbers of African Americans from the South to industrial cities in the North. Consequently, racial minorities as well as European immigrants were an important focus for intergroup educators. Intergroup educators used democratic values and their knowledge of curriculum to argue against prejudice and discrimination and to recommend changes in schools and teacher training (Taba, 1953).

The similarities between intergroup and intercultural education appear to have been more important to educators in the 1940s and 1950s than their differences (Cook & Cook, 1954; Taba & VanTil, 1945; Trager & Yarrow, 1952; Vickery & Cole, 1943). In the 1945 National Council for the Social Studies Yearbook (Taba & VanTil, 1945) the terms were used in ways that suggested they were synonymous. Perhaps the overlapping usage of the terms was a reflection of the concerns and perspectives of key leaders in the field. Some intercultural educators, such as H. H. Giles and William VanTil, were concerned about intercultural education's focus on cultural contributions. For Giles, VanTil, and other like-minded intercultural educators, *intergroup education* may have been a term that reduced the dissonance they felt about intercultural education's emphasis on culture and their desire to focus on prejudice reduction and curriculum development. Strategically, the term *intergroup education* allowed them to distance themselves from the emphasis that intercultural educators placed on culture while continuing to utilize the networks and resources associated with intercultural education. Rachel Davis DuBois, one of the founders of intercultural education, continued to use the term *intercultural education* and focus on cultural issues throughout her career.

For the purposes of this book, intercultural and intergroup education are conceptualized as one continuous egalitarian movement that began in the early 1930s with an emphasis on culture and continued into the 1950s with an emphasis on prejudice reduction. Both intercultural and intergroup education are used throughout the book. For the sake of efficiency and to reflect common usage in the literature, the term *intercultural* is often used to refer to both the intergroup and intercultural education movements. Figure I.1 provides an overview of key events in intercultural and intergroup education.

CAN WE LEARN FROM THE PAST?

Santayana (1905) said that to ignore history is to doom oneself to repeat its mistakes. As our nation grapples with diversity on an unprecedented scale, we have much to learn from intercultural educators who faced similar issues stemming from the arrival of immigrants from southern and eastern Europe in the late 19th and early 20th centuries. In August 1941, a group of intercultural educators and other concerned citizens met on the campus of Williams College in Massachusetts at an institute sponsored by the National Conference of Christians and Jews. The purpose of the institute was to discuss how schools could work with the broader community to reduce intergroup tensions and improve educational opportunities for all students. The participants at what was termed the Williamstown Institute read like a list of who's who in religion, education, politics, business, labor, agriculture, and civic affairs. About 20% of the conference participants were distinguished professors or administrators at prestigious colleges and universities. Institute participants included Ruth Benedict, of Columbia University; Arthur H. Compton, University of Chicago; Edward A. Fitzpatrick, president of Mount Mary College; Mildred McAfee, president of Wellesley College; Carlton J. H. Hayes, of Columbia University; William Heard Kilpatrick, of Columbia University; Paul Klapper, president of Queens College; Otto Klineberg, of Columbia University; Henry Noble MacCracken, president of Vassar College; Clyde R.

Figure I.1. Chronology of Key Events in Intercultural and Intergroup Education

1924   The Woodbury High Assembly Program was instituted by Rachel Davis DuBois in Woodbury, New Jersey.

1934   The Service Bureau for Human Relations began operations in New York City.

1935   The term *intercultural education* was coined when the Progressive Education Association established the Commission on Intercultural Education. The Commission was directed by Rachel Davis DuBois. Ruth Benedict served as a member of the commission's board.

1938   The first national workshop on intercultural education was held for classroom teachers. The workshop was held at Sarah Lawrence College in Bronxville, New York.
The New York City Board of Education required all of its schools to hold assemblies and implement classroom activities designed to teach tolerance.
Louis Adamic's influential article entitled "Thirty Million New Americans" was published.

1939   "Americans All—Immigrants All," a 26 weekly 30-minute radio program, was aired on CBS. The program was supported by the U. S. Office of Education and the American Jewish Committee.
The first in-service course for New York City teachers in intercultural education was taught during the spring term at New York University.
The Springfield Plan was implemented.

1941   The Intercultural Education Workshop was founded by Rachel Davis DuBois after she left the Service Bureau.

1942   *When Peoples Meet,* a path-breaking book in intercultural education edited by Alain Locke and Bernard J. Stern, was published.

1945   Summer workshops were held at the University of Chicago to provide teachers with the skills and knowledge necessary to implement intergroup education programs.
The Project on Intergroup Education in Cooperating Schools was established at the University of Chicago.
The College Study in Intergroup Relations was implemented by Lloyd Allen Cook at Wayne University (now Wayne State University).

1947   The Bureau for Intercultural Education cooperated with the John Dewey Society in the production of the society's ninth yearbook entitled *Intercultural Attitudes in the Making.*

1948   The Center for Intergroup Education at the University of Chicago was established.

1954   *The Nature of Prejudice* by Gordon Allport was published.
The Service Bureau for Intercultural Education ceased operations.

Miller, of Teachers College, Columbia University; and George N. Shuster, president of Hunter College.

Deliberations from the Williamstown Institute were compiled in a book entitled *The World We Want to Live In* (Clinchy, 1942). The title of the book presents readers with two implicit questions: "What kind of world do you want to live in?" and, "Are you willing to take an active part in creating that world?" Mildred McAfee answered the first question when she said, "The fundamental and primary problem of education for the world we want to live in, is that of enlarging the group to which men consciously belong . . . We need to enlarge our conception of ourselves to include membership in a world group whose interests, therefore become our interests" (Clinchy, 1942, p. 56). McAfee was essentially arguing for a broader understanding of who we are as Americans. Today elements of that issue are being debated under the rubric of patriotism. Martha Nussbaum (1996) argues that pride in national identity and citizenship are morally dangerous and should be replaced by an allegiance to human beings throughout the world. Nussbaum uses the term "cosmopolitan" to capture the idea of a commitment to and identifying with a broad worldwide moral community. Although the meaning of cosmopolitanism goes beyond McAfee's concern with internal divisions among groups in the United States, contemporary debates about the role of the social studies in fostering patriotism make McAfee's statement and the concerns of intercultural educators as relevant today as they were in the mid-20th century.

During deliberations at the Williamstown Institute, William Kilpatrick argued that when students are encouraged to think their interests are the only interests that should be considered, neither the nation nor the student is well served. The aim of education, according to Kilpatrick, had to be refocused from the selfish interest of the individual to preparing students to work for the common good, thus creating better human relations (Clinchy, 1942). Kilpatrick noted that accomplishing that kind of transformation would require knowledgeable and committed teachers who understood social science concepts such as race, culture, and democracy. He argued that very few teachers had the kind of training and background that would enable them to embrace the idea of education as means to creating better human relations or the skills and knowledge necessary to accomplish that task (Clinchy, 1942).

Kilpatrick's statement sums up the incredibly difficult challenge faced by intergroup educators in the past and multicultural educators today. It is in that spirit that I use the title *Improving Multicultural Education: Lessons From the Intergroup Education Movement* for this text. The title connects the work done by intergroup educators to issues confronting educators today. It also highlights the importance of a long-term commitment to equity.

Closing the gap between ideal American Creed values and the reality of those values as they are reflected in the daily lives of individuals on the margins of American society is a task that cannot be accomplished in just one generation. It must be passed on to future generations, with each doing its part to close the gap. As individuals who are committed to equity today read about the work of intergroup educators, they will know that they are not alone. They are part of a long tradition of educators and social activists who envisioned a better world and worked to create it.

Part I

INTELLECTUAL LEADERSHIP AND THE DEVELOPMENT OF THE INTERCULTURAL EDUCATION MOVEMENT

E ACH of the three chapters in Part I of this book illustrates how key elements of intellectual leadership influenced the development of intercultural education. Chapter 1 describes the historical and sociopolitical milieu in which intercultural education began. It highlights the reasons why intercultural educators believed that schools needed to be reformed, and describes the ideas, concepts, and theories of intellectual leaders who challenged the status quo. In Chapter 2, readers are introduced to three intercultural educators who, as intellectual leaders, inspired their colleagues, garnered resources, created intercultural organizations, and implemented change in schools. This chapter highlights a key characteristic of intellectual leadership—the connection between the personal lives of intercultural educators and their work as professionals. Readers will learn about the biographical journeys, values, and beliefs that three intergroup leaders brought to the programs they created. Chapter 3 gives readers an opportunity to see intercultural education in action. The chapter focuses on Benjamin Franklin High School, a school that was an important site for intercultural and community-centered education in the 1930s. Leonard Covello, who served as the principal of the school, used his skills as an intellectual leader to encourage teachers to redesign the school curriculum, rethink their relationship with their students, and develop and implement community outreach programs.

1

Responding to Diversity in the Early 20th Century

BETWEEN 1881 and the beginning of World War I, almost 22 million immigrants settled in the United States (Hutchinson, 1949). Immigration continued at an unprecedented rate throughout the early 20th century, peaking in 1914 when 1,218,480 immigrants entered the United States. (U.S. Bureau of the Census, 1975). Between 1860 and 1930, more people emigrated to the United States than the entire U.S. population in 1860. An overview of U.S. immigrants at the turn of the 20th century is included in Table 1.1.

The new immigrants were ethnically and religiously diverse. Before 1880 most U.S. immigrants came from northern and western Europe and were primarily Protestant. After 1880 most of the new immigrants came from southern and eastern Europe and were Catholics, Jews, Muslims, and members of the Greek and Russian Orthodox Church. Over half a million of the immigrants who arrived in 1914 came from Russia, the Baltic States, and Italy (U.S. Bureau of the Census, 1975). By 1910, communities known as "Little Russia," "Little Poland," "Little Hungary," and "Little Italy" could be found in large cities throughout the nation.

Most immigrants who came to the United States stayed, but some returned home. Before 1920 about 30% percent of U.S. immigrants returned home (The World Book Encyclopedia, 1998, p. 82). Some of those returning to their homelands were sojourners who had never intended to stay in the United States. Their plan was to come to the United States to work, save their money, and then return to their homelands. Others intended to stay but eventually returned to their homelands because their experience in the United States wasn't what they had expected. Of those who returned to their homelands, some resented the way they were treated. Others couldn't adjust to life in the United States. Still others preferred the familiarity of life in their country of origin where they understood the language, customs, and values of their fellow countrymen (Fleming, 1970; Seller, 1977).

Table 1.1. Immigration to the United States at the Turn of the 20th Century

Region	1880–1889 [1]	1890–1899 [2]	1900–1909	1910–1919
Northern Europe	3,982,722	1,826,717	1,811,616	1,112,638
Central Europe	357,697	641,904	2,036,027	1,181,907
Eastern Europe	189,920	460,456	1,620,479	1,191,713
Southern Europe	298,718	629,701	2,165,849	1,570,302
Asia	6,986	57,738	237,980	198,587
South and Central America	524,826	37,350	277,809	1,070,535

[1] Before 1880, most of the immigrants who came to the United States were from northern and western Europe. Following the potato famine of 1845–1849 in Ireland, thousands of Irish immigrated to the United States. They were followed by Germans and Scandinavians, who came primarily between 1840 and 1860. During that same time period, thousands of Chinese immigrated to California during the 1849 Gold Rush. They were joined during the 1860s by almost 200,000 of their brethren who helped build the Union Pacific railroad. In 1869, the Central and Union Pacific railroads linked the country from the Atlantic Ocean to the Pacific.

[2] Pogroms against Jews in Russia resulted in Russian Jews immigrating to the United States. Many arrived at the new immigration center, which was opened on Ellis Island in 1892.

Source: Ziegler, B. M. (Ed.). (1953). *Immigration: An American dilemma*. Boston: D. C. Heath & Company.

NATIVISTS DEFINE WHO IS AND WHO IS NOT AN AMERICAN

The new immigrants, many of whom were Italian and Jewish, did not enjoy the privilege of being seen as White and were frequently viewed with suspicion by old stock Americans (Jacobson, 1998). They spoke alien languages and had political beliefs, religious practices, and cultural characteristics that were viewed as un-American. As immigration increased, antialien sentiments and fears escalated (Hutchinson, 1949). The new immigrants were seen as a drain on American society in much the same way as the Germans and Irish had been viewed in earlier years. The new immigrants, however, were not viewed sympathetically by the Germans and Irish. Even though they themselves had been victims of prejudice and discrimination when they first arrived in the United States, many Germans and Irish embraced nativist perspectives and spoke out against the new immigrants.[1]

Nativists argued that the new immigrants from southern and eastern Europe were threatening American values and institutions and jeopardizing the White race (Grant, 1918). Woodrow Wilson captured the anti-immigration sentiment of his day when he said, "The immigrant newcomers of recent years are men of the lowest class from the south of Italy, and men of the meaner sort out of Hungary and Poland, men out of the ranks where there was neither skill nor energy, nor any initiative of quick intelligence" (quoted in Kessner, 1977, pp. 25–26). In addition, the Bolshevik Revolution, which overthrew the Russian czar, increased concerns about the extent to which immigrants embraced revolutionary ideologies, as well as their ability to understand and appreciate American democracy (Ross, 1914). Nativists exploited fears about the stability of American institutions and their vulnerability to outside radical forces as they argued for restrictions on immigration. The American Protective Association, a nativist organization, used the availability of newer and less expensive forms of transatlantic transportation to raise fears about immigration. The association's leaders argued that unrestricted immigration would flood American institutions with "$9.60 steerage slime" (Ziegler, 1953, p. 7). Nativism reached its zenith in the early 1900s in organizations such as the Ku Klux Klan, which was anti-Catholic, anti-Jewish, antiforeigner, and anti-Black.

Nativist Perspectives in Academic Texts and School Curricula

In addition to politicians and opportunists, academic and school leaders also embraced nativist sentiments. Henry Pratt Fairchild, a well-known sociologist, expressed nativist sentiments in two books—*The Melting Pot Mistake* and *Immigration: A World Movement and Its American Significance* (Fairchild, 1913, 1926). Fairchild argued that immigrants were responsible for lowering the American standard of living, increasing crime, burdening society with a disproportionate number of people in insane asylums, and for the declining quality of American life. Commenting on crime, he noted that two forms of crime, the Mafia and White slave traffic, were connected to immigration. He associated the Mafia with Italians and White slave traffic with Jewish, French, and Belgian immigrants. He was particularly concerned about the native-born children of immigrants. He used statistics to argue that they had a much higher inclination toward criminal behavior than mainstream native Whites. Although he acknowledged the complex causes of juvenile delinquency, he concluded, "Whatever the cause, this tendency toward lawlessness among the second generation of immigrants is indisputable, and is one of the most disturbing elements in the whole situation" (Fairchild, 1953, p. 49).

Nativists' perspectives, such as those articulated by Fairchild, were incorporated into school textbooks, materials, and curricula. The statement from a 1931 curriculum guide for social studies teachers in Houston, Texas, is an example of nativist ideas in the curriculum.

Migration from the foreign countries has become a problem. The immigrants who were so freely welcomed as long as land was abundant became a menace to our higher standards of living when they remained in cities where already there were more persons than jobs. Consequently, the number of immigrants that may enter our country in any one year has been cut to a very small fraction of the number of persons from any given country who were in the U.S. in 1890. This regulation has tended to lessen the immigration from southern Europe. Before 1890 most of our immigrants had come from England, Germany, Sweden, and other countries of northern Europe. (Houston Curriculum Guide, 1931, p. 7)

The *Houston Curriculum Guide* provided teachers with a rationale for explaining why immigration was restricted and a way to draw a distinction between mainstream Americans, whose ancestors were drawn to the rich prairie land in the West where they started small family farms; and the new immigrants, who settled in cities, lived in ethnic communities, and took jobs in mines and factories. Interestingly, the distinctions between old and new immigrants that were made in the *Houston Curriculum Guide* were essentially the same as those used by nativists to justify immigration restrictions.

The *Houston Curriculum Guide* illustrates the extent to which concerns about immigration weren't limited to people on the East Coast. Houston and Galveston, Texas were two important stopping points for immigrants who were moving west. Large numbers of immigrants arrived in those cities in the early 1900s. Many stayed in Texas and established homes there, while others moved on to other cities in the west.

The Move to Curb Immigration

In 1924, Congress passed the Johnson-Reed Bill. This far-reaching bill shaped U.S. immigration policy into the 1960s. A chronology of U.S. immigration laws from 1917 to 1990 is included in Table 1.2. The Johnson-Reed Bill was the culmination of years of concentrated effort to stem the flow of new immigrants. Senator Ellison DuRant Smith voiced a nativistic perspective on immigration when in 1924 he delivered an impassioned plea to the 68th Congress to "shut the door" of immigration to the United States. He asked his colleagues in the U.S. Senate to think about who they would like to represent as a typical American:

If you were to go abroad and someone were to meet you and say, "I met a typical American," what would flash into your mind as a typical representative of that new Nation? Would it be the son of an Italian immigrant, the son of a German immigrant, the son of any of the breeds from the Orient, the

Table 1.2. A Chronology of U. S. Immigration Laws From 1917–1990

The 1917 Immigration Act	This act prevented most Asians from immigrating to the United States. However, since the Philippines was an American territory, Asians living there could immigrate to the United States. This act also required immigrants to be able to read.
The National Origins Act of 1924	This act established a total quota limiting immigration to the United States to about 150,000 immigrants per year. The law provided for a disproportionate number of people from England and Northern Europe to immigrate to the United States. Very few slots were allotted to people from southern and eastern Europe. None was given to Asians.
1952 McCarran-Walter Act	This act allowed small numbers of Asians to immigrate to the United States.
1965 Immigration Act	This act opened up immigration to the United States to people in Third World nations. It allowed 20,000 people per country to immigrate to the United States. Spouses, dependent children, and parents of U. S. citizens were exempt from the country limits.
Immigration and Control Act of 1986	This act provides for sanctions against employers who hire illegal immigrant workers. However, provisions are made for employers to hire "guest workers" who can work in the United States but are not given the same rights and benefits as U. S. citizens. It also provided amnesty for undocumented aliens who could prove that they had lived in the United States since January 1982.
Immigration Act of 1990	This act reaffirmed the importance of family reunification.

son of the denizens of Africa? . . . Thank God we have in America perhaps the largest percentage of any country in the world of the pure, unadulterated Anglo-Saxon stock; certainly the greatest of any nation in the Nordic breed. It is for the preservation of that splendid stock that has characterized us that I would make this not an asylum for the oppressed of all countries. . . . The time has come when we should shut the door and keep what we have for what we hope our own people to be. (Smith, 1924, pp. 5961–5962)

While many Americans did not embrace Smith's vitriolic views, he was not an isolated, lone individual voicing an opinion that did not have strong support. Smith represented North Carolina in the U.S. Senate from 1909 until his death in 1944. Like many others who wanted to limit immigration, Smith used Madison Grant's (1918) popular theories about race to add intellectual credibility to his arguments. In his book *The Passing of the Great Race*, Grant argued that liberal immigration policies were essentially "suicidal ethics, which are exterminating his own race" (p. 81). He believed that the United States could only absorb a small number of Slavs, Jews, and members of the Iberian races. According to Grant the idea of America as a great melting pot was flawed and race mixing would ultimately weaken the bloodline of old-stock Americans. Grant's ideas about racial hierarchies not only provided an intellectual rationale for the Johnson-Reed Bill; they legitimized racist depictions of White ethnics and minorities in the popular culture. Movies such as *The Birth of a Nation* and *The Jazz Singer* helped shape the way Americans thought about race then and continue to think about it today (Jacobson, 1998).[2]

Only six senators voted against the Johnson-Reed Bill. The forces against immigration, which included the Ku Klux Klan and labor organizations, were stronger than the American Jewish Congress and other organizations and individuals who supported immigration (Congressional Record, 1924). The Johnson-Reed Bill restricted immigration to 2% of a group's population in the United States in 1890. The national origins quotas in the Johnson-Reed Bill, which were essentially a proxy for racial and ethnic quotas, ensured that future U.S. immigrants would primarily come from northern and western Europe.

A NEW BEGINNING: INTERCULTURAL EDUCATORS CHALLENGE NATIVIST PERSPECTIVES

Nativist ideas like those articulated by Smith, Grant, and Fairchild were not universally accepted by Americans. They were challenged by academics such as Horace Kallen (1924), Julius Drachsler (1920), and Randolph Bourne (1920). They and other like-minded scholars argued that it was possible for immigrants to assimilate into American society while maintaining important elements of their ethnic cultures. Kallen (1924) and his colleagues called this idea *cultural pluralism*. They believed that cultural and ethnic diversity would enrich American society.

European immigrants challenged nativist perspectives through ethnic societies like the Knights of Columbus, the Polish National Alliance, and the Serb National Federation, as well as through ethnic newspapers. In addition to advocating for changes in immigration policies, they advocated for changes in school curricula. White ethnics wanted their children to see themselves reflected in the school curriculum. They wanted their voices, perspectives, and heroes to be visible in school texts and materials

(Zimmerman, 1999). The growth of parochial schools was in part a response by White ethnic parents to public school curricula and texts that did not reflect their values, concerns, and histories.

Rachel Davis DuBois (1928), a teacher at Woodbury High School in Woodbury, New Jersey, also rejected the idea that the new immigrants were inferior to mainstream Americans. In the late 1920s she began developing school assembly programs on ethnic groups in her local community. DuBois worked with parents and members of the community to organize the assembly programs, identify artifacts that could be displayed at school, and solicit speakers who could present information on ethnic groups. The assembly programs were designed to affirm the values, customs, and contributions of ethnic students in the school, improve intergroup relations, and dispel negative images of the new immigrants (DuBois, 1928). DuBois's assembly programs at Woodbury High School served as a prototype for what later became known as intercultural education.

Major Characteristics of Intercultural Education

Intercultural educators developed and implemented projects and programs in schools, colleges, and teacher training institutions through the Service Bureau for Intercultural Education in New York City directed by Rachel Davis DuBois (DuBois, 1930, 1939); the Springfield Plan, under the leadership of John Granrud (Alland & Wise, 1945; Bresnahan, 1971; Chatto & Halligan, 1945); the Intergroup Education in Cooperating Schools Project, led by Hilda Taba (1953); and the College Study in Intergroup Relations Project organized by Lloyd Cook (Cook, 1951; Cook & Cook, 1954). These and other intercultural education projects and programs were based on the assumption that there were more similarities than differences among people and that when people from different racial, ethnic, and religious groups had an opportunity to get to know each other they would learn to accept and respect each other (Kilpatrick & VanTil, 1947; Taba & Elkins, 1950). William Heard Kilpatrick and William VanTil (1947), two influential scholars who were involved in intercultural education, defined intercultural education as follows:

> Intercultural education aims at the best possible achievement of the values of participation with, acceptance of, and respect for others. It is an effort to bring education to bear as constructively as possible on actual and possible intercultural tensions and on the evils of any and all bias, prejudice, and discrimination against minority groups. In short, the effort of intercultural education is to ensure to all the adequate realization of these social values and to remove and cure the bias and prejudice leading to such discriminations. This is the fundamental meaning of intercultural education, and it

explains the presence of intercultural education as an integral part and aspect of modern democratic education. (p. 4)

Intercultural education was a broadly conceptualized movement that wasn't limited to schools. Intercultural educators recognized that education took place in the community as well as the classroom (Cook, 1938). Mounting effective programs to reduce intergroup tension and increase the self-esteem of the second generation required work in the community as well as in schools. Intercultural education programs were implemented in community organizations such as the Young Men's Christian Association (YMCA) and the Young Women's Christian Association (YWCA) as well as entire cities such as Springfield, Massachusetts, where the Springfield Plan was initiated.

Another important characteristic of intercultural education was the way that it linked theory and practice. Even though intercultural education was an applied field, it wasn't limited to classroom practice. It also involved research. Intergroup educators researched ways to help teachers gain the skills and knowledge they needed to work with students from diverse groups (Cook, 1950; Cook & Cook, 1954; Taba, 1953) and to reduce student prejudice (Trager & Yarrow, 1952).

Intercultural education had many variations representing different populations, sites, strategies, and activities. There were, however, several common threads that linked intercultural educators together. They included a clear focus on education as a means to address intergroup tensions, the centrality of democratic values and responsibilities in American life, and the recognition that education took place in the community as well as in schools.

Intercultural Educators Offer an Alternative to Nativism

By 1945 there were over 200 organizations working in intercultural education (Giles, 1945). The number of intercultural organizations mushroomed after riots in Detroit and Los Angeles in 1943. Many of these organizations were national in scope. However, there were also a large number of local and regional intercultural education organizations. In a survey identifying intercultural organizations throughout the United States, H. Harry Giles (1945) found that 60 were located in the Northeast, 51 in the South, 44 in the Midwest, and 20 in the West. The number and location of intercultural organizations was consistent with the population distribution of immigrants, the second generation, and people of color.

Intercultural education programs were implemented throughout the United States, but were primarily and most extensively implemented in New York City. Population demographics in New York City made it a logical center for intercultural education. Millions of immigrants landed at Castle Garden in New York Harbor and later at Ellis Island. Castle Garden, the country's first immigration station, opened in New York City in 1855. The Ellis Island station operated in New York Harbor from 1892 to 1954. Prior to the mid-1800s, Philadelphia was the nation's chief port of entry for immigrants.

As in New York City intergroup education was popular in Chicago, Philadelphia, Syracuse, Los Angeles, San Diego, and other cities that had large immigrant and minority populations (Committee, 1949; Taba, Brady, Jennings, Robinson, & Dolton, 1949). However, intergroup education was not implemented for as long a period or as comprehensively in other cities as it was in New York City.

Intercultural Education in New York City. The New York City schools provided intercultural training for teachers, developed intercultural curricula, and purchased intercultural materials for teachers to use in their classrooms. The implementation of intergroup education in New York City, however, was not steady. It had peaks and valleys reflecting the politics of diversity in New York, teacher indifference and resistance, and the school board's concerns about the quality and impact of intergroup education (Chase, 1940; Zitron, 1968).

New York City educators' ideas and perspectives about immigrants largely mirrored those that were prevalent in U.S. society. Political concerns about ethnic diversity were among the most important factors that influenced the readiness of teachers to embrace intercultural education. Intercultural education came into being when the memory of loyalty oaths and attacks on teachers who were critical of the United States were still fresh in the minds of educators. When the United States entered World War I, anti-immigrant forces raised concerns about the possibility that teachers and university professors were subversives. People who were pacifists or critics of the war were viewed with suspicion. Concerns about the extent to which educators were patriotic supporters of the United States led to the requirement that teachers take loyalty oaths. In 1917, New York State passed a law that called for teachers to be dismissed for using seditious words or engaging in seditious acts. The New York City Board of Education required teachers to take the following loyalty oath:

We the teachers in public schools of the City of New York declare our unqualified allegiance to the government of the United States of America and pledge ourselves by word and example to teach and impress on our pupils the duty of obedience and patriotic service as the highest ideal of American citizenship. (cited in Zitron, 1968, p. 163)

Community groups also influenced the speed and scope of the implementation of intercultural education in New York. A broad range of ethnic groups and organizations supported intercultural education, but there were also widespread concerns about how to present ethnic groups in the curriculum as well as concerns about who could legitimately speak for a group. The American Jewish Committee clashed with intercultural educators over content on Jews. Jews were frequently presented as an ethnic group in intercultural education materials and programs. The American Jewish Committee insisted that Jews be presented as a religious group (Montalto, 1982). During the 1930s, the committee gradually withdrew its support for intercultural programs that persisted in identifying Jews as an ethnic group. Catholics and Protestants also had concerns about the way their religious groups were presented in intercultural education programs and materials (Zimmerman, 1999). When Mary L. Riley, who worked for the New York City Board of Education, received a list of speakers for an upcoming intercultural education program, she protested the inclusion of Bishop G. Bromley Oxnam. In a letter to Mrs. Lily Edelman of the East-West Association, the organization sponsoring the intercultural education program, Riley noted that Oxnam had made offensive remarks about the Roman Catholic Church and that he should be removed from the program. Riley went on to recommend other speakers who were more acceptable to the Catholic Church. These and other conflicts reflected how ethnic and religious groups jockeyed for power by using their connections with school and political leaders to exert pressure on intercultural educators, and when necessary, by withholding their support for intergroup programs.

DIVERGENT VIEWS WITHIN THE MOVEMENT

While there was consensus among intergroup educators that discrimination and hostility toward immigrant groups should be kept in check and that immigrants should be assimilated into mainstream American society, leaders in the intergroup education movement did not speak with a single voice (Montalto, 1982; Olneck, 1990). Beyond consensus on several broad goals, leaders in the intergroup education movement embraced different ideological perspectives and points of view on the direction and philosophy that should guide the movement. The movement was marked from its inception with internal conflict about how to achieve racial harmony and assimilation.

Americanization

Americanization was one of the most salient and visible ideological perspectives to influence the education of immigrant groups. However, Americanizers did not have a uniform perspective on diversity. Their perspectives ranged from conservative to moderate. Americanizers included individuals who were intolerant of diversity and believed that immigrants from northern Europe were superior to immigrants from southeastern Europe. They also included moderates. Montalto (1982) uses the term *Scientific Americanizer* to describe moderate Americanizers. Scientific Americanizers, according to Montalo, supported a limited program of ethnic and cultural education, mostly in the form of folk art performances and handicraft displays. Such programs were intended to raise the status of immigrant parents in the eyes of their children and reestablish the social control function of the immigrant family. They were not, however, designed to divert immigrant children from recognizing the importance of becoming Americans. In an effort to reduce the burden of marginality for immigrants and their children, scientific Americanizers set up classes to teach English to immigrants and provide other forms of support to help them adjust to U.S. society. Montalto (1982) concluded that "their goal was to instill an identity without substance, a sentimental attachment to the superficial aspects of cultures." (p. 54). Even though there were differences among Americanizers, they shared the belief that ethnic and religious diversity could potentially fracture U.S. society and that schools should work to assimilate immigrants into mainstream society as soon as possible.

Cultural Pluralism

Another important ideological strand in intercultural education was cultural pluralism. Rachel Davis DuBois, Leonard Covello, and other cultural pluralists believed that schools should be linked to students' communities and that students should be taught to appreciate their parents' culture and their ethnic heritage. Cultural pluralists also believed that all students should be taught to appreciate cultural diversity and to recognize that ethnic and religious diversity were an important part of being an American (DuBois, 1945). Because of her zeal in promoting the cultural heritage of immigrants, Americanizers accused Rachel Davis DuBois of trying to turn intercultural education into a social movement. DuBois rejected that criticism. From her perspective, it was essential that all students understand the values, beliefs, customs, and other important characteristics of American ethnic and racial groups.

During the 1930s, members of the second generation began to assume leadership roles in the intercultural movement. Second-generation intercultural educators were born in the United States and spoke English as their first language. With members of the second generation in leadership positions, the movement began to focus more directly on the school's role in instilling all students with a sense of pride and appreciation for ethnic culture. Even though second-generation intercultural educators had many of the cultural characteristics of mainstream Americans, they were not strangers in ethnic communities. They understood and identified with ethnics as a result of their early socialization in immigrant communities and as a result of their ongoing contacts with family members who remained in the communities.

Cultural pluralists created educational programs that went beyond tolerance. Their programs called for positive appreciation of immigrant culture and for incorporating ethnic cultural characteristics into the U.S. national identity (DuBois, 1945). Americanizers challenged cultural pluralists with the following question: "Are you not, by singling out first one culture group and then another for special attention in assembly programs and classroom discussions, developing rather than reducing a sense of separateness among groups?" Rachel Davis DuBois responded by pointing out that many members of cultural groups were already compartmentalized in people's minds in a negative way. Since members of culture groups are already viewed in a negative way, DuBois asked, "Shouldn't we set them off in a positive way in order to counteract that negative influence?" (DuBois, 1945, p. 158).

Cultural pluralists saw American culture as dynamic and open enough to embrace the values, beliefs, and other cultural characteristics of immigrant groups. They believed that both old as well as new immigrants would need to make adjustments as a more authentic American identity was constructed. Cultural pluralism, however, never gained widespread acceptance. Even though it was consistent with liberal ideology, cultural pluralism was unacceptable to many liberals. Intercultural educators who embraced cultural pluralism ultimately found themselves on the margins of a movement that they helped to create.

Variations in Intergroup Programs

In addition to ideological differences, intercultural education programs varied in their scope, target population, and content. This is somewhat understandable given the location of ethnic population centers. The content of intercultural education curricula, like multicultural education curricula today, frequently focused on local ethnic and racial groups and local intergroup tensions and concerns. Intercultural programs in New York City and other East Coast cities generally focused their attention on White ethnics from southern and eastern Europe and on religious groups. Many of the Italian immigrants who entered the United States through Ellis Island remained on the East Coast. Approximately 97% of the Italian immigrants who arrived in the United States after 1880 settled in New York City

(Nelli, 1983). The remaining 3% spread out to other cities such as Philadelphia, New Castle, and Chicago in search of job opportunities (Allen & Turner, 1988).

Intercultural education programs in San Diego, California, and other cities on the West Coast included more content on ethnic minorities such as Japanese Americans and Chinese Americans. People of Asian descent primarily entered the United States through Angel Island and settled in cities on the West Coast. Many of their early settlements were in San Francisco, Los Angeles, Seattle, and Portland. However, there were Chinese and Japanese settlements in New York City as early as the 1920s and significant numbers of Chinese in Chicago and Boston in the early 1900s (Allen & Turner, 1988).

The organization and content of intercultural programs also varied. For example, some programs looked more like international education than intercultural education. Intercultural education programs that had an international focus were often affiliated with organizations such as the East and West Association. Pearl Buck founded the association in 1942 and dedicated its work to cultural exchange and understanding between Asia and the West. Other intercultural education programs sought to educate the "whole child" and borrowed key ideas from progressive education. Leonard Covello (1942), the principal at Benjamin Franklin High School, reflected that perspective when he said, "Life and learning in school should be continuous with those experiences out of school, with free interplay between the two" (p. 4). Many of the people who were involved in intergroup education were also actively involved in progressive education. Leonard Covello was a frequent speaker at Progressive Education Association conferences. William Heard Kilpatrick, who was well known for his seminal contributions to progressive education, also served on the board of the Bureau for Intercultural Education. This is an example of another linkage between progressive education and intercultural education.

SOCIAL SCIENTISTS PROVIDE INTELLECTUAL ARGUMENTS FOR INTERCULTURAL EDUCATION

Intergroup educators, such as Rachel Davis DuBois, Leonard Covello, and Hilda Taba were deeply influenced by social science knowledge. They studied with the leading social scientists of their day and completed their doctorates at institutions where new ideas and key social science concepts were being discussed and researched. Social science concepts such as culture, assimilation, cultural pluralism, discrimination, and prejudice were woven into their thinking and provided an intellectual foundation for their work.

During the early 20th century, biological determinism, which claimed that racial minorities and certain White ethnics were inferior to northern Europeans, was widely accepted and used to explain status differentials between old and new immigrants (Gould, 1981). It also provided a rationale to justify the unequal treatment of particular ethnic and racial groups. Differences in the status and attainments of old and new immigrants could be explained by the fact that people of Northern and Western European ancestry were superior (Gould, 1981). Social scientists, many of whom were racial minorities and White ethnics, began to develop knowledge that challenged biological determinism and offer alternative explanations for White dominance.

African American scholars, such as W.E.B. DuBois and Carter G. Woodson, were among the first scholars to challenge biological determinism. W.E.B. DuBois's (1899/1973) study of African Americans in Philadelphia challenged the idea that Blacks were poor because of their inherent deficiencies. His work illustrated how the social context in which Blacks lived influenced their life chances and attainments. DuBois's work not only provided an alternative explanation for differences among groups; it served as a model of social science research.

Research on Assimilation

Some of the most troubling questions faced by intergroup educators were related to assimilating southern and eastern European immigrants and racial minorities into mainstream U.S. society. Social science knowledge provided insights on those questions. It suggested that culture was a much more persistent psychological and social reality than many people had previously thought and that assimilation could not be accomplished overnight. It could take several generations (Park, 1935). Some social scientists such as Robert Ezra Park believed that the second generation would never completely become Americanized (Park & Miller, 1921). Instead, they would serve as a bridge between the older unassimilated generation and the younger assimilated generations.

Park (1928) used the term *marginal man* to discuss the psychosocial conflicts experienced by many second-generation immigrants. He believed that when society opened up opportunities for minorities and immigrants, they would leave the geographical, social, and psychological boundaries of their ethnic communities. However, even though they were attempting to embrace a new way of life, they would remain psychologically tied to their ethnic communities and to the old ways of their mothers and fathers. According to Park, the dilemma for the *marginal man* is that he would never be able to fully return to his ethnic community and old way of life because he would see the community and people living there from a more detached and rational perspective. Sadly, having given up his old ways, he would never be fully accepted into his new cultural group because he could not or would not change his values, perspectives, or his fundamental sense of himself. Consequently, the *marginal man* would be destined to live in the borderlands in between two cultures, unable to be fully integrated into either. Over time, the term *marginal man* became a synonym for the second generation. However, Park used the term in a more limited way. The Jewish intellectual and the educated mulatto were used by Park as prime examples of *marginal man* when he coined the term (Cahnman, 1978).

Park and his students—who included eminent social scientists such as E. Franklin Frazier, Pauline Young, Frederick Thrasher, and Louis Wirth—developed knowledge that revealed that culture had both positive and negative effects. Culture restrained antisocial behavior, supported group cooperation as well as stifled creativity and individuality (Park & Miller, 1921). Park (1928) saw the disappearance of ethnic cultures as an advance rather than a setback. He believed that race relations could be characterized by a cycle of four inevitable phases: "contact, conflict, accommodation, and eventual assimilation" (Park, 1950, p. 150). He warned that even though it may take many years, coercive attempts to speed the process of assimilation could backfire (Park, 1955).

Park's work on assimilation reflected a long-term interest in race relations and immigration. Nine years before joining the faculty at the University of Chicago, he worked with Booker T. Washington at Tuskegee Institute. From 1905–1914, Park served as Washington's assistant, advisor, and ghostwriter (Cahnman, 1978). In 1921, he published an extensive study of American immigration entitled *Old World Traits Transplanted* in which he discussed the theoretical framework for his understanding of the assimilation cycle (Park & Miller, 1921). Park's work on European immigrants was followed in 1924 with a major survey of race relations on the Pacific Coast, which focused on Asians. Park, along with his colleagues Emory Bogardus, Roderick McKenzie, and William Carlson, used the term *Oriental* to describe Chinese and Japanese immigrants and the term *Oriental problem* to describe "the shared experiences of Chinese and Japanese in being excluded from the White experience of successful assimilation" (Yu, 1996, p. 157). Park ended his career by retiring to Fisk University, where one of his former students, Charles S. Johnson, was president. At Fisk, he was engaged in research on intercultural relations and taught courses on sociology and human ecology.

Research on Self-Esteem

The second generation was often in the peculiar position of helping their parents meditate the language, values, and other cultural characteristics of their adopted country. While playing the role of cultural translator, the second generation commonly saw their parents humiliated by people outside their communities. School wasn't any different. There they frequently experienced humiliation and a lack of understanding and appreciation of their parents and their ancestral homeland. In movies and in other forms of popular culture the language, values, and customs of their parents were frequently ignored, dismissed, or denigrated. Nearly everywhere the second generation turned, they were tacitly encouraged to reject their parents' "old ways" and become American. Consequently, it wasn't uncommon for the second generation to see their parents as hopelessly old-fashioned. Their parents' opinions could easily be dismissed as being the response of someone who was ignorant of American culture.

If parents are not seen as respected authorities, the role that they traditionally play in directing and controlling their children's behavior is muted. When members of the second generation skipped school or engaged in petty criminal activity, many of their parents were not in a position to intervene with the traditional moral authority of a parent. The social fabric of immigrant communities and families was undermined by widespread negative images of immigrants and their cultures as being at best inferior and at worst dangerous. As family control broke down and traditional values were undermined, delinquent behaviors among the second generation increased. Over time these behaviors became widely associated with the second generation and eventually became a stereotype of it (Seller, 1977).

Research by Alfred Adler (1929) and other psychologists suggested that the antisocial behavior that was associated with the second generation was a reflection of their low self-esteem. Adler and his colleagues provided an intellectual basis for intergroup educators to think about the relationship between society's rejection of immigrant culture and immigrant children's rejection of their parents and ultimately themselves. Intergroup educators hypothesized that increasing the status of immigrants and ethnic groups could ameliorate the second-generation problem. Rachel Davis DuBois and other intergroup educators used Adler's transformative ideas about the relationship between societal image and self-esteem as a rationale for creating materials, activities, and programs to enhance students' self-esteem and for changing societal attitudes about immigrants. One of the strategies that intercultural educators used to help establish a positive link between self-esteem and societal image was to acknowledge publicly the accomplishments of immigrant groups and praise symbols of their cultures, such as their songs, dances, and foods (Adamic, 1929; 1934; 1944; DuBois, 1930).

Research on Culture

Franz Boas (1928) and his students at Columbia University, who included Otto Kleniberg (1955), Melville J. Herskovits (1938; 1958), and Ruth Benedict (1934), created knowledge that encouraged people to think more deeply about the role ethnic cultures could play in improving United States society. Boas challenged the idea of racial purity and a superior race. He and his students promoted a sophisticated understanding of culture not as tangible artifacts, but as a group's way of adapting to its environments. Boas (1915) argued that people were not bound together by blood or language, but rather by ". . . the community of emotional life that rises from our every-day habits, from the forms of our thoughts, feelings, and actions which constitute the medium in which every individual can unfold freely his activities" (p. 9).

The new field of anthropology, founded by Boas and his students, developed concepts, ideas, and theories that suggested that culture wasn't unique to one society. Moreover, from the perspective of other cultures, United States society had limitations and could be improved. Anthropologists argued that contact with different peoples and cultures was characteristic of all great civilizations. Intergroup educators used that and other ideas from anthropology to argue that cultures should be blended in U.S. society (Benedict, 1934; Boas, 1928). Alain Locke and Bernard J. Stern (1942) captured that perspective in an insightful book they edited, entitled, *When Peoples Meet: A Study in Race and Culture Contacts*. This book was widely read by intergroup educators and used to help justify their work (Montalto, 1982).

Research on Prejudice

During World War II and the period immediately following it, racial and religious tensions increased. Minorities became a focal point for frustrations born out of irritations with gas shortages, rationing, separation from loved ones, and anxiety about the future. Additionally, organizations such as the German-American Bund, the Christian Front, and the Christian Mobilizers exacerbated fears about Jewish educators radicalizing young people. Those fears were reflected in newspapers, magazines, and journal articles. Zitron (1968) reports that a 1939 issue of *Social Justice* contained an article entitled "Are Reds in Control of New York City Schools?" The members of the Teachers Union were listed in the article with the notation "Jew," "Jewess," "Undetermined," and "Gentile" beside each name (cited in Zitron, 1968, p. 193).

Intergroup tensions continued to develop throughout and after the war years. In June of 1943, a major race riot in Detroit, Michigan called national attention to the deep interracial tensions that existed between Whites and Blacks. The Detroit riot was the first of several riots that occurred in what came to be known in following years as the "bloody summer" of 1945. African Americans who had left the South during the Great Migration were experiencing discrimination in a wide range of areas, including housing, education, and employment. This was also a difficult time for other ethnic minorities. Mexicans who had been invited to the United States to work in Bracero programs were seen as taking jobs from Whites and were unwelcome. People of Japanese descent who had been put into internment camps returned to western cities to reestablish themselves after the war. They experienced prejudice and discrimination as they returned to their homes. African Americans, Jews, Japanese, Mexicans, and other ethnic minorities were easy and visible targets for prejudice and discrimination.

To combat Hitler's focus on racial purity in Nazi Germany, social scientists began to develop new explanations for group differences. Before World War II social scientists had primarily focused on measuring the attitudes of Whites toward racial and ethnic groups. For example, in the 1920s Emory Bogardus (1925a, 1925b, 1933) developed an attitude scale to measure ethnic prejudice by measuring *social distance*, the feelings of acceptance or rejection for different racial and ethnic groups. In the 1940s and 1950s researchers began developing and testing a broader range of theories about prejudice. Social psychologists such as Theodor Adorno and Gordon Allport offered thoughtful explanations about the origin of prejudice and ways to reduce it. In *The Authoritarian Personality*, Adorno and his colleagues (1950) argued that prejudice stemmed from certain personality dispositions. Their theory about the authoritarian personality, which was very popular and widely accepted after World War II, was later regarded by social scientists to be a useful but limited theory about the origin of prejudice.

Noting that public opinion polls indicated that 85% of the U.S. population was psychologically prepared to scapegoat another group, Allport (1944) began to analyze the psychology of the bigot. He defined a bigot as "a person who, under the tyranny of his own frustrations, tabloid thinking, and projection, blames a whole group of people for faults of which they are partially or wholly innocent" (p. 2). Allport's theory not only offered explanations of prejudice; it provided ideas for improving intergroup relations. His theory is called the *contact hypothesis*. Allport stated that contact between members of different social groups could improve intergroup relations if the following four conditions were met:

1. there was equal status among the groups;
2. the activities the groups engaged in reinforced a sense of common interests and humanity between the two groups;
3. the groups shared mutual goals;
4. the groups' activities were sanctioned by institutional authorities. (Allport, 1954).

Allport's ideas about how to structure intergroup contact were used by intergroup educators to bring members of different ethnic groups together. His theory has been widely researched and in its revised form serves as the basis of many intergroup interventions today (Pettigrew, 2004; Stephan & Stephan, 2004).

Research Highlights American Creed Values

Myrdal's (1944) study on intergroup relations in the United States entitled *An American Dilemma: The Negro Problem and Modern Democracy* revealed a gap between American Creed Values such as freedom, justice, and equality, and the reality of those values in the daily lives of African Americans. By law and custom African Americans and other people of color were denied equal rights and were subjected to various forms of exclusion, segregation, and discrimination. Myrdal argued that the consequences of racism and discrimination were at odds with the nation's ideals. Intergroup educators were encouraged by Myrdal's finding that even though the reality of American life was at odds with its ideal values, these values had not been forgotten and still defined what Americans believed they should and could be. Ideals associated with democracy became a major focus of intergroup education during World War II and were used as a justification for prejudice reduction activities in the schools. Intercultural educators argued that prejudice reduction had a legitimate and necessary place in the school curriculum of democratic societies.

LINKING TRANSFORMATIVE KNOWLEDGE TO SCHOOL KNOWLEDGE

The transformative knowledge created by Robert Park (1928), Franz Boas (1928), Alfred Adler (1929), Gordon Allport (1944), Milton Gordon (1964), and other scholars was critically important to the intercultural education movement. It challenged mainstream knowledge about immigrant groups and prepared the public for receiving new ideas about the role that immigrants could play in American society. Most importantly, it provided an intellectual platform from which intercultural educators could challenge perceptions of new immigrants as individuals who didn't have a culture, had little to offer American society, and were inferior to old immigrants. Intercultural educators used transformative social science knowledge to argue for changes in textbooks, materials, curricula, and other forms of school knowledge so that the ancestral homelands and cultures of immigrants could be acknowledged and celebrated. They also used transformative knowledge to develop in-service training materials and programs for teachers who were responsible for implementing intercultural education in schools.

Intercultural educators increased their legitimacy by using transformative research to justify their work and to develop their programs and materials. Their association with transformative scholars and scholarship allowed them to speak with authority when they argued that intercultural education was an effective way to respond to the problems of second-generation children and youth.

2

Leadership Through Values: Learning from the Lives of Intercultural Leaders

L EADERSHIP through values is most effective when leaders appeal to values that express fundamental interests of their followers (Burns, 1978). However, appealing to the interests of followers is not a simple task (Bass, 1981). The interests of followers often involve contradictions between real and idealized values. Those contradictions reveal the dualism that often exists between self-involved interests that reflect real values such as the desire for economic security and publicly involved interests that reflect idealized values such as eliminating job discrimination. This dualism, which existed in the intercultural education movement, resulted in tension and conflict between mainstream, ethnic, and minority groups. American Creed values, which were centered in the intercultural education movement, served as a common language among intergroup educators. They allowed them to raise issues related to race and ethnicity and to close the gap between the realities of prejudice, discrimination, and exclusion in American society (Taba, Brady, & Robinson, 1952). Through an appeal to idealized values, such as justice, liberty, brotherhood, and equality, intercultural leaders gave voice to American Creed values. Using values as the foundation for their leadership, they were able to build broad-based coalitions composed of individuals who were members of a wide range of groups and organizations.

PUTTING A FACE ON INTERCULTURAL EDUCATION

Leaders play an important role in organizations by providing vision and inspiration (Burns, 1978). Their values, perspectives, and worldviews are key factors in shaping and influencing an organization's direction (Bass, 1981). For the most part, leaders in the intercultural education movement were highly educated and well-read individuals who were committed to social change. The movement was also supported by intellectual leaders such as Robert Havighurst and Kurt Lewin, who served on the Committee on Intergroup Education in Co-operating Schools; Ruth Benedict, who published books for children on prejudice and discrimination and coauthored a curriculum guide for teachers; and Bruno Lasker, who worked at the Service Bureau for Intercultural Education (Benedict & Wetfish, 1943, 1948; Locke & Stern, 1942; Taba & Elkins, 1950). It also included political, labor, and community supporters such as U.S. congressman Vito Marcantonio, labor leader Rose Russell, and the writer Louis Adamic. These leaders advocated for cultural integration and lent their support to the intercultural education movement.

The leadership in the intercultural education movement, which spanned over 3 decades, included individuals with wide-ranging expertise. Consequently, it is not possible to discuss the full range of leaders who participated in the intergroup movement. Therefore, I've selected three prominent intercultural programs and their leaders to profile: Rachel Davis DuBois, Hilda Taba, and John Granrud. The biographical journeys traveled by DuBois, Taba, and Granrud helped shape their view of social problems in U.S. society and their sense of their responsibility to respond to them. They were intellectual leaders who, for their times, mounted innovative and progressive educational programs.

Each of the leaders described in this chapter made unique and important contributions to intercultural education. Rachel Davis DuBois is widely credited with creating and sustaining the intercultural education movement (Davis, 1999; Montalto, 1982). From its founding in 1934 until 1941, DuBois served in leadership positions at the Service Bureau for Education in Human Relations. Hilda Taba was a respected leader and decisive voice in the intergroup education movement from 1945 to 1951 (Brady, 1992). Her program, Intergroup Education in Cooperating Schools, was one of the most influential programs in the intergroup education movement. John Granrud received national recognition for developing the Springfield Plan. He served as the superintendent of the Springfield, Massachusetts public schools from 1933–1945.

The Biographical Journeys of Taba, Granrud, and DuBois

Hilda Taba, John Granrud, and Rachel Davis DuBois grew up in small tight-knit communities. Taba was born on December 7, 1902 in Kooraste, a small village in southeastern Estonia. She was the oldest of nine children born to Robert Taba, a schoolmaster (Krull, 1992). Granrud was born in Decorah, Iowa on March 17, 1895. His Norwegian parents, who had experienced prejudice and discrimination, taught him to appreciate ethnic and racial diversity (Bresnahan, 1971). Rachel Davis DuBois was born January 25, 1892 on a farm in Clarkesboro, New Jersey. She was the second of six children born to Charles Howard Davis and Bertha Priscilla Haines Davis. DuBois's background as a Quaker and a pacifist taught her to appreciate the importance of the individual and to recognize that she had a responsibility to help others (DuBois with Okorodudu, 1984).

Educational Background. As women, attending college in the early part of the 20th century was a major accomplishment for Taba and DuBois. Taba graduated from Tartu University in Estonia in 1926. She went on to complete her master's degree at Bryn Mawr College and her doctorate at Columbia University in 1932. While at Columbia she studied with William Heard Kilpatrick and John Dewey. DuBois attended Bucknell University, graduating in 1914. After overcoming her shyness and discomfort in social situations, she became a student leader. She credited her experience of being an outsider at Bucknell with her ability to empathize with people of color (DuBois & Okorodudu, 1984). DuBois completed her doctorate in educational sociology at New York University in 1940. Her dissertation, *Adventures in Intercultural Education*, described the ethnic assembly program she created at Woodbury High School in Woodbury, New Jersey. Granrud grew up in a home with educated parents. His mother was a teacher and his father was a university professor. He went to college immediately after high school and graduated from St. Olaf College in 1917. After receiving his master's degree from the University of Minnesota and working as a classroom teacher and principal, he completed his doctorate in educational administration at Teachers College, Columbia University in 1922. While at Teachers College, he worked with eminent professors, including George Strayer, Nicholas Engelhardt, and William Heard Kilpatrick. Kilpatrick, along with several other professors at Teachers College, were active in intercultural education.

Hilda Taba: A Leader in Intergroup Education

After completing the requirements for her doctoral dissertation, Taba returned to Estonia and tried to secure a position at Tartu University. She was unsuccessful. Among the reasons were the following: she was a woman and in 1931 the university preferred to hire men; her doctoral degree had not been officially awarded; and in 1931 Estonians valued German degrees and educational ideas more than those from the United States. Taba's inability to secure a teaching position at Tartu University was a major disappointment and, according to Krull and Marits (1992), was an important turning point in her life. She returned to the United States in 1933. After holding a range of positions in education, she joined the faculty at the Ohio State University in 1936 as an assistant professor. In 1939, she went on to become an assistant professor at the University of Chicago. After serving in a number of posts, including as the director of the curriculum laboratory at the University of Chicago and as director of the Center for Intergroup Education and the Intergroup Education in Cooperating Schools Project at the University of Chicago, she left the Midwest for California, where she served as a curriculum consultant in Contra Costa County in California. She also joined the faculty at San Francisco State University as a professor of education, where she remained until her untimely death in 1967 (Krull & Marits, 1992).

Rachel Davis DuBois: A Leader in Intercultural Education

After graduating from Bucknell, DuBois became a teacher at Glassboro High School in Glassboro, New Jersey, where she became known to her colleagues as a dedicated and competent teacher. In 1924, she visited a school for African Americans in North Carolina and met George Washington Carver. For the first time in her life she witnessed discrimination against African Americans. DuBois with Okorodudu (1984) describes that experience as a turning point in her life. She began to read the works of W.E.B. DuBois and other African American writers. Both George Washington Carver and W.E.B. DuBois became lifelong friends.

With her new awareness, DuBois embarked on a lifestyle that was not characteristic of White women of her day. She joined the National Association for the Advancement of Colored People (NAACP) and disregarded social prohibitions against socializing with African Americans (DuBois with Okorodudu, 1984). Over the years, DuBois interacted with some of the leading figures in the Black community, including Mordecai Johnson, a former president of Howard University; the renown artist Aaron Douglas; E. Franklin Frazier, the eminent sociologist; A. Phillip Randolph, head of the Brotherhood of Sleeping Car Porters; and lifelong friend and confident W.E.B. DuBois (DuBois with Okorodudu, 1984; Lewis, 2000). As a result of her firsthand experiences with African American leaders, DuBois came to believe that intercultural education was as important for mainstream White students as it was for the second generation and minorities (Montalto, 1982). DuBois maintained her convictions about cultural maintenance through the 1940s and 1950s when there was little support for her ideas. During the 1960s she refocused her efforts and became active in the Civil Rights Movement. In 1964, she was invited by Dr. Martin Luther King to set up a program based on her work at the Intercultural Education Workshop for the Southern Christian Leadership Conference (SCLC) (DuBois & Okorodudu, 1984).

John Granrud: The Educational Leader Who Implemented the Springfield Plan

After working as a classroom teacher, principal, assistant superintendent, and superintendent of the U.S. Government Schools in the Panama Canal Zone, Granrud accepted an offer to become Assistant Superintendent of the Springfield, Massachusetts, Public School System. In 1933, he became superintendent of schools in Springfield and served in that position until 1945.

When Granrud arrived in Springfield, he noted that the student population was ethnically and racially diverse, but the teachers were Anglo-Saxon Protestants. He believed that this and other aspects of the hidden curriculum in Springfield schools worked against the district's efforts to promote brotherhood and reduce prejudice. When teaching positions opened up, he used the Placement Bureau at Teachers College, Columbia University to recruit teachers from different races and religious groups (Bresnahan, 1971). In addition to working to increase diversity in the teaching staff, Granrud worked with local leaders to reduce intergroup tensions in the school and community. He is credited with providing the vision and leadership for the development of the Springfield Plan, which is described later in this chapter.

MAJOR INITIATIVES IN INTERCULTURAL EDUCATION

Each of the three initiatives discussed in this section provides an important view of intercultural education. The Service Bureau for Education in Human Relations was the first intercultural education organization with a national audience. It advised schools throughout the nation on problems related to intergroup tensions and established programs and projects to improve intercultural relations. The bureau is an example of an advocacy group. Its founder, Rachel Davis DuBois, a New England Quaker, was a social activist who was committed to incorporating ethnic content into the curriculum and linking schools with communities. The Springfield Plan was a citywide effort to promote brotherhood and assimilation. It is offered as an example of how city and school officials cooperated with intercultural educators to create a prototype of a city free of prejudice and discrimination. The Springfield Plan illustrates the power of social networks and the role that schools can play in social change. The last program discussed in this chapter is the Intergroup Education in Cooperating Schools Project, directed by Hilda Taba. Unlike the social activist perspectives that grounded the Service Bureau for Intercultural Education and the social network that supported the Springfield Plan, Taba's work reflected her stance as a professional educator and scholar. Her work focused on prejudice reduction through research, curriculum development, and professional development for teachers.

Service Bureau for Education in Human Relations

In 1933, Professor Mabel Carney of Teachers College invited 16 academic and community leaders to a lunch where they discussed establishing a service bureau for education in human relations. Professor Carney opened the discussion by emphasizing the need for schools to address intergroup tensions and referencing the school assembly programs that Rachel Davis DuBois had begun implementing in the late 1920s. By the end of the lunch there was a consensus that the group would constitute an advisory board and work to establish a service bureau. By 1934, only months after their first meeting, the advisory group had established the Service Bureau for Education in Human Relations. The bureau grew out of the advisory board's vision for a place where educators and community leaders could turn for information and resources on intercultural education.

Rachel Davis DuBois served as the first executive secretary of the bureau and eventually became a major figure in intercultural education. She helped establish the bureau and its successors as the premier organizations in intercultural education. The bureau implemented intercultural education programs that included the study of ethnic groups, assembly programs, and club activities in Englewood, New Jersey; Washington, D.C.; Philadelphia; New York; and other cities. The bureau developed and disseminated newsletters, articles, reading lists, and curriculum materials on intercultural education, to a national audience. It also offered in-service courses for teachers, served as a network for individuals interested in working in intercultural education, and advocated for intercultural education among school and community leaders.

The goals and direction of the bureau were guided by its funding sources and the intellectual orientation of its leaders. Bureau leaders were well connected to the intellectual community in New York City and to funding sources through their positions on influential boards and organizations. Eight members of the 25-member advisory board that established the bureau were faculty or staff members at Columbia University or Teachers College, Columbia University. They provided the academic credibility necessary for the nascent intercultural education movement to have intellectual legitimacy. Bureau leaders also had connections to the American Jewish Committee and the National Conference of Jews and Christians. These groups were an important source of funding for the bureau.

Over the years the name of the bureau changed three times. It was originally called the Service Bureau for Education in Human Relations, later the Service Bureau for Intercultural Education, and finally the Bureau for Intercultural Education. Under its various names, the bureau provided intercultural support to schools from 1934 until it closed its doors in 1954. Rachel Davis DuBois was associated with the bureau under all of its names. However, with each name change she moved farther from the center of decision-making within the bureau. She also saw more of her ideas about the importance of ethnic contributions to American life, the self-esteem of immigrants, and cultural maintenance challenged.

One of the major challenges to DuBois's leadership concerned the assembly programs that she developed and which over time become closely associated with the bureau. Based on her experience with the programs and data that she collected during her years at Woodbury High School, DuBois believed the assembly programs were effective. When she administered the Newman Attitude Test to Woodbury High School seniors who participated in assembly programs and to a similar group of seniors in a nearby school who had not participated in the program, she noted that students who had participated in the program were more tolerant. (DuBois & Okorodudu, 1984).

Staff members at the bureau collected data on student responses to assembly programs. Their information, which was anecdotal, suggested that students had more positive feelings about their own ethnic groups after participating in the assemblies than before participating. For example, bureau staff reported that German students at Tenafly High School were less fearful of being identified as members of a minority group after an assembly on German Americans (Montalto, 1982). While the bureau's informal information did not convince their critics of the value of assembly programs, it inspired their supporters and became part of the folklore that increased the bureau's influence in schools (Montalto).

In June of 1939, the General Education Board (GEB) of the New York City schools budgeted $8,000 for an evaluation of the bureau's programs (DuBois & Okorodudu, 1984). The evaluation focused on the practices of teachers who were using the bureau's materials and were consulting with bureau staff. A special advisory committee composed of distinguished social scientists, including Otto Klineberg, Harry Stack Sullivan, Donald Young, and E. Franklin Frazier, was created to help organize the evaluation. The committee asked Genevieve Chase to direct the evaluation. Chase was the director of research for the district. Chase and her staff interviewed teachers, administrators, and students; observed intercultural education programs in progress; attended in-service courses; surveyed educators who used the bureau's materials; and conducted the day-to-day work required for the evaluation. The evaluation report was completed in January 1941. The report challenged the bureau's assumption that school programs based on the cultural contributions of ethnic and racial groups could reduce prejudice and increase cultural understanding. DuBois wrote a seven-page, single-spaced response to the findings in the report. She challenged the objectivity and thoroughness of the evaluation process and the accuracy of the evaluation findings. She did not receive a reply to her response and the evaluation report stood essentially unchallenged as a serious indictment of the bureau's effectiveness (DuBois & Okorodudu, 1984).

In order to promote her ideas and play a larger role in decision making, DuBois left the bureau in 1941. Later that year, she founded the Intercultural Education Workshop, which was also known as the Workshop for Cultural Democracy. A goal of the workshop was to promote the idea that cultural differences are a strength. DuBois worked with a number of notable individuals at the Workshop for Cultural Democracy, including Shirley Chisholm, the first Black congresswoman, and Lillian Smith, the social activist and author of *Killers of the Dream*.

After DuBois's departure from the bureau, other notables in the intercultural education movement, including William VanTil, who was director of learning materials for the bureau, and Helen Trager, who was director of the bureau's program on age-level studies, helped move the bureau beyond its earlier focus on cultural contributions (Kilpatrick & VanTil, 1947). Under the leadership of H. Harry Giles and other intercultural leaders, the bureau refocused its efforts on prejudice reduction. The bureau also worked to reassert its academic creditability through publications like the John Dewey Society's ninth yearbook, which was on intercultural education. The bureau provided staff support for the publication of the yearbook (Kilpatrick & VanTil).

The service bureau is an example of an organization that was influenced by both internal and external forces. The strong resolve and leadership of Rachel Davis DuBois exemplified an internal force that helped shape the goals and direction of the bureau. Funding sources illustrate the power external forces influenced over the direction of the bureau (Davis, 1999). Most importantly, the ebb and flow of support for the bureau paralleled the assimilation of White ethnics into mainstream society. The waning saliency of the bureau and its programs were a harbinger of the eventual demise of the intercultural education movement. By the 1960s when civil unrest threatened to paralyze a number of U.S. cities, the intergroup education movement was only a dim memory (Banks, 1996). The grandchildren of immigrants who had come to the United States at the turn of the twentieth century had settled conformably into the suburbs and were now part of mainstream America. The story of their parents and grandparents' early experiences in the United States with adversity and struggle had been rewritten as a narrative about the attainment of the American Dream.

The Springfield Plan

The Springfield Plan was a community-based plan designed by the citizens of Springfield, Massachusetts, to combat intergroup tensions through education. Leaders in Springfield were concerned about intergroup tensions because they recognized that limiting the ability of some citizens to fully participate in society could ultimately undermine democracy and limit everyone's freedom (Chatto, 1944). Reflecting prevalent progressive education sentiments of the day, the designers of the Springfield Plan saw the school as a place where students should not only learn about democracy; they should also experience it. That perspective was captured in a motto that was said to have been written by an elementary student and was displayed in one of the city's elementary schools. The motto read, "This is our school. It does not belong to the principal, to the teachers, to the pupils, or to the city. It belongs to all of us together" (Clinchy, 1942, p. 66). While there is scant evidence that the motto actually existed, the discussion of it in publicity materials on the Springfield Plan points to the importance that people promoting the plan placed on students exercising democracy.

The Springfield Plan was developed in 1939 and included community and school components. It was designed to help young people and adults acquire the skills, attitudes, and behaviors needed to understand and embrace the principles of democracy in a culturally diverse society (Alland & Wise, 1945; Chatto, 1944; Chatto & Halligan, 1945).

The idea for the Springfield Plan came out of a suggestion made by Professor Clyde R. Miller of Teachers College, Columbia University, to the leadership of the National Conference of Christians and Jews. He suggested that the organization try to identify a city that could serve as a laboratory to determine if it was possible for people to be accepted regardless of their ethnic, racial, religious, or class background. Miller had spent time in war-torn Germany and understood the dangers of unchecked prejudice. In August of 1939, the National Conference of Christians and Jews completed a survey that indicated that counter propaganda was not effective in reducing prejudice. The conference decided to take Miller's suggestion and look for a community where the school system could work with the community to implement democratic practices and reduce prejudice. Miller and officials of the National Conference of Christians and Jews met with John Granrud to discuss implementing an intercultural education program in Springfield. Granrud enthusiastically supported the idea.

Springfield was selected as the site for the program because it had many of the characteristics of middle-sized American communities whose demographic profiles had changed as a result of immigration and migration. Of the 130,000 people in Springfield in 1939, about 30% to 40% were considered "old" immigrants. Their descendents had come to the United States in the 1600s and 1700s (Green, 1886). The rest of the population were considered "new" immigrants. New immigrants included individuals who were Jewish, Irish, Italian, Polish, and Greek. The Springfield population also included Chinese and Filipino immigrants as well as Mexican Americans and African Americans. Springfield was also religiously diverse, with Catholics comprising approximately 60% of the population. The remaining 40% included Jews, Orthodox Greeks, and Protestants (Alland & Wise, 1945; Douglass, 1926). Although segregated housing and people with anti-Catholic and anti-Semitic feelings were present in Springfield, prejudice and discrimination weren't rampant. They were at a level that was typical for most northeastern communities of the day. The city also had several positive characteristics. Miller (1944) cited Springfield's high rating in Edward L. Thorndike's study of cities as one of the reasons Springfield was selected. In his study, Thorndike (1939) gave Springfield a high rating on his "goodness index" for its civic spirit, good newspapers, and strong school system. Ironically, a high percentage of Black families in a city was considered a negative factor on Thorndike's scale.

The first step Granrud took in initiating the plan was to convene the committee on Education for Democracy. The committee conducted surveys to determine the extent of prejudice and discrimination in Springfield and then developed an action plan to improve intergroup relations. Three key insights guided the committee's recommendations. The committee concluded that prejudice among students could not be addressed effectively by focusing exclusively on students. An effective program to reduce prejudice had to include the entire community. The committee also concluded that efforts to reduce prejudice and improve intergroup relations needed to be grounded in democratic principles with multiple opportunities for students to experience democracy both in the school and in the community. Finally, the committee recognized that teachers would need additional training to design and implement the kinds of curricular changes necessary to support the committee's recommendations (Alland & Wise, 1945). With this in mind, the committee recommended that provisions for teacher training be included in the plan.

After the committee issued its report, the Council on Adult Education and the Council of Social Agencies were formed. These groups, which included clergy of different faiths and members of business organizations, unions, and civic and social agencies, were responsible for the actual development of the plan (Alland & Wise, 1945). In addition to an extensive educational program for students and in-service training for teachers, the Springfield Plan included adult evening classes on subjects ranging from the duties and privileges of citizenship to ethnic cooking. It also provided opportunities for members of the community to attend musical concerts and forums on local and national civic problems. Perhaps most importantly, the plan provided an opportunity for people from diverse racial, ethnic, and religious backgrounds to identify common goals and work together to achieve them. The Springfield Plan exemplified the idea that tolerance could be taught (Alland & Wise, 1945).

Almost immediately after it was implemented the Springfield Plan won national acclaim as a prime example of the way to reduce intolerance. The League for Fair Play, an organization based in New York City, was largely responsible for publicizing the plan. Working with its educational consultant Dr. Clyde R. Miller, the league provided speakers, printed materials, and information on the plan's organizational procedures. Miller also personally conducted round table discussions about the plan for educators and members of civic groups. Articles about the plan were published in popular magazines such as *Parents' Magazine* and *Vogue* as well as in professional journals such as the *Journal of Education* and the *National Elementary Principal*. The plan was also discussed in newspaper articles throughout the United States and was the subject of a Warner Brothers film, *It Happened in Sprinfield*.

The Springfield Plan was considered a model for other cities to emulate. School officials from Pittsburgh and other U.S. cities sent representatives to Springfield to study the plan with the intent of implementing their own version of it. During the 1940s, community-based intercultural programs were implemented in Albany, New York; Gloversville, New York; Gary, Indiana; Detroit; and Philadelphia. The plans were not a mirror image of each other or of the Springfield Plan. They reflected the unique characteristics of each city and consequently differed in focus, organization, and sponsors. Some of the programs, such as the Philadelphia Program, began in the schools and then moved into the community. Others, such as the one in Gary, Indiana, were initiated by community organizations that worked with schools. School personnel initiated others. In describing the range of community-based programs, Mildred Biddick (1945), an administrative consultant for the Bureau for Intercultural Education, reported that the most important commonalties among the programs were that from the initial planning stages each of the programs provided the following:

1. As wide community participation as possible in planning.
2. Careful analysis of the community climate.
3. Formulation of step-by-step procedures.
4. Willingness to take the time required for the idea to mature, for people to develop a sense of personal investment in it and for a readiness for action to develop. (p. 6)

The Adult Council in Springfield evaluated the plan 5 years after it was implemented and concluded that it had a positive impact because adults and children in Springfield better understood the necessity for mutual respect. Citizens were more willing to accept the obligations of freedom in a democracy, which included living and working with people from diverse ethnic, racial, and religious backgrounds. The council also believed that Springfield citizens had a greater recognition and appreciation for the contributions that all U.S. citizens had made in building a unified nation. While many people in Springfield did not know the details of the plan, most recognized that it promoted team play in its broadest sense (Chatto & Halligan, 1945). Overall, the members of the Adult Council based their understanding of the plan's success on its role in creating a subtle change in the city's human climate.

The Springfield Plan began to come under more critical evaluation during the mid-1940s. Prior to that time, most accounts of the plan directly or indirectly promoted it. An early critique of the plan noted that describing it as a "plan" was inaccurate (Payne, 1946). The term *Springfield Plan* was a media invention, and only became popular after it was used in a *New York Times* article. Bresnahan (1971) notes that the Springfield Plan included several independent components, such as the authorization of a single salary schedule for teachers, the use of newsletters, an adult education program designed to foster stronger school–community ties, and the use of an examining board made up of administrators and members of the three major religions to select teachers.

In the early 1950s, rumors undermined the last vestiges of the plan by connecting it to subversive activities. Bresnahan (1971) reports that "A witness before the Senate's internal security subcommittee revealed that in a 1947 course for New York teachers she was told that the plan was introduced as "a softening up process done so carefully that to oppose [it] would have seemed sinful" (p. 157). Granrud resigned under pressure in the fall of 1945 amid an earlier controversy involving the plan. In the summer of 1946, Alden H. Blankenship was hired to replace Granrud. With

Granrud's departure, the plan was left without a local or national-level champion. It did, however, have critics in the Catholic community who were vying for more control of the schools and were interested in recruiting students into parochial schools. In a series of articles in Catholic publications such as the *Catholic Viewpoint* and the *Catholic Mirror*, Catholic leaders condemned public school education and promoted parochial education. Also, by the 1950s most White ethnics in Springfield were assimilating into the mainstream. Safe and secure in mainstream American society, they did not want to be reminded of their former second-class status or be associated with the ethnic and racial differences that were highlighted in the plan.

By the 1960s some elements of the plan, such as the policies on staff selection and the single-salary schedule, had been incorporated into standard practice in the school district. Other aspects of the plan, such as its intercultural education program, had faded. Its focus on a citywide response to prejudice and discrimination had also disappeared. In December of 1966 the Massachusetts State Advisory Committee reported that there was deep-rooted prejudice in the housing market in Springfield. It also noted that there was discrimination against certain religious groups in employment, education, and recreational facilities and clubs. It is ironic that only 2 decades before the Springfield Plan had been widely recognized for creating a climate that was antithetical to prejudice and discrimination.

During the 1960s, there were efforts to resurrect the term *Springfield Plan* to address intergroup tensions related to African Americans and old and new immigrants who were now both seen as Whites. However, those efforts failed to revive the plan. The intellectual and monetary support that was at the center of the creation of the Springfield Plan had moved on to other issues. The individuals who were trying to revive the plan did not have the social network necessary to finance, promote, and legitimize its resurrection.

The demise of the Springfield Plan suggests that the initiation, maintenance, and expansion of educational innovations are highly dependent on continued commitment by local political, business, civic, community, and educational leaders. They also require highly skilled individuals who can assist the school district in designing and implementing the innovation. Lastly, the personal hands-on involvement of high-level administrators can be very helpful in getting innovations to take hold in a school district. These factors are especially important in mounting effective programs in the area of intergroup education because such programs are frequently initiated in a social context marked by intergroup tension. Educational leaders who are in charge of intergroup education programs need to have the authority to hire and supervise the people who work closely with them as they implement the programs, the charisma and organizational skill to foster changes in staff attitudes, and the political acumen necessary to involve a multitude of diverse groups in a common effort. Developments associated with the demise of the Springfield Plan also suggest that educational leaders like John Grunrud face many serious challenges in their personal as well as professional lives. Therefore they must possess unusual courage and skill as they work to keep the educational ship on an even keel while navigating with, across, and often against pressures in the pursuit of their vision.

Center for Intergroup Education

Hilda Taba founded the Center for Intergroup Education at the University of Chicago in 1948 where it continued until 1951. Taba had been involved in early intercultural education activities, but her primary contribution in intercultural education occurred when the focus in the movement was shifting from White ethnics to racial minorities. Racial unrest and the ongoing assimilation of White ethnics into the mainstream precipitated that shift. Foundations and educational institutions stepped forward to respond to the widespread prejudice and discrimination that were highlighted by the riots in Detroit and other U.S. cities. Taba found support for the intellectual rigor that she brought to what was considered a national problem.

Taba (1945) approached her work in intergroup education as a curriculum theorist and scholar. She argued that intercultural issues were complex and that teachers needed to bring "the sharp tools of logic and intellectual analysis" to their work (Taba, 1945, p. 126). She feared that without a firm grasp of social science knowledge, teachers would turn to "superficial sentimentalism and the musical comedy variety of pageantry in place of a fundamental, systematic education" (p. 126).

Staff at the Center for Intergroup Education were especially interested in experimental programs in schools and communities that could help teachers diagnose the human relations needs of their students. Center programs were based on the belief that "only by studying what children know, understand, feel, and can do can teachers decide what they need to learn next" (Taba et al., 1951, p. 1). Center staff conducted research and reported their findings on effective ways to learn about the cultural backgrounds of students and the communities in which they lived. Taba also wrote about ways to evaluate methods used to reduce prejudice. One of her most important contributions was a series of books called *Studies in Intergroup Education* in which *Diagnosing Human Relations Needs* was the first volume.

Taba implemented her ideas on intergroup education and continued to research them through a series of leadership training workshops which were held at the University of Chicago from 1945 to 1950. Beginning in 1946, workshops were also held at Mills College in California and at Syracuse University in New York (Taba, 1953). Eighteen school districts participated in the leadership training workshops.

The workshops reflected Taba's appreciation for interdisciplinary approaches in intercultural education. Key concepts and ideas from anthropology, sociology, psychology, and other social sciences were brought to bear on the educational challenge of reducing intergroup tensions. Her workshops varied from those that focused on theoretical perspectives and content to those that emphasized practice and application. All of the workshops, however, had several common characteristics. They focused on teacher concerns and were organized around issues that grew out of classroom experiences. When working with teachers, Taba made sure that they had direct access to project staff, subject matter specialists, and the information they needed to refine their questions. The teachers didn't have to go through an intermediary. Additionally, they were encouraged to expand their understanding of human values by participating in community-based activities in which they could interact with people who held different values and perspectives on various issues. Finally, the workshop experiences were designed to promote cooperation among the teachers in planning and implementing projects (Taba, 1945).

In her evaluation of 3 years of intercultural workshops, Taba found that teachers needed to be actively involved with intercultural information. Knowledge alone was insufficient for reducing prejudice and creating an environment of understanding. It was important for teachers to experience what they were studying through role playing, simulations, or some other experiential avenue in which they would have an opportunity to take on the perspectives of people who were different from them and understand what others were experiencing. Taba (1945) noted that the intergroup workshops could be markedly improved if teachers had "an opportunity to first plan, secondly to practice [the planned activities] under supervision, and thirdly to re-plan in terms of practical experience" (p. 128). She also believed that provisions should be made for some component of the workshop to be conducted in a community setting where members of the community would be able to work with teachers to develop and refine the plan. Taba's carefully researched approach toward intergroup education supported the efforts of intercultural educators such as Leonard Covello and John Granrud, who linked their schools to the communities in which they were located.

The Project in Intergroup Education in Cooperating Schools was also implemented at the University of Chicago. Taba served as the director of the project from the time that it began in January 1945 until it ended in September 1948. The Project in Intergroup Education was one of the best-known programs developed by intergroup educators. During its height, it involved more than 250 local projects in 72 schools and 2,500 teachers, school administrators, and community members (Brady, 1992). The American Council on Education sponsored the project with financial support from the National Conference of Christians and Jews. Project staff worked cooperatively with classroom teachers to develop materials, approaches, and techniques to reduce prejudice and to identify ways to mobilize school and community resources to improve human relations and promote intergroup understanding (Taba et al., 1949).

Hilda Taba was an influential leader and decisive voice in the intergroup education movement (Brady, 1992). Her biographical journey in many ways marked her as what Collins (1990) refers to as "an outsider within." Taba was a woman in a man's world, an intellectual in a field characterized by social action, and an immigrant who, by many standards, succeeded in mainstream America. As an outsider within she, like other intercultural educators who were immigrants or members of the second generation, had firsthand experiences with prejudice and discrimination. She was also aware of gender discrimination. Yet there is little evidence in her writing that Taba saw herself as a feminist or believed that education could be a force for social change for women (Bernard-Powers, 1999).

LEADERSHIP MAKES A DIFFERENCE

Intercultural education grew out of a societal context in which immigrants and the second generation were in many ways considered second-class citizens. The organizations and activities discussed in this chapter provided an opportunity for individuals who had a common purpose to come together to respond to the collective needs of immigrants, the second generation, and minorities. These like-minded individuals developed bold and innovative organizations and approaches for responding to immigration, the role of immigrants in American society, and the impact of prejudice and discrimination on its perpetrators as well as its victims.

The intercultural educators and organizations that are featured in this chapter were selected because of their transformative qualities. As transformative leaders, DuBois, Taba, and Granrud were able to identify and respond to what Burns (1978) refers to as larger "end values such as liberty, equality, justice, [and] community" (p. 15). In doing so, their leadership took on a moral quality that involved them in social transformations intended to create a society in which those values could be actualized and where individuals could make the most of their human potential.

The case-study-like profiles that are presented in this chapter illustrate the extent to which values were an integral part of intercultural education. Each of the three leaders was able to communicate their values to the people around them and use values as a common foundation for creating a shared vision. Their leadership skills enabled them to use the visions to inspire others to join them in creating the three intercultural organizations discussed in this chapter. Their goal wasn't personal fame or fortune. Their goal, like that of all transformative leaders, was to grow, to be effective, and to implement principled social change (Burns, 1978).

Burns (1978) notes that leadership is part of a broader social process in which leaders and followers are connected. Consequently, transformative leadership is centered in relationships, not in positional authority. Leaders who move too far ahead of their followers run the risk of losing their effectiveness. All three of the leaders covered in this chapter ultimately lost touch with audiences that were essential for their continued success. DuBois and Granrud were asked to leave their positions as a result of internal conflict within leadership circles in their organizations. DuBois recognized that her ideas and positions were out of step with those of her funders and of the board. However, she refused to change and pushed the bureau in directions that resulted in her being forced out of the organization. Granrud's leadership was so closely linked with the Springfield Plan that when it came under fire, he was vulnerable. His profound and fundamental commitment to the mission of the plan helped to solidify and move it forward, but when it ran into problems it was easy for his detractors to challenge his effectiveness and his leadership. Ultimately, Taba left intergroup education and moved on to create a new career focus for herself. Funding to work on intergroup issues was becoming more difficult to secure when Taba left the University of Chicago. As a curriculum theorist, Taba was able to refocus her work on the social studies, where she incorporated many of her ideas from intergroup education.

Transforming Leadership

Rachel Davis DuBois, Hilda Taba, and John Granrud were transformative leaders who created innovative programs that gave a glimpse of what schools could be when they are linked to the community, what students could learn when they are engaged as respected knowers, and what teaching might become when teachers have the skills and knowledge to work effectively with a diverse population of students. The biographical journeys, values, and beliefs of these leaders influenced their thinking about schools and their understanding of the need for initiating change in them.

Their ideas and programs were initially praised and championed for their liberatory and forward-looking qualities, but as times changed their programs and ideas were challenged. We have much to learn from these leaders about the role that values, beliefs, and dedicated purpose can play in educational leadership. Their efforts are part of a long-term contribution to social change.

3

Linking Schools to the Communities They Serve

FROM the day its doors opened, Benjamin Franklin High School (BFHS) was a beacon of hope for a struggling and underprivileged community. To the immigrant and minority community it served, BFHS was their school, a school where they were welcomed, understood, and appreciated. Its location at 116th Street near the East River in East Harlem, New York City represented a new beginning for people who were on the margins of U.S. society. There was a sense among the people in East Harlem that things were changing for the better. "A new school in a new community" was a phrase heard throughout the community when BFHS opened in 1934.

Leonard Covello, an Italian immigrant, was the first principal of Benjamin Franklin High School. Covello was born in Avigliano, Potenza (Italy) and came to the United States at the age of 10 with his parents. During his childhood he lived in the East Harlem community where BFHS was located. Covello was a studious child and an outstanding student at Morris High School. After high school he entered Columbia University, where he graduated Phi Beta Kappa in 1911. Years later, he received his Ph.D. in education from New York University. Before becoming principal at Benjamin Franklin High School, Covello taught languages in New York City high schools and served as the head of the Italian Department at DeWitt Clinton High School. Covello was a sought-after speaker and was considered a gifted teacher (Perrone, 1998). While serving as the principal at BFHS he taught courses in the evenings and during the summer at New York University, Columbia University Extension, Hunter College Extension, and Montclair Teachers State College.

Covello (1939b) believed that America could be "enriched by the cultural heritage of all the world without sacrificing any degree of that which is essentially American" (p. 11). He incorporated that belief into BFHS's community outreach programs, school curricula, and teacher-student interactions. Working with a cadre of dedicated teachers and administrators,

Covello created structures that linked BFHS to the community. He also implemented an in-service intercultural education program to give BFHS teachers the support they needed to work effectively with East Harlem students and their parents.

Many of the educational issues that confronted teachers at BFHS in the early 1930s bear a striking resemblance to problems educators are grappling with in today's schools and classrooms. The ideas and practices that Covello and the teachers at BFHS designed and applied to the intercultural problems they faced are still viable today. However, their work has largely been forgotten. Consequently many people believe that the educational problems we face today are unique to our time. Teachers wonder aloud how they can be expected to teach in schools where many of their students and their parents do not speak English, where conflict between groups require that they "police" the hallways, and where the economic and family characteristics of their students seem so different from their own. This chapter transports us back to the 1930s and 1940s and allows us to see how Covello and the teachers at BFHS worked to create an educational environment in which diversity was considered an asset.

BENJAMIN FRANKLIN HIGH SCHOOL: A SCHOOL CENTERED IN THE COMMUNITY

East Harlem in the 1930s and 1940s was a low-income immigrant community in which Italian Americans were one of the dominant groups. Neighborhood studies conducted by BFHS teachers and students on the ethnic and racial backgrounds of the people in East Harlem indicated that in 1930 233,400 people lived in the community. Approximately 80,000 of them were Italians, 29,422 African Americans, 28,000 Jews, 19,000 Irish, 5,000 British, 4,000 Slavs, 4,000 Scandinavians, and 1,500 Greeks. The remaining population included Whites who were born in the United States of American-born parents, and members of other races (Covello, 1936).

Soon after BFHS opened, it was clear that the school couldn't simply focus on teaching and learning; it had to address the social and economic needs of its students. The school staff provided free lunches, carfare, clothes, shoes, and other necessities of life to the young men who attended BFHS. As the social service component of the school expanded and became an integral part of the school, a teacher was assigned to direct community outreach activities. Commenting on the economic and social needs of BFHS students, Covello (1939b) stated that ". . . the work of the school became so intimately associated with the life of the community that it became inconceivable to think of the school in terms other than a neighborhood agency dispensing not only education but many other aids necessary to a happier community life" (p. 14). Covello understood that students had a life outside of school. Problems they faced in their homes and communities didn't disappear as soon as students stepped inside BFHS.

Benjamin Franklin High School was a student-centered, rather than a subject-centered, school. As such, the school was concerned with students' home life and social background. Teachers recognized that school was not the only place where learning took place. There were powerful disruptive as well as constructive forces in their students' communities and homes that both contributed to as well as detracted from their education. Teachers used questionnaires to find out more about their students' home lives, needs, handicaps, and emotions. Students were asked questions about the following:

- Their place of birth, as well as that of their fathers and mothers;
- The number of years each parent had lived in the United States;
- The number of siblings in their families;
- The language spoken in their home;
- The employment status of their fathers;
- Difficulties they were experiencing at school;
- The cause of the difficulties they were experiencing;
- Their ideas about how they could be helped.

When problems of truancy and delinquency occurred or whenever there was a need for assistance with students, teachers had the support of a special staff of home visitors who were hired to go to students' homes and talk with their parents. The home visitors were bilingual and were familiar with East Harlem. Covello (1939a) believed that immigrant families should be communicated with in their mother tongue. He stated that talking to parents about school programs or student concerns in a language they didn't understand simply "leaves them stranded" without the information they need to support their children (p. 324). Covello also believed in nipping problems in the bud instead of letting them grow larger. He didn't hesitate to call parents and ask them to come to the school for special interviews if a problem arose. In that way the problem could be responded to quickly and positively before it became more serious.

Long before educators recognized the importance of engaging students' preconceptions about key concepts and issues (Donovan, Bransford, & Pellegrino, 1999), teachers at BFHS sought to identify and build on their students' personal and cultural knowledge. James A. Banks (1993) states that personal and cultural knowledge consists of "the concepts, explanations, and interpretations that students derive from personal experiences in their homes, families, and community culture" (p. 9). Students use personal and cultural knowledge to interpret their school experiences and their experiences in other institutions within the larger society. By building on their students' personal and cultural knowledge and by linking the school to the community, BFHS teachers were not only able to see their students as they were seen in the community; they were able to gain a better understanding of how their students saw the school. Understanding their students' personal and cultural knowledge gave BFHS teachers a basis for challenging their preconceptions. For example, teachers were able to better understand their students' ideas and beliefs about gender roles; their concerns about interacting with people who were ethnically, racially, and regionally different; as well as other preconceptions the students formed in their homes and communities. As a result of their increased understanding of their students' personal and cultural knowledge as well as through their connections with the community and the adult school, BFHS teachers were able to uncover, challenge, and ultimately provide adults and young people in East Harlem with new ways of viewing the world and their position in it.

Diversity Within the Italian American Community

Linking a school to a community requires deep knowledge of the community and the diversity within it. East Harlem wasn't a single community, and the Italian Americans who lived there didn't constitute a single group. People in the community had different perspectives, concerns, and allegiances. To outsiders, ethnic communities are frequently seen as monolithic; composed of people who essentially look and act in similar ways. Intragroup diversity can be invisible to outsiders who don't have a deep understanding of the ethnic or racial group. Ethnics, however, are very aware of their differences. Leonard Covello (1936) used his understanding of intragroup differences in the Italian American community to gain legitimacy with parents and to secure community support for his educational program. He was able to help teachers at Benjamin Franklin High School become aware of and respond sensitively to intragroup differences within the Italian American community in East Harlem.

What Teachers Needed to Know and Understand About Italian Americans. The time period in which they emigrated to the United States as well as the region in Italy they called home were important markers of difference among Italian immigrants. Four-fifths of the Italians who came to the United States came either from the *mezogiorno*, that part of the Italian peninsula south of Rome, or from Sicily. Driven by hard economic times, high taxation, and the impact of disease on the grape vineyards, they left Italy in search of a better life. Over half of the immigrants were between 14 and 49 years old. Between 1881 and 1910, four-fifths of the immigrants were male, and between 1911 and 1930 about two-thirds were male. Most of the Italian immigrants who came to the United States during the late 1800s and early 1900s were poor, uneducated, unskilled transient agricultural workers in the *mezogiorno*. When they arrived in the United States, the jobs that were available to them, such as working in coal mines, required long hours and hard work (Allen & Turner, 1988)

Immigrants from northern Italy, most of whom arrived in the United States before 1880, were comfortably settled in the United States when large numbers of immigrants from southern Italy began arriving. Unlike those from southern Italy, many of the northern Italians who emigrated to the United States came with marketable skills. They were educated professionals or skilled tradesmen such as stone cutters and masons (Allen & Turner, 1988). Their background in northern Italy, which was the most prosperous region of the country, provided a strong foundation for their assimilation into the U.S. mainstream. Over time they were integrated into the social and civic life of the communities in which they lived. Their hard-earned status, however, was threatened by the arrival of their poor and uneducated cousins from southern Italy and Sicily. Instead of embracing them, many northern Italians were ashamed of the cultural characteristics of the new immigrants and held them in disdain (Orsi, 1985).

While northern Italians and mainstream Americans may have seen the southern Italians as a single group, the southern Italians didn't see themselves as a holistic group. From their perspective, their differences were salient. To them nationality was less important than region. Southern Italians identified with their region or village. Italy, after all, did not become a unified nation until 1871. Italians came together in U.S. neighborhoods that were often made up of people who came from the same region or village in Italy (Allen & Turner, 1988). In Springfield, Illinois, for example, Italians from Abruzzi lived in Starnes Park, Venetians lived in Deveraux Heights, and Sicilians lived near 10th and Carpenter Streets (Bernard, 1976). There was a sense of kinship among people from the same region that didn't extend to people from other regions. People from different regions often spoke different dialects and couldn't easily communicate with each other. Dialects and other regional variations resulted in allegiances as well as animosities within the Italian American community.

Over time regional distinctions became less significant and ethnicity became a unifying concept. The ancestral village was less important to the second and third generation than it was to their fathers and mothers. As subsequent generations interacted with Italian Americans from different regions as well as people outside the Italian American community, their identity began to shift from the village to a larger Italian American identity. These shifts, however, were not always evident in BFHS's adult school.

Adult Education at Benjamin Franklin High School

There were two educational programs at Benjamin Franklin High School— a regular high school for boys and the adult school. While conceptually separate, the two schools were linked through school–community committees, a shared facility, and families that had siblings in the regular school and the adult school. The school building was open continuously from 8:30 a.m. to 10:00 p.m. Monday through Friday. The regular school program ran during the morning and early afternoon and the adult school operated during the late afternoon and evening. The curriculum at the adult school included English and courses designed to build vocational skills. Multilingual naturalization aides were also on staff at the adult school. Their job was to assist members of the community who were having difficulties with their naturalization papers.

In addition to providing a wide range of support to people in East Harlem, a major aim of the adult school was to increase intercultural understanding among the more than 36 different ethnic groups in the immediate community. Educators at Benjamin Franklin recognized that the attitudes, values, and behaviors of parents, older siblings, and other members of the community influenced the attitudes of students in the school. If they were going to eliminate intolerance among students in the school, they had to go out into the community and find ways to increase understanding and appreciation of difference among adults.

Covello's experience growing up in an ethnic community helped him to understand that adults did not always realize the extent to which their attitudes and opinions were reflected in the attitudes and behaviors of their children. He believed that most parents didn't understand how their intolerance and unkind behavior toward people from other ethnic, racial, regional, and religious groups could harm their children. The adult school provided a space where negative ideas about ethnic, racial, religious, and other differences could be challenged and hopefully transformed. Two approaches that were commonly used in the adult school to reduce prejudice were: first, to put members of different social groups in direct contact with each other in integrated classes. While in those classes students would work cooperatively on class projects. Consequently, students worked with people they would not have had contact with outside of school. Second, innovative curricula that could give students an opportunity to learn about and discuss information on the cultural characteristics and accomplishments of people from different ethnic and racial groups were integrated into a wide range of subjects, from cooking to citizenship education.

When the adult school opened there was some concern that people in East Harlem would not be interested in attending an afternoon or evening educational program. However, through the efforts of BFHS teachers who mounted an intense outreach program and Covello, who served as principal of both the regular and Adult School, enrollment in the adult school grew. By 1939, Covello reported that more than 1,700 adults had enrolled in English language, sewing, cooking, and other classes at the school. At its height the adult school had 46 classes and 26 teachers, some of whom also worked at the day school.

INTERCULTURAL EDUCATION AT BFHS

By the 1930s the rampant nativism of earlier years had waned and been replaced by a more benign push for assimilation. There was a sense that, with immigration restricted, the second generation would not be exposed to the ongoing reinforcement of ethnic culture and, with more sympathetic support, the second generation would be able to assimilate quickly into the American mainstream. Intercultural educators at BFHS wanted their students to assimilate into the mainstream of U.S. society. However, they did not believe it was necessary for them to abandon their ethnic culture in order to do so. Covello and the teachers at BFHS were committed to using education to reduce prejudice and discrimination and to helping students recognize and appreciate the United States as an ethnically, racially, and religiously diverse society. They worked with a broad range of groups, including ethnic organizations such as the Anti-Defamation League of B'nai B'rith, community-based groups like the Young Men's Christian Association (YMCA), educational groups like the Service Bureau for Intercultural Education, and religious groups like the Churches of Christ in America to accomplish their goals. BFHS was aligned with a number of organizations that were heavily influenced and frequently led by members of the second generation. Covello and the teachers at BFHS worked well with these groups because they shared a core value: that ethnic, racial, and religious diversity added to the richness of American life.

While assimilation remained an important national goal for most Americans, including intercultural educators, the idea that cultural maintenance could also benefit society was an important part of the educational discourse at BFHS. Covello believed that responding to ethnic groups in a more positive way could help reduce tension among members of different social groups. He was aware of social science knowledge that supported his position as well as information that indicated that immigrants would not easily relinquish their rich connection to and appreciation for their ancestral homelands and people. Stewart G. Cole (1941), director of the West Coast Office of the Bureau for Intercultural Education, echoed that perspective when he said that "it is not possible for immigrant people to forget their past; they cannot shift cultures as they would change a suit of clothes" (p. 18). With these values and beliefs as his foundation, Covello and the teachers at BFHS began thinking about how they could incorporate intercultural education into the curriculum.

What Teachers Were Taught About Intercultural Education

One of the problems that Covello faced in implementing intercultural education at BFHS was the preparation of teachers. Most of the teachers at BFHS were concerned about discrimination and prejudice and were aware of intercultural tensions in the United States and particularly those in New York City. However, for the most part, the teachers were subject-matter specialists who did not know how to deal with issues related to race and culture in the classroom.

Covello used a two-prong approach to increase the intercultural skills, knowledge, and attitudes of BFHS teachers and administrators. First he implemented a schoolwide in-service training program for teachers which focused on both teachers and students. The teacher component of the program gave teachers an opportunity to read and discuss books about ethnic and racial groups and related issues. In this way BFHS teachers were able to better understand the concepts, ideas, and rationale for intercultural education. They were also given an opportunity to learn about intercultural activities, materials, and assembly programs that were available for students and were encouraged to develop their own activities, materials, and programs. BFHS teachers integrated the new intercultural information they received in the in-service program with their subject-matter knowledge and began to transform their curricula. Intercultural ideas and perspectives were integrated into English, social studies, biology, and other subject areas. Rita Morgan and several other BFHS teachers and administrators became known for their innovative curricula through articles in subject-matter journals and through presentations given at professional meetings (Bleifeld, et al., 1939; Fields, 1938).

Intercultural Workshops. Covello worked with the Service Bureau for Education in Human Relations and his longtime friend Rachel Davis DuBois to provide intercultural training for teachers at BFHS. BFHS teachers and administrators met in Covello's office with representatives from the service bureau to design an in-service training plan for the school. The teacher component of the plan involved small group meetings between representatives from the bureau and BFHS teachers. They discussed intercultural education, read material on the contributions of immigrant groups, and were trained in the intercultural program that was implemented with students. The student program employed a three-level approach:

- *An Emotional Approach*:
    This approach included assemblies with guest speakers and performances. The goal of this approach was to give students a chance to see the rich cultural traditions of their classmates.
- *A Situational Approach*:
    The situational approach provided an opportunity for students to engage in informal conversations with community members who could talk about ethnic or cultural issues. The conversations were arranged to give students a chance to get to know people on a personal basis who were from a different ethnic group.
- *An Intellectual Approach*:
    This approach focused on content. During homeroom, students read and discussed information about the cultural characteristics, contributions, and experiences of various ethnic groups. This information wasn't covered in their school texts and was new information for most of the students. The information was provided in the form of pamphlets and booklets produced by the service bureau. Examples of intergroup booklets are listed in figure 3.1.

In commenting on the in-service training at BFHS, Covello noted that it was vital, alive, real, and, most importantly, it was popular with teachers. Covello's leadership at BFHS was instrumental in the success of the intercultural in-service training program. He was able to calm the fears of people who did not support the program as well as overcome other expected and unexpected difficulties. Covello was encouraged by the success of his initial efforts to train BFHS teachers in intercultural education (Covello, 1937). His approach toward school change could be summed up in one of his old sayings: "The job could be done – if we willed it strong enough." Covello had a will of steel and was totally committed to linking BFHS to the community. Intercultural education was a critical part of his vision of community schooling.

In addition to the in-service education programs offered at BFHS, teachers were encouraged to attend summer workshops in human relations.

Figure 3.1. Examples of Intercultural Education
Materials Developed at Teachers College,
Columbia University

German Contributions in Physics;

Italians in Chemistry and Physics;

Poles in American Agricultural Life;

Jewish Orchestra Conductors in American life;

Lue Gim Gong: A Chinese American Horticulturist;

Jewish Participation in Colonial America;

Mexican Mural Painters and Their Influence in the United States;

The Negro Contribution to Folk Music in America;

Japanese Flower Arrangement.

Source: Montalto, N. V. (1982). *A history of the intercultural educational movement 1924–1941* (p. 95). New York: Garland Publishing.

Scholarships covering registration fees, tuition, and room and board were offered to New York City teachers who attended intercultural workshops, which were held at Stanford University, the University of Michigan, and other major U.S. universities. The summer programs focused on helping teachers learn how to work more effectively with racial, religious, class, national, and ethnic groups.

Intercultural Education in the Classroom. Covello and the teachers at BFHS used social science knowledge and research techniques to design their curriculum. One of their first steps in formulating new curricula was to investigate how BFHS students felt about each other. Covello purchased a questionnaire from the Service Bureau in Human Relations for 30 dollars (a significant amount at that time) and used it to survey BFHS students about their attitudes toward diverse groups. In later years, the faculty developed their own questionnaire. Covello noted that in order to mitigate prejudice and intolerance in both the school and the community it is necessary to:

- ascertain how students feel about one another,
- identify the nature and cause of interracial conflicts,
- find out how different social groups are perceived in the community,
- identify facts and values that can help students increase their tolerance of people who are different from them,

- investigate the extent to which information given to students is retained and used in decision-making, and
- investigate the extent to which interventions alter previously held attitudes.

The information collected in the questionnaire was used to design curricula that could address gaps in student knowledge and focus curricular attention on areas where there were misunderstandings about social groups. To get some insights on the effectiveness of their curricula, BFHS teachers assessed students at the end of curriculum units dealing with diversity. They used their data on student learning to create teaching units directly related to the intercultural needs and problems of students both in the school and in the community. They also used the data to develop new school policies.

In 1944, "Living Together with Others," "Mankind Grows Up," "Understanding America," and "The Literature of Moral Attitudes and Social Problems" were themes that were woven through the BFHS English curriculum. Joseph Gallant, the head of the English Department at Benjamin Franklin High School, believed that these themes gave teachers enough flexibility to explore a range of issues related to race relations, nationality, prejudice, stereotypes, and the interrelationships of world religions. In addition to exploring these issues, English teachers at BFHS helped students become critical readers. Readings such as *The ABC's of Scapegoating*, *The Footprints of the Trojan Horse* by the Citizenship Educational Service, and *Divide and Conquer* by the Office of War Information were used at BFHS to teach students how to analyze propaganda.

The Races of Mankind by Ruth Benedict and G. Wetfish, along with its companion 35-minute silent filmstrip titled "We Are All Brothers," was used in biology classes to challenge the myth of the supremacy of the Aryan race. *The Races of Mankind* was a widely disseminated booklet that simply yet scientifically explained why it wasn't possible for positive human traits such as intelligence, character, and others to be present in only one race. BFHS teachers believed it was important to confront racial stereotypes because at that time it was widely believed that there was a hierarchy of races. Information about race that was covered in biology classes was reinforced in English, math, and other classes. To a great extent, BFHS students received a consistent message throughout the curriculum about race and the importance of respect, recognition, and positive intergroup relations.

Teacher Research at BFHS

Teachers at Benjamin Franklin were involved in research to improve their practice. For example, with support from the Rockefeller Foundation they investigated the influence of motion pictures on young people. The teachers were particularly interested in the extent to which films could be used to help students discuss personal and social issues and the extent to which talking about those issues could influence student attitudes and behaviors. Several English classes were identified for the study. Scenes from *Black Legion, Fury, The Life of Louis Pasteur, Men in White,* and other popular movies were shown to the students. Information drawn from surveys and observations was used to critically evaluate student responses to the movies. Insights from the surveys and observations were used to generate discussions with students and to identify areas where additional readings and information was needed.

Another example of teacher research at BFHS involved program evaluation. To determine the effectiveness of intercultural education at BFHS, a study was conducted in which an experimental group and a control group were identified. The experimental group included several hundred BFHS students who had completed an intercultural course that lasted from September 1938 to January 1939. The course was designed to combat prejudice and intolerance. It included a series of facts about the cultures and contributions of BFHS's largest ethnic groups: African Americans, Jewish Americans, Italian Americans, and Puerto Ricans on the mainland. The course gave students an opportunity to discuss stereotypes and misunderstandings about the groups that were widespread in East Harlem. For many of the boys, it was their first exposure to the idea of "brotherhood" and the commonality of cultures. The control group, which consisted of a similar group of boys who attended school at the 79th Street Annex, did not receive intercultural instruction. At the end of the experiment, the two groups were given a questionnaire designed to measure attitude changes that may have occurred. While these studies showed the positive impact of intercultural education, they weren't definitive. They did, however, illustrate the BFHS faculty's concerns about the effectiveness of their curricula and the professional and scientific way that they approached their work.

Teachers at Benjamin Franklin High School had many questions that could only be answered with research. They were particularly interested in finding out more about the following questions:

1. *When should intercultural education instruction begin? What causes people to respond negatively to people on a purely racial basis?* These were also questions that social scientists were raising. Social science research ultimately showed that children's racial attitudes are influenced much earlier than was commonly expected (Goodman, 1952; Lasker, 1929; Minard, 1931; Williams & Moreland, 1976). This research supported the contention of BFHS educators that intercul-

tural education had to begin in the primary years and continue through adult classes.

2. *What types of educational programs best prepare high school students to assume civic and social responsibilities and contribute to intercultural harmony?* This question reflected the staff's understanding that community improvement was an important goal of schooling. It also highlighted the faculty's commitment to education that included civic and social goals as well as academic ones.

3. *What is the most effective way to involve the community in a school-based intercultural education program?* This question was based on the assumption that there should be a strong connection schools and the communities in which they are located. There was an understanding at BFHS that when planning a school-community intercultural program all elements in the community should participate in order to benefit the whole community.

INFORMING SCHOOL KNOWLEDGE
THROUGH COMMUNITY INVOLVEMENT

The second component of Covello's plan to implement intercultural education at BFHS involved linking the school to the community. He believed that there were several reasons why schools and communities should be in partnership. First and foremost, many intergroup educators saw the community as an extension of the school. According to Covello (1939a), the community was "the larger classroom of people in which the school assumes the role of leader" (p. 326). There was also a sense that the school could not be effective in educating students without understanding their homes and communities. Covello (1939a) argued that "a child's brain cannot be dissociated from the sum total of his body and its many experiences, and that, likewise, it is impossible to subtract the child as a whole from the sum total of his experiences as a part of a family, a community, and the nation" (p. 326). According to Covello, education had to reach into the home and draw it to the school. He argued that the language teacher, perhaps more than anyone else, could play an important role in drawing the home to the school. Figure 3.2 contains a list, developed at BFHS, of recommended ways that teachers could work with the community. The list illustrates how teachers can gain a better understanding of how parents interact with their children, what parents expect of their children, and the competencies children demonstrate in the community that may not always be evident at school.

Linking the school to the community was more difficult for Covello to organize and execute than implementing an in-service program for BFHS

Figure 3.2. Recommended Ways to Link the School with the Community

1. Make a study of the community in which you are teaching.
2. Choose one, or more, of the ethnic groups that attracts your interest and make a special study of its history, literature, music, and art.
3. List material that would be adaptable for use in an intercultural program.
4. Plan a series of lectures, entertainments, or plays through which information may become available to other nationality groups and through which members of a particular ethnic group may derive pleasure and satisfaction.
5. Offer to serve on school-community committees working on the community program.
6. Become a member of a Speakers Committee to speak in a familiar language to special community groups.
7. Offer to be in school at times to assist in interviewing non-English-speaking parents.
8. Volunteer to be present now and then at public school affairs where a receiving committee speaking many languages would make all comers feel welcome in the school.
9. Organize field tours for groups of the foreign-born, taking them to museums and points of interest outside their isolated community boundaries.
10. Keep in touch with all organizations working in the field of intercultural education and make the results of your personal experience known to them.
11. Offer to meet at regular intervals with children's groups in the neighborhood, giving them something of their own cultural background and interpreting to them more fully the America of which they have become a part.
12. Aid in collecting books of special interest and value to the foreign-born for use in a neighborhood reading room.
13. Prepare selected bibliographies for adults and children, both in a native language and in English and list also books of particular interest to others who wish to acquaint themselves rapidly with the cultural background of the particular ethnic groups in which you may have become interested.
14. Write books that you believe are needed.
15. Keep in touch with libraries in the community and help make their services know to people in the community.
16. Stress at all times the significance of language as a factor in adjustment and the need for a wider study of languages and heritages of the various ethnic groups.
17. Organize and sponsor language clubs in which English and the familiar language would be spoken, aiding thereby in securing more rapidly a more fluent use of English.
18. Prepare material of value to the school-community program for use in the foreign-language press.
19. Emphasize the fine things in various foreign cultures, but also help the foreign born to realize that not all contributions from foreign cultures are adaptable in a democracy. There must be a clean-cut line of demarcation between cultural propaganda with political objects inimical to the ideals of democracy and the presentation of desirable values in the various cultural heritages.
20. Strive to create leadership and to guard young people against the confusion that necessarily arises when the clean-cut line of embarkation between educational and political objectives in cultural programs is not observed.

Source: Covello, 1939b, pp. 331–332.

teachers. Covello had to set up structures that would allow and encourage community members to work closely with teachers. A wide range of community–school committees composed of parents, community members, teachers, and administrators were developed to link the school to the community. Covello also had to convince BFHS teachers that the committees were important enough for them to support and staff. Many, though not all, of the teachers at BFHS were committed to working both in the school and in the community. Securing community members to work with the school was relatively easy. A strong and well-organized community effort had been underway in East Harlem for several years. Civic groups were instrumental in advocating for a new school in East Harlem. Consequently, many individuals and groups in East Harlem saw BFHS as the community's school. They felt comfortable in voicing their perspectives and concerns about school curriculum, texts, and activities to Covello. For them, Covello's efforts to institutionalize community involvement at BFHS was expected and welcomed.

The difficulty in linking the school to the community was that East Harlem wasn't a single community. It was a diverse community composed of encapsulated social groups with norms that discouraged social interactions with outsiders. However, to the extent possible, Covello made sure that BFHS was a place where diverse groups could feel at home and be respected; a place where people believed they would be treated fairly. As the community's school, everyone in the community had a stake in making sure that BFHS succeeded. The school was a focal point for the community and as such helped pull the diverse community together.

Working with Parents and Other Members of the Community

Teachers at BFHS faced a tremendous challenge when they tried to involve parents in the school. Many of their students' parents were foreign-born, did not speak English, and couldn't read letters or school brochures written in English. Moreover, they weren't interested in attending meetings where all of the business was conducted in a language they didn't understand. In addition to language barriers, some parents, as a result of negative experiences at school or the formality of the school setting, did not initially believe they were welcome at BFHS.

In an effort to break down those barriers, communications to parents were sent out in several languages, including English, Italian, Spanish, German, and Yiddish. Covello and other educators at Benjamin Franklin High School who were multilingual made presentations to community groups in the language of the members of the group. In many cases, when parents came to the school they were able to work with staff members who knew their language. Covello and several members of the BFHS staff were fluent in Italian. Communicating with parents in their mother tongue allowed the school staff to talk directly with parents without using children as intermediaries. Most importantly, it helped to restore parents as the heads of their households by giving them the information they needed to make good decisions for their children and to influence their behavior.

Working effectively with the community required not only a multilingual staff, but a staff that was visible in the community. Soon after BFHS opened Covello began working to make the school and the teachers who worked there more visible in the community. He joined community organizations and encouraged the teachers to become active in the community. He also made sure that the school had networks in the community. BFHS was an institutional member of several community organizations, including the East Harlem Council of Social Agencies, of which Covello was vice president. When teachers needed to meet with parents, they were encouraged to meet at community sites. For example, parent conferences were held in a wide range of places in the community, including the East Harlem Health Center, the Neighborhood Music School, and the Union Settlement House. Covello believed that by getting outside the school and going into the community, teachers would be able to broaden their knowledge of the community and to make valuable personal contacts.

Covello also established the BFHS Association of Parents, Teachers, and Friends. He believed working with parents and members of the community were among the most important aspects of his work at Benjamin Franklin High School. In addition to the association, Covello established the Friends and Neighbors Club, a family club where parents, grandparents, and young people could meet and plan activities. Club activities included art, sewing, and cooking classes. When school committees met on Saturdays or after school hours, they would meet at the club. At other times they would meet at the school. Members of the association helped maintain the club and acted as hostesses at neighborhood meetings.

Not everyone at BFHS supported Covello's commitment to community schooling. Some of Covello's strongest opposition resulted from his effort to acknowledge and respond to the wide range of languages spoken in the community. Educators who believed it was important for immigrants to learn English were afraid that the school's validation of multiple languages would discourage people from learning English. Covello did not yield to the opposition he encountered. He believed that in order for parents to understand and ultimately support the goals of the school, they had to understand them. He also believed that when possible, the mother tongue of the student's family should be used during school conferences. This would, according to Covello, reduce the parents' tension during conferences and encourage them to be active participants who could share their concerns and perspectives.

Even though Covello believed the school should have staff who could communicate with parents in their mother tongue, he also believed that non-English-speaking parents should be encouraged to learn English. As the parents learned English they would have an opportunity to gain a greater respect and appreciation for American ideals, customs, and values. Covello also thought that the second generation should be encouraged to learn their parents' language. This would enable parents and children to share experiences and strengthen their bond with each other. When parents and children share a language they can share experiences with each other, children can gain a sense of their ethnic heritage, and parents can gain increased ability to provide supervision and direction to their children.

Students as well as teachers were involved in community outreach activities. Through school committees like the Speaker's Committee, BFHS was able to take its message out to the community. Members of the committee spoke to community groups about school programs and services, and to student groups, the latter whom they encouraged to support each other. Committees such as the Big Brother and Juvenile Aid Committees provided an institutional structure that encouraged older students to help younger ones. Students who served on the committees were selected by their teachers. The teachers primarily used two criteria—leadership and high grades—to identify students to serve on committees. Committee work was seen as a way to help students develop critical judgment, self-discipline, and decision-making skills. By helping students develop these skills, teachers believed they were preparing students to be successful both in school and in life.

Covello believed that when students worked with adults in the community, both the adults as well as the students benefited. The give-and-take of the working relationship allowed for a bond to be established between the older and wiser adult group and the younger, more idealistic, student group. Moreover, the type of educational experience that resulted from working on a school-community committee could not be provided in school classrooms. The affirmation, attention, informal discussions, and counseling offered by elders in the community gave BFHS students direction and a sense of importance.

Social Action at BFHS

Linking the school to the community went beyond simply working with community members and parents to gain support for the school's goals. Covello believed teachers should be advocates for positive change in East

Harlem. This aspect of Covello's philosophy was reflected in the establishment of two BFHS committees: the Housing Committee and the Guidance Committee and Placement Bureau.

Housing was a problem in East Harlem. Many of the residence apartments in the congested community were old tenement houses that were badly in need of repair. The Housing Committee's charge was to help secure better housing for low-income families in East Harlem. The committee, which was composed of teachers, students, and community members, conducted a study of housing needs in East Harlem and used their data to advocate for a low-rent housing project. In addition to grounding their argument for improved housing in empirical data, the committee also organized a grassroots campaign to advocate for better housing in East Harlem. Figure 3.3 illustrates the interconnected way that the committee was linked to the community. The committee worked to make housing a visible and important community issue by holding community forums and encouraging people to get involved on the committee. In January 1939, for example, BFHS sponsored a community theater party at the Adelphi Theatre. *One-Third of the Nation*, a play dramatizing the problem of poor housing, was performed for parents, teachers, students, and community members. The play presented the housing issue in an accessible and galvanizing way to people from many different walks of life. The committee's efforts eventually resulted in some, though limited, improved housing in East Harlem.

BFHS's Guidance Committee and Placement Bureau was also involved in social action. However, instead of addressing issues outside of the school, this committee provided support to BFHS students. Teachers, counselors, and community members worked with BFHS students to help prepare them for the world of work. They also established a network among New York City businessmen who could employ BFHS students. The committee developed a list of job openings by contacting businessmen to identify their labor needs. This committee was particularly helpful given the scarcity of jobs. BFHS developed such a good reputation with local businesses that when job openings occurred employers frequently called the school for qualified applicants.

Addressing Racial Conflict Through School-Community Committees. Covello believed that the tensions and overt conflicts between various racial and ethnic groups that occurred in the community had to be addressed at school. Therefore, during the first year of the school's operation, a committee was formed to promote racial understanding and cooperation. The process that Covello used to link the committee to the community is an example of his philosophy and his power in the community. The commit-

Figure 3.3. The Role of the School in a Housing Program for the Community

```
                ┌─────────────────────────────────────┐
                │     BENJAMIN FRANKLIN HIGH SCHOOL     │
                └─────────────────────────────────────┘
                          ┌──────────────────┐
                          │    COMMUNITY      │
                          │    ADVISORY       │
                          │    COUNCIL        │
                          └──────────────────┘
        ┌──────────────────────────────────────────────────┐      ┌──────────────┐
        │        SCHOOL–COMMUNITY COMMITTEES                │      │   HARLEM     │
        └──────────────────────────────────────────────────┘      │ LEGISLATIVE  │
              REPRESENTED BY 1. STUDENTS                           │ CONFERENCE   │
                             2. FACULTY                            └──────────────┘
                             3. PARENTS                            ┌──────────────┐
                             4. COMMUNITY REPRESENTATIVES          │  COMMITTEE   │
                                                                   │  OF HOUSING  │
  (Racial      (Citizenship) (Adult      (Leadership) (Housing   (Health)
   Cooperation)               Education)                Committee)            ┌──────────────┐
                                                                              │    JOINT     │
                                                                              │   HOUSING    │
                                                                              │  COMMITTEE   │
                                                                              └──────────────┘
```

Activities of the School Housing Committee	*Activities of the Joint Committee*

Activities of the School Housing Committee

1. Housing exhibits and films in school (for students and public)
2. Discussion in classroom and writing of compositions on housing
3. Prize essay contest on housing
4. Scale modeling of their own block by neighborhood children at the Friends and Neighbors Club or BFHS
5. Building of model village by students in art department class
6. Painting of pictures and posters on housing by art department students
7. Projection of program for better housing in East Harlem
8. Housing questionnaire for students of the school (study of student's reaction to housing conditions)
9. Study of local land values and use of land
10. House rallies in school
11. Housing forums with authoritative speakers
12. Sponsorship and participation of faculty and students in radio broadcasts on housing
13. Community gardens, beautification of neighborhood ("The Block Beautiful")

Activities of the Joint Committee

1. Mass meetings of East Harlem Residents; Adoption of resolutions
2. Appointment of a continuance committee to confer with authorities on a housing unit for East Harlem
3. Community signatures to housing petitions; establishment of petition signing stations
4. Publicity (press, pamphlets, buttons, etc.)
5. Housing parade and mass meeting, March 22, 1939
6. Establishment of information service on housing; low-rent housing unit known as East River Houses allocated to East Harlem (appropriation: $7,390,000)
7. Victory parade and mass meeting October 15, 1939, to celebrate securing of unit
8. Initiation of course on community planning and housing in adult school at BFHS
9. Groundbreaking ceremonies for East River Houses, March 2, 1940
10. Application for tenancy (distribution of blanks, advisement on procedures)
11. 56th meeting of the Housing Committee held
12. Housing Committee inaugurates campaign for East Harlem Municipal Hospital

Note: This figure is based on a diagram prepared by the School–Community Research Bureau of Benjamin Franklin High School, New York City, Leonard Covello, President.

tee began as a school committee. However, to strengthen it, Covello decided it needed to include members of the community. He invited several visible and well-connected East Harlem leaders, along with a few people from outside the community, to a meeting to discuss racial discord in the community. The first meeting of the newly established group looked like a who's who of East Harlem. It also looked like a meeting of the United Nations in that all of the major ethnic and racial groups in East Harlem were represented. Covello was able to pull the diverse group together because of his knowledge of East Harlem, his political savvy, his connections in East Harlem and at City Hall, and his ability to articulate a vision that could be understood and appreciated by a wide range of groups. The group was told that the committee for Racial Co-operation needed to plan ways to counteract racial tension and discrimination in East Harlem. The meeting resulted in a coalition of parents, teachers, students, and community leaders who were willing to join together to publicly voice their concerns about racial discord in the community. The newly reorganized Committee for Racial Co-Operation decided to:

- meet periodically to maintain open lines of communication between the school and the community,
- organize a group of speakers who would visit various community organizations to make presentations in the language of the group on the intercultural goals of BFHS,
- present radio addresses on intercultural education that were designed to reach audiences that were larger and more diverse than those that attended community meetings,
- publish articles on intercultural education in local foreign-language newspapers and other publications.

The Committee for Racial Co-Operation was a visible statement to the community about the values of the teachers, students, and parents at BFHS. However, it did not eliminate intergroup conflict in the school. Conflict between ethnic and racial groups surfaced again and again throughout the years the school was open. However, the committee representing a coalition of teachers, students, and parents was always there to express the values of the school and to temper intergroup tensions. For example, in 1945 students threatened to strike following a series of incidents between African American and White students at BFHS and James Otis Junior High School. Covello immediately convened a committee of teachers to investigate the incidents and draft a statement of facts. The statement was written in English and Italian and was shared with students and parents. In a letter inviting parents to attend a meeting where they would be able to hear factual reports on the incidents in English and Italian, Covello implored the school community to work together:

> For eleven years I have worked all year 'round, day and night, seven days a week—motivated only by my deep interest in the welfare of your children and families. I have always been willing to assume the responsibility of the school's program. The responsibility, however, is not mine alone. It is a joint responsibility—yours as parents, ours as teachers. I know that I can count on your help. (Covello, October 5, 1945, letter to BFHS parents)

The meeting with parents was followed with an all-day student assembly, where it was decided that students would work with their English teachers to draft slogans that would be used in the upcoming Columbus Day Parade. Teachers were asked to encourage their students to write brief slogans that expressed:

- The democratic spirit of the unity of races
- Respect for all individuals
- BFHS school unity

Figure 3.4 contains examples of the slogans BFHS students created for the Columbus Day Parade.

The Columbus Day Parade, which was a major community event, became a focal point for BFHS to reassert its values and commitment to racial harmony to the people of East Harlem. The parade was an event that Covello knew would be well attended. It was essential that BFHS make a strong and united showing. Therefore, in addition to encouraging students to attend the parade, Covello worked to get a large turnout of BFHS teachers. Among his many actions, he sent a memo to the faculty in which he said,

> A week ago Friday our school went through a difficult and trying experience. Every member of the faculty stood by fully, allaying the fears of our boys and of their parents and thus making it possible by the middle of last week for us to have normal attendance and normal programs. Let us again stand by as a group by marching with our boys on Friday. Let us affirm by positive action how deeply we feel on the question of segregation, discrimination, and the fermenting of race hatred. (Covello Archives, October 9, 1945)

The Columbus Day Parade was a tremendous success for Covello, BFHS students and teachers, and for East Harlem. The school reclaimed its position of leadership in the community and distanced itself from another incident of racial discord. The ongoing challenges that Covello and the teachers at BFHS faced with racial discord suggest that issues related

Figure 3.4. Slogans for Columbus Day
        Parade

Christian, Jew, Negro and White
Americans All
Unite and fight race-hate

Race-Hate
Has no place
In America

Drive Race-Hate out of our city!

Our boys—of every race, color, and creed—
Laid down their lives over there,
So that we could live together in peace over here
In communities Free From Fear

No man is safe unless ALL are safe.
No man is free unless ALL are free.

Race-Hate
Is Un-American

We drove those Nazis to their graves
Because they aimed to make us slaves.
Their stooges hope they'll soon come back
By splitting Americans—White from black.
DON'T LET IT HAPPEN HERE!

Race-Provocateurs beware!
We won't take your filthy poison!

Public Menace Number 1
Is the race-Baiter.
Put him where he belongs
In the Insane Asylum!

Keep Bilbo-ism out of our fair city!

Source: Covello Archives MSS40; Covello; 54/4

to intergroup tensions cannot be fixed in a final sense. When they are addressed in one area, they may surface in another. The committees and procedures developed by Covello and his staff were designed to enrich the lives of their students through intercultural knowledge, contacts, and experiences. The lessons of open communication with parents and students, taking advantage of teachable moments, not being afraid to state your values and commitments, and of working together as a school and community are as sound today as they were in the mid-20th century.

Being Accountable to the Community. During the 1930s when BFHS was established, it was not uncommon for educators to voice concerns about the intellectual ability of the second generation. Immigrants from southern and eastern Europe were widely believed to be incapable of reaching high levels of academic achievement. This idea was turned on its head at BFHS. Teachers were expected to teach and students were expected to learn.

As a community school, the staff at BFHS was accountable to the community. Covello and several BFHS teachers made themselves available to the community by holding an open house at BFHS every Wednesday evening. They met with parents who had concerns, and in many cases were able to find solutions to problems that could have become serious if they had been left unattended. Over time the school became a familiar and comfortable site for community meetings and activities.

While the concept of accountability was not used in the way that it is used today, there was a clear sense at BFHS that teachers needed to understand the cultural backgrounds and challenges of their students in order to provide classroom environments, curricular materials, and the interpersonal support students needed to be successful in school. This message was communicated in several ways. Students evaluated teachers and felt comfortable complaining to Covello if they believed a teacher was unprepared or not performing at an expected level. Students who dropped out of school were interviewed to find out why they left school and whether the school had failed them in some way. In the summer of 1937 a corps of men and women paid by the Works Progress Administration interviewed all of the students who had dropped out of BFHS during the previous year. The interview schedule included questions on the former students' employment status, reasons for leaving school, what they liked best about school, and what they liked least. In essence, the corps found that the boys primarily left school to go to work because they

- were older than the other students in the school,
- felt uncomfortable in relation to their teachers and fellow students,
- were discouraged due to bad grades or a lack of interest,

- began associating with a "bad" element,
- did not find the type of classes at BFHS that fitted their capabilities.

This information resulted in a recommendation that BFHS establish a way to maintain communication with these students. It was hoped that the students would, at a later date, enroll in the adult school or make themselves available to help in school programs designed to encourage students to stay in school. With this in mind, Covello worked with teachers to organize the Old Friendship Club. A major goal of the club was to maintain contact with boys after they left BFHS. The club included students who had dropped out as well as those who graduated from BFHS. The club held periodic meetings in which the boys and their families and friends were invited to the school or a school clubhouse for entertainment, advice, and fellowship.

Rethinking Community Involvement. Once the community school committees were organized, teachers took a leadership role in staffing and running them. By October 1937, it was becoming increasingly clear that the strain on teachers was too great. In addition to carrying heavy teaching loads, teachers were chairing or serving on several school-community committees. Due to growing unrest among teachers, Covello appointed a subcommittee to review the entire community–school committee structure. The subcommittee recommended that the committees be reorganized and that committees that overlapped be eliminated. Committees that did similar work were merged and others that were no longer needed were retired. The total number of committees was reduced to 18. The focus of committees at BFHS changed over the years, but committees remained an important organizational structure for linking the school to the community until the early 1950s.

THEY MADE A DIFFERENCE

The aims of Benjamin Franklin High School, to the extent that they were achieved, resulted from the dedicated commitment of socially minded teachers and the visionary leadership of its principal, Leonard Covello. The student was paramount at Benjamin Franklin. Each student was important and viewed as a complex human being. Covello believed that students should not be viewed as clay to be molded in the hands of skilled craftsmen. They were alive, vibrant, ever-changing young people who were being shaped by forces both within and outside the school.

Commenting on intercultural education at Benjamin Franklin, Ione S. Eckerson, field secretary for the New York State Board of Higher Education, said,

"There is no doubt that the minority groups in this school have already become more interested in and proud of their own backgrounds. They seem to have gained a new conception of American culture and what their people have contributed to it. The inferiority complexes sublimated in bravado and mischief will gradually fail away. . . . The so-called majority group is having an eye-opening experience, finding out how very unique and rich American culture and life is because of its gifts from many lands and races" (MSS 40, Covello, 60/13).

Many educators viewed Benjamin Franklin High School as a successful example of how to educate students who were on the margins of society. Covello and several of the BFHS teachers were sought after as experts who provided insights to educators, politicians, the business community, and others about teaching "underprivileged students." In 1944, when the editors of *Educational Leadership* decided to devote the March 1945 issue to intercultural understanding, Ruth Cunningham contacted Leonard Covello to ask for his support. The editors at *Educational Leadership* wanted to craft an issue that would be appealing and represent the perspectives of young people. Cunningham asked Covello to identify students who could write about intercultural education at Benjamin Franklin High School and share their understanding of the nature of intercultural problems and possible solutions to them. Ten years earlier no one would have believed that students from East Harlem would be asked to write for a national publication. In a relatively short period of time, a dedicated group of educators had helped to improve the lives of young people in East Harlem and the community in which they lived.

Leadership through values was at the base of Covello's work at Benjamin Franklin High School. This is a difficult kind of leadership because values are often in conflict. As the community and student population changed, it became harder for Covello and the teachers at Benjamin Franklin to identify and utilize common values to motivate people to come together. The momentum that Covello and the teachers at BFHS initiated in the early 1930s began to wane by the late 1940s as African Americans and Puerto Ricans became a more sizable component of the student population. By the late 1950s, community schooling at BFHS was only a shadow of what it had been in the 1930s and 1940s (Johanek, 1995). Covello retired from the New York City schools in 1956 and in 1972 returned to Italy. By the end of the 1982–83 school year, BFHS, the school on the hill, was no more. It closed amid accusations about its failed programs, high dropout rate, and declining teaching quality.

Part II

THE ACHIEVEMENTS AND FAILURES
OF INTERGROUP EDUCATION

INTERCULTURAL EDUCATION was, in many ways, a prototypical American movement. Its origins as a grassroots movement located it within the American tradition of efforts that reflect creativity, ingenuity, and a "can-do" spirit. Additionally, its social justice message was consistent with democratic principles and American Creed values. Yet it was not uncommon for intergroup education programs to be viewed with suspicion and even characterized as un-American. The irony of espousing American ideals and being challenged as being un-American is at the center of the achievements and failures of intergroup education. Within educational, political, and social circles, there was both an approach and an avoidance response to intercultural education. During World War II, intergroup education was seen as a means to help prevent the nation from fracturing into competing ethnic and racial groups. However, by the 1950s, it was seen as at best unnecessary and at worse subversive. The two chapters in Part 2 discuss the impact that social context had on the perception of intergroup education and its reception as well as its achievements and ultimate demise.

Chapter 4 includes an overview of the major characteristics and principles of intergroup education. That overview serves as a backdrop for the second part of the chapter, which highlights the contradictions that students in the Seattle Public Schools experienced when they were taught about democracy and brotherhood—two important concepts in intergroup education—as their Japanese American classmates were sent to internment camps. Student comments about that experience are used to reveal the inconsistency between the formal and implicit curriculum.

Chapter 5 discusses the extent to which the achievements and failures of intercultural education were influenced by tensions within as well as outside the movement. Erickson's (2004) definition of cultural *boundary* and *border* is used to frame the chapter and to describe three important tensions: multiple voices within the intercultural education movement, the McCarthy hearings' chilling effect on projects promoting cultural pluralism, and intercultural educators' response to people of color.

4

Teaching for Tolerance and Understanding: The Meaning of Intergroup Education

THE WAR YEARS were particularly challenging for intergroup educators who must have been struck by the irony of fighting Nazism abroad and racism at home. Nevertheless, they maintained their belief in the power of education to change minds and hearts. Intergroup educators were committed to making democratic values and ideals more of a reality for U.S. ethnic, racial, and religious groups. They argued that if the gap between the rhetoric of democracy and the realities that contradicted it weren't closed, democracy would be seen as a pretense and empty words (Clinchy, 1942). Their social philosophy promoted tolerance, an appreciation and understanding of ethnic, racial, and religious groups in U.S. society, and the cultivation of democratic attitudes and values. Teaching for tolerance and understanding was at the heart of their work.

USING THE MEDIA TO REDUCE INTERGROUP TENSIONS

Radio broadcasting became distinguished as a new and important form of media after World War I. Radio executives, such as Merlyn Aylesworth who was head of NBC, recognized the power of radio in shaping popular culture and influencing social cohesion. He noted that to create a common culture, "We must know and honor the same heroes, love the same songs, enjoy the same sports, and realize our common interest in our national problems" (Lacey, 2002, p. 29). Aylesworth believed radio could play an important role in accomplishing that goal. During the war years, radio was used to help reshape national identity by projecting a positive image of race and ethnicity in the United States. Two programs in particular, Freedom's People and Americans All-Immigrants All, captured the nation's attention.

Freedom's People was developed with the support of the Federal Radio Education Committee and aired by NBC over a thirteen week period in

1941–1942. The programs featured A. Philip Randolph, Paul Robeson, and other African American notables talking about the contributions made by African Americans to education, science, the arts, and other fields and the challenges they still faced. The programs were designed to inform in a positive and entertaining manner. Music was incorporated into narratives describing the role of African Americans in American life, and issues relating to prejudice and discrimination were presented with great care so as not to anger Whites. One of the challenges that the program's producers faced was that the program drew multiple audiences. Each had different sensibilities and were listening for different things. Many Blacks wanted a hard-hitting plea for equal rights and were critical of programs that seemed to dilute that message with entertainment. On the other hand, even Whites who were open to hearing about racial problems in the United States did not want Whites to be presented in a negative light. Moreover, they were accustomed to programs like The Amos N' Andy Show which had begun airing in 1928. Amos N' Andy along with a few other programs that presented Blacks as minstrel characters, stereotypes, and simpletons were the only representations of Blacks on the radio at that time (Savage, 1999). Susan Douglas (1999) notes that Whites had become fascinated with Black English and that certain phases and pronunciations associated with Blacks found their way, as a form of humor, into the everyday language of White listeners. This perspective was in direct contrast to that of members of ethnic and racial groups who saw the programs as a means to promote social justice and reduce prejudice. African Americans were especially concerned with promoting ideas that called for an end to segregation and discrimination. They were also aware of the importance of presenting images of African Americans that contradicted the Amos and Andy image that was so prevalent at that time. The producers of Freedom's People were able to successfully reach both Black and White audiences. Several segments of the program were very well received and got positive feedback from listeners all over the country including those in the South (Savage, 1999).

"Americans All-Immigrants All," which ran from 1938 to 1939, was a nationally broadcasted series of twenty-six weekly dramatic and factual programs on the contributions and challenges of various American ethnic and racial groups in American society. After it was turned down by NBC, the program was picked up by CBS and aired coast to coast on Sunday afternoons. Executives at NBC turned it down because they feared that the program's focus on race and ethnicity would be offensive to some of their listeners and sponsors. In the end, the program received critical acclaim and was a tremendous success. Unlike Freedom's People, which focused on African Americans, Americans All-Immigrants All primarily focused on European ethnic groups and only contained one episode on African Americans.

In Americans All-Immigrants All, the United States was presented as a nation made up of immigrants. Individuals who were descendents of "colonists" who came to North America before 1776 generally did not define themselves as immigrants. However, in Americans All-Immigrants All, colonists along with Hispanics, the descendents of Spanish settlers who established colonies in what later became the southwestern part of the United States, Africans who were enslaved and forcibly brought to North America, Near Eastern Peoples, Asians, and southern and eastern Europeans who came to the United States at the turn of the twentieth century were all considered immigrants. Americans All-Immigrants All was designed around the theme that "American civilization is a historical composite of the toil and thought and blood of nearly all the races and nations of the world, and therefore belongs to all" (Covello Archives, 1938).

Rachel Davis DuBois and other bureau staff members researched and provided the data for program scripts. Scholars and writers such as Alain Locke also served as consultants to the project and helped prepare and review scripts. After the series was developed, DuBois and the bureau staff worked with the New York public schools to disseminate the program as part of a series of school assemblies on "tolerance and democracy" (DuBois with Okorodudu, 1984). Bureau staff also developed curriculum units on the American ethnic and racial groups covered in the broadcasts and implemented in-service courses designed around them (DuBois with Okorodudu, 1984). They made listener aids and follow-up activities available without charge to schools and community groups. In the public's mind the bureau became closely associated with the broadcasts as a result of advertisements on them that listed the Service Bureau for Intercultural Education as an agency that had pamphlets, bulletins, and other material on U.S. ethnic and racial groups (Covello Archives, 1938). The Office of Education made arrangements with CBS to make both 33 and 78 rpm. recordings of the programs available for classroom use. The Linguaphone Institute, which at that time was the largest distributor in the world of speech records in English and in twenty-seven languages, made a set of the programs consisting of 3 12-inch double faced records at $4.75 a set. With each order the institute also provided a copy of a manual prepared by J. Morris Jones entitled "Handbook for Listeners." The manual contained material for classroom teachers on how the records could be used, suggestions on the grades, classes, and subjects they could be used in, rationale for the programs, information on which recordings were suitable for school assembly programs, and follow-up activities (Jones, 1938). DuBois in her position with the Service Bureau for Intercultural Education encouraged listeners to get together with friends and form "listening-in groups." She suggested that people from different ethnic, racial, and cultural groups be invited to the gatherings to share their perspectives during discussions following the programs.

Americans All-Immigrants All and Freedom's People were not altruistic attempts to highlight ethnic and racial groups in the United States. They were designed to remind listeners that all Americans were all immigrants and thus shared a common status. Moreover, the programs highlighted an important intercultural education message: that all of the ethnic and racial groups in the country had contributed to the development of the nation. John W. Studebaker, U.S. Commissioner of Education at that time, stated the programs, "Seek to promote better understanding for and among all the cultural and racial groups in this country through a knowledge of the contributions made by each." He went on to say "Europe's desperate plight, with neighbor set against neighbor, cannot be suffered in the United States. We in this country do not know racial or national boundaries. Although composed of many immigrant strains, we are one people! All Americans, all born of immigrant forbearers" (Covello Archives, 1938, p. 2).

The program's sponsor, the U.S. Office of Education, was very pleased with the programs because they believed the program could be used to reduce intergroup tensions and secure broad-based support for the war effort. The program's focus on race and ethnicity provided a means for the government to strengthen national unity by quieting racial unrest and drawing a distinction between the United States and the growing threat of fascism abroad (Savage, 1999). However, even though the government wanted to raise the morale of African Americans and other ethnic minorities, it was not willing to use programs like Americans All-Immigrants All and Freedom's Children to promote racial reforms such as putting an end to racial segregation. Ultimately, Americans All-Immigrants All and Freedom's Children did not change deeply held interracial attitudes in the United States. They were too little too late. They can, however, provide us with some insights into the role the media can play in influencing public discourse during times when societal conflict is widespread. They also illustrate the close relationship between politics and the media.

Americans All-Immigrants All and Freedom's People reflected both assimilationist and cultural pluralist perspectives. By highlighting the contributions minorities and immigrants made to American society the programs embraced the cultural pluralist goal of legitimizing immigrant groups. However, it also helped calm mainstream Americans' concerns about minorities and ethnic cultures by creating an atmosphere of tolerance for diversity. This was an important goal for assimilationists. Intercultural educators who leaned toward assimilation as well as those who embraced cultural pluralism both supported the media's treatment of race and ethnicity in these two programs.

INTERGROUP EDUCATION AS A WAY TO TEACH FOR TOLERANCE AND UNDERSTANDING

School knowledge developed by intercultural educators helped bridge the gap between real and ideal American Creed values. James A. Banks (1993) defines school knowledge as "the facts, concepts, and generalizations presented in textbooks, teacher's guides, and other forms of media designed for school use" (p. 11). Examples of school knowledge, such as information on the cultural contributions of various ethnic groups and information on prejudice and discrimination, were included in books and materials written by intercultural educators for teachers (DuBois, 1939) and students (Benedict & Wetfish, 1948) and in guides used to develop curriculum (Taba et al., 1949). These aspects of school knowledge were integrated into intergroup curricula.

Taba, Wilson, and other intergroup educators defined curriculum as "The total set of experiences into which schools direct pupils" (Taba & Wilson, 1946, p. 19). This broad definition of curriculum gave intergroup educators a basis for investigating and responding to a wide range of issues and student activities. Intergroup curricula addressed both the affective and the cognitive domains and were used to help students learn about as well as understand their attitudes and behaviors toward people who were different from themselves. For example, in her investigations of group life in schools Taba examined how residential segregation and stratification paralleled segregation and stratification in school club memberships and cross-group associations (Taba, Brady, & Robinson, 1952). This kind of information provided a basis for teachers to incorporate real-life issues into the school curriculum and for students to consider the ways in which racial attitudes that were prevalent in the community were also present at school. Intergroup educators linked those factors together by providing opportunities for students to become involved in community-based social action projects.

Students who lived in low-income communities not only researched social issues such as poor housing; they could advocate for improved housing in these communities. Linking school knowledge to social action was also used to improve intergroup relations in communities. Intergroup educators argued that schools should be sites where people from different racial and ethnic groups could learn from one another (Covello, 1937; DuBois, 1936). However, bringing people from different racial and ethnic groups together had to be done thoughtfully because when groups were put together conflicts could and often did occur.

Instead of ignoring or denying intergroup tensions that were present in a community, intergroup educators argued that they should be studied by conducting surveys and interviews with community leaders (Taba & Wilson, 1946). The data from the surveys and interviews could be used to identify common concerns and lead to social action activities such as letter writing to officials and journalists, holding mass meetings, and organizing forces and resources for worthy causes. These kinds of social action projects, which could benefit a wide range of groups, helped bring students and community members together to create a more encompassing and common identity as they worked to achieve their goals.

PRINCIPLES UNDERGIRDING THE WORK OF INTERCULTURAL EDUCATION

The four principles discussed in this section served as the foundation for most intergroup programs, materials, workshops, and curricula. While all of the principles were not universally included in all intergroup efforts, they were reflected in much of the school knowledge developed by intercultural educators.

Principle 1: Schools Should Be Linked to Their Students' Communities

Intercultural educators believed that schools should be linked to their students' communities. This principle is illustrated in the way intergroup educators saw and tried to respond to intergroup tensions. Concerns with intergroup tensions were particularly troubling during World War II when the nation needed but did not have a united front. In certain localities in the United States, there was open hostility between Protestants and Catholics, Gentiles and Jews, Blacks and Whites, and among other ethnic, racial, and religious groups. *The New York Times* reported that juvenile gangs in New York City were involved in mobbings and raids, the windows of synagogues were broken, and "KKKs" were written on the walls of Catholic churches. Intervening and helping students develop more positive attitudes toward out-group members required attacking nondemocratic attitudes at their source: in students' homes and communities. Intergroup tensions could not be reduced solely through school interventions. Schools in isolation of other community institutions lacked the power to influence human relations. The well-known intercultural educator Everett Ross Clinchy

(1942) summed it up well when he said that helping people learn to live together required "all the forces that influence human behavior—the family, the church, the school, companions, the museum, the library, the theatre, the newspaper, all of life" (p. 57).

Community Councils Help Reduce Intergroup Tensions. Community councils were frequently sites for social action projects that were designed to reduce intergroup tensions in communities. Social action projects initiated by community councils were sometimes combined with student projects, such as the ones discussed in the previous section. However, unlike school-based social action projects, adults provided the leadership, identified the focus, and generated the funding for social action projects initiated by community councils.

During the 1940s, Mayor LaGuardia and the New York City Board of Education encouraged educators to help organize neighborhood community councils. Once organized, the councils held town meetings, initiated neighborhood projects, organized handicraft classes, and developed numerous interfaith and intercultural activities that brought people together to work on common goals. The community councils provided a way for neighbors to come together and talk about the kind of community they wanted for themselves and their children.

The councils approached interfaith and intercultural issues indirectly by focusing on concrete concerns such as education, housing, and recreational facilities. Once the issues were identified, the members worked together to find solutions for them. In doing so, members of the council got to know each other on a personal basis and instead of only focusing on their differences they were often able to see their similarities. While educators generally did not lead these efforts, they were frequently members of the councils and provided crucial support in the form of expertise, meeting facilities, and other resources.

Councils were widely supported by politicians, civic leaders, and educators as a means to combat prejudice. Alexander J. Stoddard, who was superintendent of schools in Philadelphia, captured the power of community councils when he said,

> Yesterday the battlegrounds of freedom were in the streets, in the field, on the beaches, in the mountain passes, on the snow-capped mountains, in the trees, in fox-holes, in the trackless jungles, in the seas, in the skies—all over the world. Today, the battlegrounds of freedom are in the schools, the churches, the homes, the places of business, on the sidewalks, in our clubs, at our shows, in our night clubs—wherever we are at the time we are there. As we learn to live together as free men in the smaller everyday affairs of

life, we will build the kind of country of our dreams. (Stoddard, cited in
Brameld, 1947, p. 73)

By 1946, there were community councils in major cities throughout the
United States. The New York State Citizen's Council held its fourth annual
state conference at Saratoga Springs, New York, on November 10–12, 1946.
The council included key individuals from state and civic associations
as well as educational leaders such as Everett Case, president of Colgate
University; Rufus Day, president of Cornell University; and Howard
McClusky, assistant to the president of the University of Michigan. Mary
Riley, who at that time was the secretary of the New York City Board of
Education's Advisory Committee on Human Relations, was also present,
and submitted a seven-page report on the conference to John E. Wade,
superintendent of the New York City public schools.

The attendees at this meeting didn't simply gloss over intergroup tensions and focus on their success in pulling diverse groups together. One of
the key ideas that was highlighted at the conference came from Dr. Julius
Schreiber, a psychiatrist. He said,

> Americans are the greatest hypocrites in the world as there is a profound
> discrepancy between the things we talk of as being in our American tradi-
> tion and the things we do. (The Bill of Rights, the equality of man, etc.) . . .
> The kind of community I want is one where democracy really works, where
> hypocrisy is recognized for what it is. (Covello Archives, November 20, 1946)

Dr. Schreiber wasn't alone in his feelings about the contradiction between
American Creed values and the reality of prejudice and discrimination
experienced by White ethnics and minorities. In a study on minority groups
in the United States, Brameld (1947) found that segregation and discrimination existed throughout the United States. He noted that in California
there was an especially "poisonously anti-Japanese" attitude (p. 69). Mexican Americans in the Southwest often held a lower status than Blacks.
Brameld observed that Mexican Americans "lack both leadership and
militancy of any sort; and prejudice against them is sometimes so strong
that one again finds segregated schools in certain communities" (p. 69). He
also found blatant anti-Semitism in his study. He concluded that Jewish
citizens were often denied jobs, excluded from membership in certain
clubs and organizations, and in some cases they were "forced into semi-
segregation" (p. 69). Brameld argued that this was especially serious because anti-Semitism was insidious and that it was difficult to identify its
source. Race riots, lynchings, and attacks on synagogues during the 1940s
highlighted the extent to which the fight against prejudice and discrimination in the United States was far from over.

The attendees at the New York State Citizen's Council's fourth annual meeting recognized that much more needed to be done to reduce intergroup tensions. The group needed to work with educators in order to move the process forward. Several speakers at the conference argued that promoting intergroup cooperation was the responsibility of all citizens and institutions within U.S. society, but even so they believed that schools had a special responsibility to help build bridges between groups. Unlike religious institutions, settlement houses, labor organizations, and other groups that had socially educative programs and aims, schools had several characteristics they lacked. These included compulsory attendance laws, which required students to attend school; the diversity of the student population, which held the potential for social groups to come together and interact; and the high esteem in which teachers were held, especially by immigrant parents. Intergroup educators had long argued those points. They believed that the primary aim of public schools was not to "facilitate the success of individuals in the struggle for economic or social advancement, but rather to strengthen and promote the democratic ideals and institutions of American life" (Worlton, 1940, p. 1).

The relationship between the school and the community illustrated in the Springfield Plan and at Benjamin Franklin High School highlight the importance that intergroup educators gave to community involvement. However, even though many intergroup educators believed community involvement should be an integral part of the school experience, many mainstream educators remained unconvinced. Educators who supported community involvement in schools received support from reports such as the 1938 Report of the Joint Committee on Maladjustment and Delinquency. That report recommended that schools provide new and suitable recreational activities for community use and that teachers and principals establish closer ties between the home and school. These recommendations, which were adopted by most secondary schools in New York City, encouraged schools to open their doors to community groups and allow their gymnasiums, swimming pools, and other facilities to be used in community-based programs and to require teachers to visit their students' homes in order to learn more about the communities in which the students lived.

Leonard Covello and other intergroup educators worked through the teachers union to keep community involvement visible among their colleagues. In 1939 Covello, working with the New York Teachers Union, helped organize a forum on the school and the community. The purpose of the forum was to encourage dialogue among teachers surrounding these three questions:

1. Should there be cooperation between the school, the home, other agencies, and the community in educating for democracy?

2. What should be the nature of this cooperation?
3. How should cooperation be achieved?

These broad questions opened the door for educators to talk about specific aspects of community involvement such as the role of teachers in community-based activities, how to develop leaders for school-community programs, the role of foreign languages in school-community programs, and why so many teachers and principals were hesitant to develop and implement school-community programs.

Principle 2: Social Science Knowledge Is a Requirement for Effective Intergroup Teaching

An important goal for intergroup educators was to help students learn to think clearly and act "constructively where the problem of cultural coexistence in America was concerned" (Covello Archives, 1943). Accomplishing this goal required teachers who were not only committed to the goals of intergroup education but who also had the skills and knowledge to use concepts like culture, ethnic group, and prejudice effectively. DuBois (1984) and Taba (Taba, Brady, & Robinson, 1952) believed that classroom teachers should be involved in creating the curriculum they taught. They felt that teachers who helped create a curriculum would be more likely to support its implementation. However, in order for teachers to be meaningfully involved in creating curriculum they had to have subject-matter knowledge as well as a deep understanding of intergroup education. With an informed understanding of intergroup education and a firm background in their disciplines, teachers would be well positioned to rethink their curriculum, develop materials, and write curriculum units and lessons (Committee, 1949; Cook & Cook, 1954; Taba & Wilson, 1946).

To provide teachers with the knowledge and skills they needed to develop and implement intergroup curricula, intergroup educators such as Rachel Davis DuBois (1984) taught intercultural education courses at Boston University; Teachers College, Columbia University; The University of California, Berkeley; and New York University. An example of intergroup curricula taught at the university level is a course taught at Teachers College entitled "Education in American Culture." The course was designed to help students better understand the social pressures and issues confronted by immigrant and minority students. Students read Allison Davis's (1948) work on social-class influences on learning, *The Negro Family* by E. Franklin Frazier, St. Clair Drake and Horace Cayton's *Black Metropolis*, as well as other progressive texts. Using course readings and class discussions, the course provided a foundation for students to gain insights into unfamiliar communities and to better understand the educational problems of students from diverse communities.

In addition to university courses on intercultural education, teachers were also given opportunities to study abroad. New York University offered a course at the College of the Apennines, an intercollegiate school in Rome for Italian language teachers. The course focused on Italian grammar and composition, advanced conversation, Italian history and literature, and classical art. After the 4-week course ended, students participated in guided tours to Florence, Sienna, Venice, and Milan. These kinds of experiences gave teachers a closer, though not completely representative, view of their students' ancestral homelands.

Intergroup educators were also involved in organizing and implementing in-service courses for teachers. In 1945, Helen Trager, as a representative of the Bureau of Intercultural Education, worked with New York City teachers in a course entitled "Techniques for Projects which Promote Democratic Living." In this and other in-service courses, teachers were encouraged to examine and assess their own attitudes and beliefs about Americanization theories and classroom practices with respect to immigrants. Trager asked her students to think back to their own childhoods and reflect on the extent to which they were afraid of being ridiculed because of their parents' broken English, their fathers' menial jobs, the foods they ate, or because people in their community were called guinea, wop, dago, or other pejorative names. She also asked students if they had changed their name to increase their social status or to avoid letting their friends know their ethnic background (Covello Archives, 1945). These kinds of discussions gave students an opportunity to make a personal connection between ideological and theoretical perspectives on diversity.

Lloyd Cook (1950), another intergroup educator, mounted an extensive 4-year national project called the College Study. The purpose of the project, which began in 1945 and ended in 1949, was to train teachers in intergroup education and impress "prospective teachers with the importance of their role in the elimination of prejudice among their pupils, and to equip them with the tools and the methods to deal with intergroup prejudices" (Cook, 1950, p. vi). An important goal of Cook's project, which was funded by the American Council on Education and the National Conference of Christians and Jews, was to improve teacher education by implementing national workshops for faculty members from the 24 colleges and universities. Figure 4.1 contains a list of the institutions that participated in The College Study. The College Study may well have been the first national effort to provide teacher educators with skills and knowledge in intergroup relations (Cook, 1951; Cook & Cook, 1954).

Figure 4.1. Colleges and Universities That
Participated in the College Study

Atlanta University

Arizona State College, Tempe

Central Michigan College of Education, Mt. Pleasant

Central Missouri State College, Warrensburg

City College, New York City

Colorado State College of Education, Greeley

University of Denver

Lynchburg College, Virginia

Marshall College, Huntington, West Virginia

New Jersey State Teachers College, Trenton

New York State College for Teachers, Albany

Ohio State University, Columbus

Roosevelt College, Chicago

San Francisco State Teachers College

Southwest Texas State Teachers College, San Marcos

Springfield College, Massachusetts

State Teachers College, Eau Claire, Wisconsin

State Teachers College, Milwaukee, Wisconsin

Moorhead State Teachers College, Minnesota

Talladega College, Alabama

University of Florida, Gainesville

University of Pittsburgh

Wayne University, Detroit, Michigan

West Virginia State College

Source: Cook, L. A. (1951). *Intergroup relations in teacher
education* (p. 8). Washington, DC: American Council on Education.

Intergroup educators also conducted workshops at Harvard University; Sarah Lawrence College; New York University; Teachers College, Columbia University; Wellesley College; and other universities during the 1940s. According to Vickery & Cole (1943) four major purposes of the workshops were to

1. Use social science knowledge to develop practical projects that addressed real problems in schools, institutions, or communities.

Projects that were developed included curriculum units, guidance plans, and action plans to address community problems.

2. Make social science information and expertise available to a broad range of educators. After defining a problem, workshop participants were able to work with intergroup experts who would help them examine the context in which the problem existed. This included examining the background of the problem and the underlying issues related to intergroup tensions. Participants, for example, clearly understood that riots were a problem, but may not have been aware of the issues that led to riots. Students also learned how to use role playing and other practical "how-to" methods that could help them address intergroup problems.

3. Provide opportunities for firsthand experiences that could help shape and influence teachers' attitudes and perspectives about immigrant groups. An important component of most of the workshops included contacts and interactions with people outside the teachers' social group.

4. Help teachers deepen their knowledge base. Intergroup educators such as Taba believed that teachers didn't need more strategies. Instead, they encouraged teachers to read and discuss social science literature. In that way they could become familiar with arguments that could be used to refute claims of racial superiority, better understand the ways in which culture influences behavior, and develop an understanding of prejudice as a complex and nuanced phenomenon.

Principle 3: Intergroup Curricula Should Be Broad and Integrated

Intergroup educators argued that the field should be broadly conceptualized because it had to challenge long-held beliefs and values that were reflected in many aspects of American life. Prejudice against certain ethnic and racial groups did not wane during the 1940s. Rather it was refocused on new groups and grew at an alarming rate. Taba and Elkins (1950), as well as other intergroup educators, believed that integrating critical thinking throughout the school curriculum could help reduce prejudice. They argued that students should be taught to critique, evaluate, and solve problems for themselves. With the skills to engage in these behaviors they would be able to change their opinions when presented with convincing evidence (Bismarck, 1931). To that end, Taba and Elkins argued that intergroup curricula should be conceptualized as a holistic process, not as an add-on. When planning intergroup education programs, Vickery and Cole (1943) noted that it was important that the teachers on curriculum committees represent several different disciplines. This would help ensure that intergroup education was not viewed as the exclusive concern of one discipline or group of subjects. Intergroup tensions were so complex that an interdisciplinary approach was needed to understand and respond to them. Consequently when dealing with intergroup issues, teachers were encouraged to draw information, key concepts, and perspectives from anthropology, sociology, psychology, and other social science disciplines.

Ideally intergroup educators believed that intergroup experiences and activities should be woven throughout the curriculum, at all grade levels, and in all subjects (Taba & Wilson, 1946). In that way the strength of each part of the curriculum could be multiplied as each part supported and reinforced other parts. Intergroup educators argued that isolated efforts, no matter how effective, would not achieve the impact needed to challenge long-held beliefs and values about ethnic and racial groups. Even so, intergroup issues were frequently relegated to the social studies curriculum in units that focused on "community problems" (Cheney, et al., 1935; Shepard, 1925). The approach for teaching about immigrants in Ironwood, Michigan, is an example of how the social studies curriculum was used to help students understand ethnic diversity in their communities. Inez B. Petersen (1937), the elementary supervisor in Ironwood, Michigan revised the fourth- and fifth-grade social studies curriculum to include content on immigrants. In 1935, 78.4% of the parents of Ironwood students spoke a foreign language and 43.6% were born outside the United States (Petersen, 1937). The curriculum units that Petersen developed on immigrants included sample lessons, suggested assignments, and references for students and teachers that included magazines, songs, stories, records, and books. Her goal was to give teachers the tools to help students develop a better understanding and appreciation for the ancestral homelands of immigrants in Ironwood.

One of the finest examples of integrated intercultural curriculum was at Benjamin Franklin High School. Teachers in math, fine arts, science, English, social studies, and foreign language classes integrated content on racial issues into their curricula. Teachers from these subject areas worked together to design the integrated curriculum. In English classes, for instance, students studied about the contributions that various cultural groups had made to the United States, read at least one book on their own cultural group, and read at least three additional books that dealt with cultural groups other than their own. The students also conducted research on their family histories and wrote their autobiographies. They posed and discussed questions such as, "What is prejudice?" "Why are people prejudiced?" "What do we mean by *racial justice*?" and "To what extent does racial justice actually exist in the United States today?" (Covello Archives,

1939). Students also gave reports on the contributions and achievements of people who were members of groups other than their own.

The English curriculum was the primary focal point for intergroup education at BFHS. Teachers in other subject areas built on the depth of knowledge that students developed in their English classes. Nancy D. Zito, who taught Italian at BFHS, incorporated information on the contributions Italians made to the world in her curriculum. Curriculum units in BFHS's Elementary Business Training Course included ten lessons that were designed to highlight the contributions people from foreign countries made to banking and communication. Maurice Bleifeld, a biology teacher at BFHS, developed curriculum units that integrated social science knowledge into biology units on race (Bleifeld, 1939; Bleifeld, et al., 1939). The units were so successful that the Anthropology Study Group of the New York Association of Biology Teachers distributed them to teachers who were interested in implementing similar units. Bleifeld's unit outline showed teachers how to integrate social science knowledge into a biology unit. Teachers were given an extensive list of activities, but were encouraged to evaluate the activities and think about which ones were best suited for their students before they selected or created one to use. The teachers were also given information on films, library materials, museums, periodicals, and other teaching materials and resources (Covello Archives, 1939).

Even though most schools were not systematically concerned with improving intercultural relations and understandings, superficial elements of intercultural activities were woven into the standard curriculum of a number of schools. In music classes, for example, students frequently sang Negro spirituals. Immigration was a typical topic in social studies classes. In science classes, students confronted commonly held beliefs about biological differences among racial groups. However, even though these efforts were well intended, in isolation they lacked the power to influence intergroup dynamics.

Principle 4: Democracy Was a Key Concept in Intergroup Education

Democracy was an important concept in intergroup education. Some intercultural educators went so far as to argue that intercultural relations were synonymous with the most basic objective of democracy: that of "congenial, workable, and equal relations among all groups who make up the democratic order" (Brameld, 1947, p. 67). Figure 4.2 contains a list distributed by the New York City School Board on the characteristics of democracy. The Committee on Practical Democracy in Education compiled the list with input from students, teachers, and administrators. The committee encouraged

Figure 4.2. Some Fundamental Characteristics of Democracy as It Pertains to Education

1. Democracy has for its purpose the long-time interests, welfare, and happiness of all people, not merely of those who for various causes have previously been privileged.

2. It develops a steadily increased sense of obligation to a constantly enlarging social group.

3. It carries an obligation to be socially informed and intelligent.

4. It expects and requires informed and responsible participation in making decisions on broad social policies.

5. It induces a willingness to sacrifice personal comforts for the recognized public welfare, and also active cooperation in the support of policies legally adopted.

6. It requires that each individual actively, intelligently, and conscientiously help to choose those to whom responsibility will be given.

7. It expects every individual to render willingly and with such skill as he possesses services that his fellows assign to him for the general welfare.

8. It offers opportunities for voluntary, self-initiated acceptance of responsibilities.

9. It respects the personality of every individual (whatever his origin, present status, or natural gifts):
   a) develops in him a sense of "belongingness,"
   b) assumes that the maximum development of each individual is for the best interests of all, and
   c) both furnishes an environment and provides opportunities for stimulating, encouraging, and directing him to respect himself and to make the best of his own natural gifts and to develop his own unique personality.

10. It ensures equality of treatment by those to whom authority has been entrusted.

11. It ensures freedom
    a) of acquiring information by direct but unhindered inquiry,
    b) of coming to independent conclusions, using the ideal of honesty, fair-mindedness, and scientific method,
    c) of speech and press to exert such influence as he can over his fellows,
    d) of criticism,
    e) of proposal and of advocacy of plans for the general betterment,
    f) of assembly to consider means of attaining rights or greater general welfare,
    g) of petition for the redress of what he considers to be wrongs
    h) of worship

12. It respects the rights of minorities, but compels them to conform to the program approved by the majority when nonconformance would interfere with progress toward general welfare and happiness, leaving to minorities the right to agitate peacefully for desired changes.

13. It believes that an individual becomes free and effective by exercising self-restraint and reasoned self-direction rather than by having restraint or arbitrary direction imposed by external authority, and therefore it appeals to reason and to an educated conscience rather than to force for the promotion of its desired ends.

14. It guarantees the right to the pursuit of happiness in any ways that do not materially interfere with the happiness of others.

15. It encourages initiative.

16. It offers opportunities for individuals to learn under guidance the use of their rights and privileges, alone and by active participation with others, always for the ultimate good of the social group.

17. It attempts a general diffusion among its people of the ideals, knowledge, standards of conduct, and spirit of fair play, which promote a sense of equality and of responsibility.

18. It renews its strength by continued education as to its means and purposes, by education for the effective realization of the democratic faith.

schools to use the list to engage students, teachers, administrators, parents, and members of the school community in an open dialogue about the degree to which democratic characteristics were present in their school.

Continued discrimination against second-generation individuals who were born and educated in the United States helped intergroup educators to understand that their work needed to be more closely aligned with democracy. Intergroup educators believed that democracy was a means through which they could argue for the interests and welfare of all people and for causes that didn't simply benefit privileged groups in society. The Project in Intergroup Education in Cooperating Schools is an example of an intergroup program that directly linked intergroup education to democratic values and ideals. (See Chapter 2 for a detailed discussion of the characteristics and components of the project.)

The Service Bureau for Intercultural Education also linked several of its programs directly to issues in democratic education. Democratic education was of particular concern during World War II when the bureau received calls from educators for materials and resources that teachers could use to help reduce prejudice. The calls frequently voiced naive demands for materials that were "guaranteed" to reduce prejudice. Such requests highlighted the extent to which educators did not understand the need for in-depth and sustained efforts to reduce prejudice. Intergroup educators frequently worked with teachers who had naive perceptions about what was necessary to reduce prejudice. It was not uncommon for educators to silently support within-school segregation and exclusion of certain groups from school activities and organizations while teaching about democracy. Intercultural educators argued that minorities should not be relegated to the margins of school life, and that schools should make a conscious effort to ensure that all groups are able to participate in athletics, school government, clubs, and other elements of social life in schools. (Taba & Elkins, 1950; Taba & Wilson, 1946).

Intergroup educators argued that democracy had to be experienced to be fully understood and embraced. Consequently classrooms should be structured so that the school was a democratic community. In that way students could experience and not simply read about democratic behavior. Helping students experience democracy required that teachers give students opportunities to develop decision-making skills, work cooperatively with people they liked as well as those they disliked, and consider different points of view when forming their opinions (Covello, 1942). Intergroup educators also linked students with people in the community. Working together, the students and community members could try to solve educational, social, and civic problems that could only be solved through cooperative work.

Many intergroup educators believed that recognizing ethnic identity and giving status to ethnic groups was an important part of educating students in a democracy. Through guided discussions students could learn tolerance, respect, and restraint from their teachers and from each other. Covello (1942) argued that in order for the school to have credibility in teaching about democracy it had to work with community leaders who may not embrace democratic ideology, be prepared to use foreign languages when English wasn't the language used within the community, and when necessary make concessions to non-American ways of life in an effort to reach out to all students. He noted that when students experienced that kind of open environment they had an opportunity to learn about the true meaning of democracy.

Intergroup educators encouraged teachers to use materials that could help their students understand the effects of prejudice on both prejudiced people and their victims. Teachers were also encouraged to explore topics that challenged students to examine their values, behaviors, and attitudes toward people who were outside their social group (Benedict, 1942; Taba & Elkins, 1950; Trager & Yarrow, 1952). Children's books were often used to introduce these kinds of topics. Books dealing with the physical characteristics and family patterns of out-group members as well as books that addressed relationships among people and feelings of fear and rejection were used with children as early as the primary grades (Stendler & Martin, 1953). Intergroup educators argued that these kinds of topics and materials could help reduce stereotypes.

Benedict and Wetfish's (1948) book for children, *In Henry's Backyard*, is an example of a book that was used to break down stereotypes by highlighting similarities among people. Henry, the protagonist, looks for and finds answers to questions about people who are different from him. He also thinks about why differences cause people not to like each other and why people who are prejudiced are also often fearful and anxious. Intergroup educators used this book to help reduce student prejudice.

Intergroup education was also used to help students better understand key concepts such as *segregation* and *scapegoat*. Teachers at BFHS challenged their students to think deeply about prejudice and discrimination by giving them opportunities in several subjects to identify and discuss ways in which immigrants were used as scapegoats and blamed for behaviors in which they were not involved. Concepts such as democracy, culture, race, religion, acculturation, prejudice, and other related concepts were used at BFHS to help students think critically about how prejudices were formed, who benefited from them, and how they could be reduced (Vickery & Cole, 1943). Teachers were encouraged to help students develop the skills and knowledge needed to examine prejudice and its implications from a legal perspective, its effect on group and individual mores, its broad impact on society, and the extent to which it was consistent with American creed ideals (Taba & Wilson, 1946).

The school knowledge constructed by intergroup educators may seem inappropriate or inconsequential today. However, it is important to note that throughout the first half of the 20th century, ethnocentric views were widespread in U.S. society and immigrants and people of color were generally seen as strange and different, genetically inferior, and incapable of fully participating in U.S. society (Bennett, 1988; Smedley, 1993). Institutionalized racism and legally sanctioned segregation were widespread throughout the United States, particularly in the South and its border states. The idea that immigrants and people of color had cultures that should be honored, histories that merited study, and that they should become first-class U.S. citizens were perspectives that many mainstream Americans rejected outright or found challenging at best.

Even though democratic environments were integrated into the framework of some schools, students and parents typically saw teachers as authority figures. No mater how humane and open teachers were, it was rare that a true democratic relationship existed between teachers and students and between teachers and members of the community. For many immigrants and their children, teachers represented the power of the state. Covello noted that many a school situation that was objectively a democratic one "is considered by the boys as a sham, a make-believe imitation of a real democratic situation." Democracy was more apt to be viewed as an ideal rather than a real state for many ethnic and minority students. The internment of Japanese Americans during World War II in the midst of students being taught about democracy, intolerance, and brotherhood is an example of the mixed messages about democracy that were given to students and preservice teachers.

MIXED MESSAGES TO STUDENTS AND TEACHERS

"Mr. Dwight Davis' civics class did not prepare me for Executive Order 9066" (Omoto, 2001, p. 2). This was among the many thoughts that Sadayoski Omoto had when he reflected back to the day over 60 years ago when he and more than 200 of his Japanese and Japanese American friends, neighbors, and relatives were sent to relocation camps. On March 30, 1942, Omoto and the other Japanese detainees stood at the old Eaglesday ferry dock on Bainbridge Island in Washington State awaiting the Kehloken, a ferry that would take them away from their homes, businesses, and friends. From Bainbridge Island, they would be sent to the Assembly Center on the fairgrounds in Puyallup, Washington. From there they would go to Manzanar, an internment camp in the California desert and other relocation camps scattered throughout the western part of the United States. However, by the early months of 1943, most of the group would be reunited with their Seattle friends and neighbors at the Minidoka Relocation Center in Hunt, Idaho just outside Twin Falls (Omoto, 2001). Table 4.1 contains a list of the assembly centers and internment camps and their locations.

There were 10 relocation campus and 15 assembly centers. The assembly centers served as temporary housing for the evacuees while the War Relocation Authority built relocation camps in the interior of the United States. In addition to the camps listed in Table 4.1, there were five smaller camps in Missoula, Montana; Bismarck, North Dakota; Santa Fe and Lordsburg, New Mexico; and Crystal City, Texas. The U.S. Department of Justice operated these camps. The Crystal City Camp housed Americans of Japanese descent from the mainland as well as Germans, Italians, 300 Indonesian sailors, Peruvian-Japanese, and Japanese from Hawaii. The Crystal City Camp, which closed in 1947, was the last camp to close (Uno, 1974).

People of Japanese descent had been living on Bainbridge Island in Washington State since 1883. About 227 lived there in 1942. Approximately two-thirds were born in the United States and were U.S. citizens. Of the remaining one-third, most were Japanese immigrants who had lived in the United States for more than 30 years (Kitamoto, 2002). Most of the people of Japanese descent on Bainbridge Island were sent to relocation camps. However, about a half-dozen men joined the armed forces and three families were allowed to relocate to Moses Lake, Washington (Kitamoto, 2002).

Omoto was born on Bainbridge Island and in 1941 graduated from Bainbridge High School where he was class president. Thinking back to that day when he was forced to leave his home, Omoto wondered how he would have felt if he had seen his friends and classmates being forced to leave the community where they had lived since they were born. He said, "Only a day previous we were friends and classmates and now we were the enemy. Did President Roosevelt have the right to deny my Nisei classmates and me those rights guaranteed to all citizens?" (Omoto, 2001, p. 2). Lessons about democracy, tolerance, brotherhood, and other concepts embraced by intercultural educators and commonly taught in civics classes were inconsistent with the reality Omoto experienced.

Some Bainbridge students left school the day the Japanese were taken away so that they could go to the ferry dock and say good-bye to their classmates. Gena Clinton Ritchie described that spring day in 1942 in a poem, "The Saddest Day of My Life."

Table 4.1. Japanese Assembly Centers and Relocation Camps

THE ASSEMBLY CENTERS

Location of Center	Dates of Operation	Maximum Population
Fresno, California	May 6–October 30, 1942	4,120
Los Angeles	May 7–October 27, 1942	18,719
Marysville, California	May 8–June 29, 1942	2,451
Mayer, Arizona	May 7–June 2, 1942	245
Merced, California	May 6–September 15, 1942	4,508
Pinedale, California	May 7–July 23, 1942	4,792
Pomona, California	May 7–August 14, 1942	5,434
Portland, Oregon (Livestock Exposition Hall)	May 2–September 10, 1942	3,676
Puyallup, Washington (Fairgrounds)	April 28–September 12, 1942	7,390
Sacramento, California	May 6–June 26, 1942	4,739
Salinas, California	April 27–July 4, 1942	3,586
Santa Anita Racetrack		
Stockton, California	May 10–October 17, 1942	4,271
Tanforan Racetrack (near San Francisco)	April 28–October 13, 1942	7,816
Tulare, California	April 30–September 4, 1942	4,978
Turlock, California	April 30–August 12, 1942	3,661

JAPANESE RELOCATION CAMPS

Name of the Camp	Dates of Operation	Maximum Population
Gila River, Arizona	July 20, 1942–November 11, 1945	13,348
Granada, Colorado (Amache)	August 8, 1942–October 15, 1945	7,318
Heart Mountain, Wyoming	August 12, 1942–November 10, 1945	10,764
Jerome, Arkansas	October 6, 1942–June 30, 1944	8,497
Manzanar, California	June 1, 1942–November 21, 1945	10,046
Minidoka, Idaho	August 10, 1942–October 28, 1945	9,397
Poston, Arizona	May 8, 1942–November 28, 1945	17,814
Rohwer, Arkansas	September 18, 1942–November 30, 1945	9,475
Topaz, Utah	September 11, 1942–October 31, 1945	8,350
Tule Lake, California	May 27, 1942–March 20, 1946	18,789

Source: Edison Uno, 1974.

The Saddest Day of My Life
by
Gena Clinton Ritchie

It was an ordinary day
At Bainbridge high
Or so we thought.
My classmates and I.

When along came an order
From the US Gov't.
An order so misguided
We were all in wonderment.

Our very best friends
From first grade on
Were ordered to leave
And would soon be gone.

It was World War II and
Our friends were "the Japs"
Who were born in the US
And now were trapped.

In "relocation" camps
Along with their parents
Who had never done wrong
As was very apparent.

School was dismissed
That "ordinary day"
So we could all go say
"Please come back—we pray."

With the signing of Executive Order 9066, according to Ritchie, people who had been considered friends since first grade were now transformed into "the Japs."

Other people who were also at the ferry dock that fateful day in 1942 noted how democratic values clashed with the reality of their lives. In describing the day when he left Bainbridge Island for the Manzanar camp, Frank Kitamoto (2002) said,

> As we marched down this road, we were in shock, [and] disbelief. We didn't know where we were going, we didn't know how long we would be away, we didn't know if we would ever come back. Heads of families had already

been taken away. It fell to the Nisei, all in their 20s, to make family decisions. The tough New Jersey soldiers with their rifles, fixed bayonets, and funny-sounding accents were carrying luggage for women and carrying children. The soldiers had tears in their eyes that rolled down their cheeks (p. 1).

Like Omoto, the young soldiers' civics classes had not prepared them for Executive Order 9066 and the day that they, as soldiers in the U.S. Army, would force U.S. citizens from their homes.

The recollections of people who witnessed that tragic day on Bainbridge Island reveal the extent to which teaching for tolerance and understanding is a complex undertaking. In communities throughout the western part of the United States, students could not ignore the empty seats in their classrooms that only weeks before had been filled by Japanese American students. The empty seats carried a powerful unspoken message about the fragility of democratic principles and values in the face of fear and politically legitimized prejudice and intolerance.

With people of Japanese descent interned and the nation at war, civics education in many schools throughout the United States became a place where patriotism was equated with unquestioned support for the United States and demonizing its enemies. However, even during this time of great unrest and fear, intergroup educators worked to reduce intergroup tensions and spoke out against undemocratic actions. They continued to believe that schools could make a difference and were one of the few groups that advocated for young people to be taught to think critically and to distinguish fact from opinion and propaganda. Working with John E. Wade, superintendent of schools in New York City, intergroup educators implemented curricula to reduce prejudice. Commenting on the need for such curriculum, Wade said,

> No longer can we afford to ignore or minimize the danger that will inevitably follow if prejudice is allowed to spread unchecked. Enemies of democracy at home and abroad neither minimize nor ignore it, but utilize every opportunity to widen the gap that exists between the racial, religious, and nationality groups in American life. Let us learn to bridge the gaps between groups and in so doing defeat the enemy and strengthen democracy. (Covello, 1943)

The National Education Association (NEA), which had over 775,000 members in 1943, took a similar position. It argued that schools should not teach students to hate the enemy. In a policy statement entitled "What the Schools Should Teach in Wartime," the NEA took the following stand.

> We shall not attempt to state whether it is either desirable or necessary for a soldier in combat to be motivated by hatred and revenge. However, if such emotions are in fact necessary or desirable for soldiers, we believe their

cultivation is a responsibility that should be assumed by the Army rather than by the schools. We especially deplore the cultivation of such traits among the younger children and others who are not likely to see military service. The spiritual casualties of war will be great enough and lasting enough without any help from the teaching profession. (NEA, Press Release January 16, 1943. MSS 40, Covello 50/4)

Intergroup Education in a Frontier City

Seattle is only a short ferry ride from Bainbridge Island where Sadayoski Omoto stood and reflected on the gap between the ideals of democracy that he was taught in the classroom and the undemocratic reality that he experienced. To better understand the complex and often mixed messages that students receive about democracy, we will turn to Seattle, Washington, for a closer look at a city where students had to personally confront mixed messages about democracy when their Japanese classmates were interned.

Seattle, Washington, in the early 1900s was a prototypical 20th-century city. It had burned to the ground in 1889 and was in subsequent years literally rebuilt from the ground up. Compared to New York City, Seattle, with its muddy streets and highly transient population, was a small frontier town in the "wild" west. However, by the turn of the 20th century, Seattle had begun to transform itself into a bourgeois city with a first-rate school system. By 1910, it had a population of 237,000 and a reputation for schools that were committed to developing students' "character, good citizenship, and morality" as well as their intellectual skills (Nelson, 1988, p. 4). Seattle schools, like the city, were built from the ground up after the 1889 fire and were centered in neighborhoods. Neighborhood schools reinforced community identity and after 1910 provided a focal point for local activities (Nelson, 1988). Some Seattle neighborhoods were multiethnic. Yet many, because of restrictive covenants, were not. Consequently, neighborhoods were often identified with particular ethnic groups.

During the early part of the 20th century, Seattle's ethnically and racially diverse population included Asians, Blacks, and Native Americans as well as European immigrants, particularly Scandinavians and Germans. Although Seattle was a multiethnic city, minorities represented a very small portion of its population. People of Japanese descent represented the largest group of minorities, followed by Blacks and then Chinese. In 1920 there were 7,874 Japanese living in Seattle, which was 2.5% of the city's population. The 2,894 African Americans made up 1% of the total population. Minority school enrollment was similar to the population statistics in the city. During the 1919–20 school year, there were 892 Japanese, 301 Black, and 185 Chinese students enrolled in Seattle schools.

Night schools were established in Seattle to provide elementary, secondary, and vocational classes to adults, immigrants, and young people who had to work during regular school hours. The night schools had an open-door policy, with no age restrictions or tuition requirements. By 1908, there were more than 3,000 students enrolled in night schools. With the addition of night schools, the Seattle school district became a symbol of unity for the city. Schools were the place where the community came together not only during the day but also at night and during the summers. The schools tried to reflect the message that everyone was a part of the community. Immigrants could use the schools to help them become naturalized citizens and racial minorities could assume they would receive a quality education.[1]

By the 1940s, elements of intergroup education and progressive education had found their way to Seattle and were reflected in Helen Laurie's work. Laurie served as the supervisor of elementary education in the Seattle public schools. In August 1939, she attended the Congress on Education for Democracy, which was held at Teachers College, Columbia University, and reported the proceedings to her colleagues in a series of articles published in the *Seattle Principals Exchange*. While at the conference, Laurie had an opportunity to interact with people from progressive groups such as the National League of Women Voters and the NAACP and to hear presentations by respected scholars such as Ralph W. Tyler, George S. Counts, George D. Strayer, and Harold Rugg (Laurie, 1940a).

Seattle teachers also had opportunities to interact with educators outside of the city through teacher exchanges. Virgil Anderson, a teacher in the Seattle school district, reported that his exchange experience in Birmingham gave him an opportunity to learn more about African Americans. Leta Young, another Seattle teacher, visited schools in Hawaii where she learned more about the Japanese. Some teachers were able to learn and grow from those experiences. For others their experiences simply reinforced the idea that people from different ethnic and racial groups were strange and different (MacDonald, 1940). Seattle teachers also maintained good contacts with educators outside the district through their summer work at universities. During the 1940s, Seattle teachers joined summer faculties at Harvard University, New York University, the University of Texas at Austin, Stanford University, the University of Washington, and other leading universities (Summer Teaching, 1941).

Spring festivals, which were similar to DuBois's assembly programs, were held in several Seattle schools during the 1940s. Students at Concord Elementary School were taught folk dancing in conjunction with their social studies classes. The dances were used to teach students about the countries the dances represented as well as to help students appreciate the contributions of immigrants (Luch, 1940; Merrick, 1940). Principals were encouraged to use materials supplied by the Association for the Study of Negro Life and History (ASNLH) in their history classes. An article in the *Seattle Principals Exchange*, announcing that Negro History Week would be observed February 9–16, 1941, quoted Woodson, the founder of ASNLH:

> We are not trying to focus attention solely on the Negro. We would study this race in relation to others, and others in relation to the Negro. Hitherto the Negro has studied others and ignored himself and others have studied themselves and ignored the Negro. To be liberally educated students must learn to grasp all things in their proper relationships. To proceed otherwise paves the way toward narrowness and intolerance. (Negro History Week, 1940, p. 9)

THE HUMAN COST OF THE INTERNMENT

Following the Japanese attack on the naval base at Pearl Harbor on December 7, 1941, the United States was in a state of fear and hysteria. While there was no evidence that persons of Japanese descent in the United States were involved in sabotage or espionage, there was concern that the Pacific Coast would be attacked. Within this atmosphere, some Seattle educators were concerned about the negative attitudes toward Japanese Americans and encouraged their colleagues to "cling to a common sense and tolerant attitude towards children whose parents came from countries now at war with us" (Seattle Principals Exchange, 1942, p. 4). Teachers in schools with Japanese students faced the problem of how to prepare their students for the internment. The teachers at Washington Elementary School under the leadership of their principal A. G. Sears were committed to promoting positive intergroup relations. Their commitment was reflected in their curriculum, their interactions with parents and community members, and their expectations that students would interact positively. The student population at Washington Elementary School was multiethnic. It included David Foy, who was born in Canton, China; Michael Sidermann, who was from Hamburg, Germany; and Judith Kahin, a rabbi's daughter from Munich, Germany. Thirty-three percent of the students at Washington were Japanese Americans.

Teachers at Washington asked their students to write compositions about how they felt about the Japanese evacuation. They didn't use the term *internment*. The students expressed regrets about losing their friends and talked about how studious, punctual, and cooperative they were. They also mentioned how their Japanese American classmates had served on the Seattle Junior Safety Patrol, made contributions to the American Red Cross, the Junior Red Cross, and participated in the War Bond Campaign and the

Conservation Waste Paper, Tinfoil, and Metal Tube Drives. The Japanese American students also wrote compositions. One girl wrote about how hard it would be for her to leave the trees in her yard. Her grandfather had planted them in 1893. Another child ended her composition with a prayer: "Please keep my family together for the duration, and then make it possible for me to come back to my school, my home, and my friends" (cited in Mortenson, 1942, p. 7).

The loss of the Japanese American students along with the enrollment of new pupils from the Yesler Hill Project and from the homes of defense workers changed the demographic profile of students at Washington Elementary School making it more African American. The teaching personnel also changed. Three male teachers resigned to enter the service or the defense industries. A chronology of events leading to the evacuation is included in Table 4.2.

Japanese Americans lost their civil and constitutional rights during the internment and were forced to live in camps that were surrounded with barbed-wire fences with guard towers. It was a harsh experience, but like in all groups there were a wide range of opinions and responses within the Japanese American community to the internment. Once it was over and they had begun to rebuild their lives, some Japanese Americans preferred to put the internment behind them or focus on the positive aspects of the relocation experience. *Shikata ga nai*—It can't be helped. Don't dwell on it. Accept it. Make the best of it. *Gaman*—perseverance. Find inner strength. Don't blame others. Endure. These are sayings that many Issei (first generation) lived by and used to guide their responses to the internment (Kitamoto, 2002). Others, primarily *Nisei* (second generation) or their children, who are called *Sansei*, saw the internment camps as American-style concentration camps that resulted from racism and hysteria (Uno, 1974).

Table 4.2. Chronology of Events Leading to and Including the Japanese Internment

December 7, 1941	Japan bombed Pearl Harbor and the United States enters World War II.
February 19, 1942	President Roosevelt issues Executive Order 9066, which resulted in the internment of over 100,000 Japanese Americans and people of Japanese descent.
March 24, 1942	Notices were posted stating that all persons of Japanese ancestry would be evacuated from Bainbridge Island.
March 30, 1942	All persons of Japanese ancestry living on Bainbridge Island were evacuated to the Puyallup Fair grounds where they waited until the internment camps were ready for occupation.

LEARNING FROM THE PAST AND ACKNOWLEDGING OLD WRONGS

Most Japanese American students who were graduating from high schools on the West Coast in June of 1942 were not allowed to participate in their school's graduation ceremonies. One exception occurred in Puyallup, Washington. Perhaps because they were in a camp in the same city, the students were permitted to leave the Puyallup Assembly Center so that they could graduate with their classmates at Puyallup High School. After graduation, they returned to the camp.

Mary Koura, a bright and active high school senior, was prevented from graduating from Mount Vernon High School in June of 1942 because she was Nikkei, a person of Japanese ancestry. Koura, who was an honor student, had been an active member of the school community throughout her 4 years at Mount Vernon High. She edited the school yearbook, played in the orchestra, and was a class officer her sophomore, junior, and senior years. An 8 p.m. curfew for people of Japanese descent was in effect on the evening she should have received her high school diploma. Koura and the other Japanese American senior, Isaac Sakuma, received their diplomas at a school assembly while their classmates received their diplomas the following evening at the school's graduation ceremonies. Being excluded from her high school graduation ceremonies haunted Mary Koura for the next 50 years.

She and her family lost most of their personal belongings when they were sent to Tule Lake, an internment camp in northern California. Everything happened very quickly. They had very little time to sell their potato farm and other belongings; consequently, they were sold below market price. In February 1943, almost a year after arriving at Tule Lake, Koura left the camp to continue her education at St. Olaf College in Minnesota. Her family was able to join her in 1945. She and her husband Knob Koura returned to Washington and opened a berry farm on Bainbridge Island and raised two children in 1946. About half of the people from Bainbridge Island who were interned returned to the island after the war.

In 1992, Mary Koura's daughter, Carole Kubota, who had heard the story of how her mother had been barred from her graduation ceremonies and knew how deeply it had affected her, mentioned the story to John Summers, a science teacher at Mount Vernon High School. When he shared Koura's story with the students in his classes, they insisted that she be invited to march at their graduation. Kubota's letter to the Mount Vernon students is in Figure 4.3.

The officers of the senior class sent an invitation to Mary Koura asking her to participate in the 1992 Mount Vernon High School graduation ceremonies. At first she was reluctant to accept the invitation. She didn't

Figure 4.3. Open Letter to the Students at Mount Vernon High School

May 29, 1992

Dear Students,

Fifty years ago, when the United States and Japan went to war, a curfew was imposed on all Japanese whether or not they were U. S. citizens. One evening fifty years ago a young girl, Mary Hayano, went to bed weeping because of that curfew. On that evening her high school classmates were attending their graduation ceremonies. Although her principal and teachers vouched for her [and] would have escorted her to the ceremonies, the federal authorities had deemed that this seventeen year old girl, simply because of her heritage, would not be allowed to violate that curfew. What should have been an evening of joyful celebration turned into an occasion that would haunt her for the next fifty years. She would be unable to speak of that night without tears coming into her eyes. She would have nightmares.

You students have given this girl an incredible gift—an opportunity to celebrate what was denied her so long ago. She is a grandmother now and she and her family are most deeply touched by the generosity of spirit displayed by the students of Mount Vernon High School. Your sensitivity to the injustice of that time and your determination to help heal a hurt [has] persuaded her to accept the invitation to participate in the present joyful celebration.

Your invitation to her symbolizes your connection to the past and your vision for the future. You are large in heart, sensitive of soul, and fair of mind. To include her in your June 5th ceremonies will be the end of something for her and wonderful beginning for you. You are to be honored for what you have done; your act attests to the fact that you are truly the hope of the future.

Thank you very much.

With deepest gratitude,

Carole Koura Kubota
The daughter of Mary Hayano Koura

want to detract from the seniors' "big day. " After being assured that this was what the seniors wanted she agreed to go back to Mount Vernon and take part in the graduation ceremonies. At 68, Mary Koura, Class of 1942, received her diploma to the sound of thunderous applause and shouts of approval. Commenting on the experience, she said, "This is something I never thought I would get" (Bianco, 1992, p. 8).

Mary Koura's sister-in-law, Sachiko Koura Nakata, faced a different situation in 1942 when she was scheduled to graduate from Bainbridge

High School. By the time of her graduation, she and the other 13 Japanese members of the senior class had been interned. Bainbridge Island was the first place in the United States where people of Japanese descent were forced to leave their homes and were sent to internment camps. By February 1942, 34 people of Japanese ancestry on Bainbridge Island had been arrested. Sachiko Koura's family was among the first to be detained. Her father, H. Otohiko Koura, was arrested on January 21, 1942, by special agents of the FBI on a presidential warrant, which was issued for the apprehension of alien enemies. He was detained at Fort Lincoln in Bismarck, North Dakota. FBI documents obtained through the Freedom of Information Act note that H. Otohiko Koura's "crime" was serving as an officer in the local Japanese Association, being an influential person among the Japanese on Bainbridge Island, and being an un-Americanized type of Japanese. Koura remained under arrest until April 17, 1942, when the alien enemy hearing board of Seattle at Missoula, Montana, recommended his release.

Sachiko Koura Nakata and her Japanese classmates at Bainbridge High School were allowed to complete their coursework through correspondence classes. They received their high school diplomas at an informal ceremony organized by their parents at the camp. Nakata recalled that the day she should have been graduating with her class at Bainbridge High School, she sat on her bunk at the internment camp and cried (Hartstone, 1992).

After hearing about Mount Vernon's plans to include Mary Koura in their graduation ceremonies, Mr. Ellick, the principal of Bainbridge High School, invited Nakata to march in their graduation ceremonies. Like Mary Koura, Sachiko Koura Nakata didn't want to detract from the students' graduation. Moreover, she didn't want to participate in graduation ceremonies if her other Japanese schoolmates couldn't march at the graduation. She was eventually convinced to participate in the graduation ceremonies by her grandson, Ed Nakata, and Mr. Ellick, who told her that her participation in the ceremonies would send an important message to the students and would be a way of "touching history." On Saturday, June 6, 1992, 5 decades late, Sachiko Koura Nakata and two of her classmates, Nobuko Sakai Omoto and Sueako Nishimori Yonemitsu, marched with the high school seniors at Bainbridge High School and received the diplomas that they had been denied in 1942.

These are only two stories of Japanese Americans who were prevented from attending their high school graduations. Altogether hundreds of students of Japanese descent were barred from their high school and college graduation ceremonies. In Seattle, Japanese students had their names listed on their schools' graduation programs, but instead of allowing the students to receive the diplomas at their graduation ceremonies, the school district mailed the diplomas to the students' internment camps. Students graduating from the University of Washington who were interned received their degrees *in absentia*. Many were honor students. Phi Beta Kappa memberships went to George Kumasaka, Mary Toribara, Kazuko Umino, and Kiyoshi Yamashita. Kazuko Umino was one of four women accepted into the women's chemistry honorary society, Iota Sigma Pi (Seattle, University of Washington Archives, n. d.).

UNLEARNED LESSONS

By reaching out to Japanese Americans who were denied the opportunity to graduate with their classmates in 1942, the students, teachers, and administrators at Mount Vernon High School and Bainbridge High School were engaging in social action. They identified a problem and worked to find a way to respond to it. In an indirect sense, they were embracing aspects of the principles that are discussed at the beginning of this chapter. Their efforts to try to redress an injustice that occurred during World War II highlights the potential of historical events such as the internment to serve as case studies about the nation's complex and complicated receptivity to ideas about tolerance and understanding. It also reveals the extent to which ideas, such as those promoted by intergroup educators, can be muted by current events.

Fear, an emotion that fueled nativist attacks on immigration at the turn of the 20th century, resurfaced during the war years and was implicated in the internment of Japanese American citizens. Intergroup educators challenged students to think about the real meaning of democracy and to recognize the potential consequences of unbridled fear. However, when Japanese Americans were interned, most U.S. citizens were unable to see how the internment itself was an attack on democracy. This was a powerful unlearned lesson from intergroup education. The lesson was not learned because Americans were unconcerned with democracy. Americans were very patriotic and believed they were fighting for democracy during World War II.

On June 6, 1944, when the Normandy invasion hung in the balance, Seattle residents, like people throughout the country, went to their churches and synagogues; athletic teams canceled their games; stores were closed; and Worth McClure, then superintendent of schools in Seattle, asked students to say a silent prayer during school assemblies. Americans commonly engaged in these kinds of acts, which were considered patriotic. Yet few Americans saw any inconsistency between fighting to free the French from the Nazis and forcing Japanese Americans to go to internment camps. For most Americans, our domestic policies with respect to Japanese Americans were unexamined or seen as irrelevant.

After the war, fear continued to grip the nation as we identified and fought a new enemy, communism. In 1947, the Washington state legislature passed an Un-American Activities bill. A year later, Washington State Senator Albert Canwell began using his state-based Canwell Committee to ferret out communists in Seattle. His efforts were supported by the Red Squad, a unit in the Seattle city police department. Canwell held hearings in Seattle and remained in the city until he won five convictions for legislative contempt and secured the dismissal of three University of Washington faculty members.

Teaching for tolerance and understanding is a difficult lesson when the implicit, and in some cases explicit, curriculum throughout society sends a powerful and contradictory message. Intergroup educators not only had to contend with ideological resistance to their message; they had to be prepared to respond to current events and issues that had the potential to render their message irrelevant. Perhaps it was the power of their message about democracy, the enduring quality of the values they embraced, or their belief in their work that gave them the courage and strength to continue in the face of great odds. As the movement entered the 1950s, internal as well as external tensions threaten the continued viability of the movement.

5

Borders and Boundaries in Intercultural Education

THE POLITICS of difference illustrated by *boundaries* and *borders* was reflected in the interactions and activities of intergroup educators. Erickson (2004) defines a *cultural boundary* as the presence of some kind of cultural difference. He states that "when a cultural boundary is treated like a cultural border, differences in rights and obligations are powerfully attached to the presence or absence of certain kinds of cultural knowledge" (p. 42). The intercultural education movement was associated with immigrants who had to cross multiple cultural borders in order to participate in mainstream U.S. society. The cultural borders that divided them from mainstream Americans included language and religious differences. These and other differences were barriers between mainstream Americans and immigrants who did not have the cultural capital necessary to participate in mainstream U.S. society. Moreover, immigrants were commonly viewed by mainstream Americans as being culturally deprived. By celebrating cultural differences, elevating the cultural characteristics of immigrants, and making information about their cultural characteristics and histories known to people outside their social group, intergroup educators hoped to change the borders between mainstream Americans and immigrants into permeable cultural boundaries. In doing so, cultural knowledge previously only known to immigrants was made available in a way that allowed it to be known, understood, and experienced by the second generation as well as by mainstream Americans.

As discussed in Chapter 2, there were also differences among intergroup educators. Leaders in intercultural education did not speak with a single voice. Rather, they expressed diverse perspectives and points of view about the purpose, direction, and audience for intergroup education. These differences, which were initially framed as boundaries, over time, became more solidified and impermeable borders. This chapter examines the cultural borders and boundaries that existed within intercultural education as well as those that existed between various groups in American society.

TRANSFORMING CULTURAL BORDERS INTO BOUNDARIES

The task of transforming cultural borders within the intercultural education movement into boundaries was extremely complex, given the diverse ideological perspectives within the movement. In a 102-page report on intercultural education in New York City public schools, Louis E. Yavner, the commissioner of investigations of the City of New York, expressed concern about divergent views in intercultural education. Yavner (1945) concluded that there wasn't agreement among intercultural educators on acceptable practices and procedures. The report was issued in response to concerns about the saliency of intergroup training and curricula that surrounded the resignations of Frank E. Karelsen, Jr., and 28 of the 40 members of the city's Advisory Committee on Human Relations. Karelsen and several other members of the advisory committee resigned to protest what they believed was inaction and confusion in the field of human relations. At Mayor LaGuardia's request, Yavner investigated the charges and issued the 102-page report (Special Collections, Milbank Memorial Library, n. d.).

While Yarver's conclusions were somewhat of an overstatement given the number of books and articles written by intercultural educators and the published definitions of the term, his critique captured the elastic quality of the movement. That quality had both positive and negative implications. On the positive side, its broad base enabled intercultural educators to focus their attention on efforts ranging from curriculum development to parent involvement and from teacher training to reducing intergroup tension in communities. That positive quality, however, also had negative implications. The broad base of intercultural education made it difficult to identify its center. Without a clearly defined focus, intercultural education was difficult to evaluate. Consequently, its quality and impact could easily be called into question.

Yavner (1945) also observed that intercultural education had taken on the character of a social movement. That observation captured concerns that intercultural educators—such as service bureau director Stewart Cole and Bruno Lasker, a noted social scientist—had raised in the early 1940s about the field's focus on cultural contributions (Chase, 1940). Even though Yavner's report had political overtones and was used to undermine the influence of intergroup educators who embraced cultural pluralism, it revealed an important element of dissent within the movement.

The Intercultural Education Movement's Encounter with Progressive Education

Differences within the intercultural education movement are illuminated by its encounter with the progressive education movement. The two movements came together in the 1930s. The American Jewish Committee decided to discontinue funding the Service Bureau for Intercultural Education after 1935. At that time DuBois was able to secure funding from the New York Foundation (DuBois with Okorodudu, 1984). The bureau staff was able to use its connections with faculty at Teachers College, Columbia University, to link its work with the work of the Progressive Education Association (PEA). George Counts and Willard W. Beatty, who were on the board of the Service Bureau for Intercultural Education, were influential members of PEA, which was selected to supervise the bureau's New York Foundation grant. The bureau's work was subsumed under PEA's Commission on Intercultural Education, which later became the Committee on Intercultural Education. DuBois was named the director of the commission, with Ruth Benedict as one of its 10 members (DuBois, 1984; Montalto, 1982).

On the surface, intergroup education and progressive education would seem to be a perfect match. The bureau and PEA had overlapping memberships in their organizations. Additionally, intergroup educators shared many of progressive education's tenets, which, according to Graham (1967), included concern for the development of the individual child, stimulation of the creative impulses and unique capacities of each child, and the development of a curriculum relevant to the needs and problems of the times. The experience of Rachel Davis DuBois with the Progressive Education Association, however, revealed important points of tension between the two organizations.

During its first year, the Commission on Intercultural Education was less financially successful than was expected. Members of the PEA criticized the bureau's program of ethnic assemblies. Seminars that were arranged by the Commission on Intercultural Education at regional PEA conferences were not popular with PEA members. PEA board members were concerned about DuBois's focus on the cultures and contributions of ethnic groups. They feared it would lead to what was termed "unwarranted cultivation of group pride." Some members of the PEA were also concerned about DuBois's insistence on treating Jewish Americans as an ethnic group instead of a religious group (DuBois, 1984). By 1937, PEA board members were openly discussing their concerns about DuBois's emphasis on ethnic groups. DuBois's critics believed intercultural education should focus on concepts such as democracy and brotherhood, not on ethnic groups.

Ruth Benedict's Perspectives on Intercultural Education. Ruth Benedict (1942), who was a member of the Commission on Intercultural Education, felt that Old World "idiosyncrasies" were given up voluntarily by most groups and that second- and third-generation students resented being singled out for special attention in the curriculum. She spoke for many in the PEA when she stated that while it was important to "keep alive our pupils' pride in their fathers' people, . . . this could best be done by firmly integrating cultural content into existing course syllabi" (p. 22). The chief thrust of intergroup relations programs, according to Benedict, should be on fair play and providing full opportunity to members of all groups.

Benedict and DuBois also held different opinions about the appropriate audience for intercultural education programs. DuBois believed the programs should primarily be directed to members of ethnic, racial, and religious groups. Benedict (1942) argued that children "on the hill," not children "across the tracks" should be a central focus for intergroup educators (p. 22). The term *children on the hill* was Benedict's way of referring to mainstream Americans. She believed that social upheaval and chaos could result from the intergroup tensions that existed in society (Benedict, 1942). She believed that to reduce those tensions, educators should help children on the hill understand the inconsistency between discrimination and democracy. She argued that intergroup educators needed to reach people who lived in "those areas where most Poles, Italians, and Negroes never go except as servants" (Benedict, 1942, p. 22). She noted that "intercultural programs which are based almost entirely on exhibiting national folkways in school assemblies or members of other periodic exhibitions [had] little to offer on the hill" (pp. 22–23). Benedict pointed out that most students would not make meaningful connections between real-life problems like poor housing and job discrimination simply because a group of Italian American boys or members of another ethnic group were brought to "the hill" for a 2-hour performance. The children on the hill, according to Benedict, would simply see the Italian boys and other ethnics as strange and different. She believed that a program based on human worth would be more effective in changing attitudes on "the hill" than presentations on ethnic "folk" culture.

DuBois and the PEA Part Ways. The PEA catered to a middle-class clientele and did not have many minorities, immigrants, or children of immigrants within its ranks. In general, PEA members did not share intergroup educators' passion for diversity and inclusion. This was evidenced, in part, by the small numbers of individuals who attended seminars arranged by the Commission on Intercultural Education at regional PEA conferences. Many progressive educators identified with and supported the democratic strand that was a part of intergroup education. However, the day-to-day problems of immigrants were of concern to many progressives only insofar as they threatened social stability and national unity.

By early 1938, DuBois's services were considered expendable by leaders of the PEA. At the April 1938 meeting of the association's board of directors, Commission Chairman Borgeson informed DuBois that her services would no longer be needed after September 1, 1938. The PEA's Commission on Intercultural Education was downgraded to a committee, and after 2 years it disappeared. DuBois's effort to unite intercultural education and progressive education had failed (DuBois, 1984).

DuBois tried to address a set of problems not clearly perceived by, nor consistent with, the interests of the PEA. Problems of social growth within a multiethnic society, emotional conflicts arising from pressures of assimilationists, and cultural revitalization were not high on the agenda of social concerns embraced by members of the PEA. When intergroup educators addressed issues such as assimilation and brotherhood they were understood and accepted by the PEA leadership. However, the PEA leadership viewed programs that focused on ethnic groups as divisive. There was also a tremendous social class divide between intercultural education and progressive education. Even though progressive education was touted as a means to educate every child to his or her full potential, low-income students, particularly in large school districts, were at a disadvantage. It was not uncommon for low-income students to be viewed by educators as having less ability than middle-class students. When students engaged in group work, low-income students were frequently relegated to more mundane tasks while middle-class students were able to engage in more intellectually rigorous tasks (Zitron, 1968). Progressive education was most effective with middle-class students. They had the cultural capital and parental support to take full advantage of the freedom and openness it allowed. It was less effective with the low-income students who were the focus of intercultural education.

Conflicting Perspectives on Ethnic Affirmation.[1] A related point of dissention, and ultimately the case for the creation of borders between intergroup educators, was the degree of ethnic affirmation they were willing to endorse. Intercultural educators recognized that some degree of ethnic affirmation was necessary to support a sensitive and humane transition into American society. They did not, however, agree on the level of ethnic affirmation that was needed. Frank Trager, who was an administrator with the American Jewish Committee and a member of the service bureau board; William Kilpatrick, the noted progressive educator and chair of the service bureau board; and Stewart Cole director of the service bureau,

were among the intercultural educators who argued that problems associated with nativism would disappear as immigrants and their children assimilated into American society. They used the term *cultural democracy* to
suggest that "the American people must learn to respect and encourage
meritorious cultural differences, while at the same time insure the cultivation of over-all purposes and co-ordination of activities which give uni-
tary vigor to our democracy" (Kilpatrick & Cole, 1943). Kilpatrick and Cole
believed that a weak level of ethnic affirmation would help speed the assimilation process, and therefore they did not support programs and materials that focused on isolated ethnic histories and contributions. They were
concerned that ethnic histories and contributions would highlight differences instead of similarities among groups. They encouraged immigrants
to learn English and to acquire the social and cultural practices of mainstream Americans while holding on to symbolic elements of their ethnic
groups. This is described in Chapter 1 as *scientific assimilation*. Once assimilated, it was assumed that the sons and daughters of immigrants would
be indistinguishable from mainstream Americans. Kilpatrick held a similar position with respect to African Americans. His biographer, John A.
Beineke (1998), notes that Kilpatrick "believed that desegregation would
be fully won only when the Black population as a whole became more fully
integrated throughout the entire country" (p. 377).

Other intercultural educators, such as Rachel Davis DuBois, George
Graff, bureau field worker; and Leonard Covello, principal at Benjamin
Franklin High School in East Harlem, embraced a stronger form of ethnic
affirmation. Although they agreed that immigrants needed to experience
some degree of assimilation, they didn't believe they should completely
abandon their cultures. Covello wanted immigrants to learn English but
also to maintain their mother tongue. He worked to get Italian listed as one
of the languages that would satisfy the high school foreign language requirement in New York City schools (Zimmerman, 1999). Covello believed
ethnics would be able to maintain important elements of their culture and
history, such as language, music, and art, if those elements were incorporated into the U.S. national culture. He and his colleagues not only supported ethnic affirmation; they worked to incorporate ethnic content into
the curriculum. They believed that ethnic content in the regular school
curriculum would send a message to both ethnic and mainstream students
that the school valued information about All-American ethnic groups.

Conflicting Perspectives on Strategies. Intercultural educators also
used different strategies and approaches. Rachel DuBois focused her work
on issues related to culture, race, and religion. She and like-minded colleagues believed students needed to have accurate information about eth-

nic groups and their cultures. Consequently they provided students and teachers with information on the contributions and cultures of ethnic and minority groups. Hugh Hartshorne, a board member of the Service Bureau for Intercultural Education, and Bruno Lasker, the social scientist, raised two major concerns about intergroup materials. Hartshorne was concerned about the impact of the materials. He argued that focusing on ethnic studies would be divisive and potentially lead to separatist tendencies (Chase, 1940). Lasker was concerned about the quality of the bureau's materials. He thought they were superficial, emphasized insignificant contributions, and included inaccurate information on the role ethnics and minorities had played in U.S. history (Chase, 1940). Intergroup educators who shared Hartshorne's and Lasker's perspectives preferred for students to focus on concepts such as brotherhood, prejudice, and discrimination. In that way teachers would be able to refute claims of racial superiority as well as teach students about the ways that prejudice undermined democracy (Cole, 1946; Vickery & Cole, 1943). Intergroup educators with these perspectives focused on providing teachers with the skills and knowledge they needed to reduce student prejudice and increase positive intergroup relations.

FUNDING FOR INTERCULTURAL EDUCATION

Diversity within intercultural education mirrored its funding sources. Funding for the intercultural education movement came primarily from organizations that were concerned with groups on the margins of U.S. society. The American Council on Education, the American Jewish Committee, the Council on Cooperation in Teacher Education, the Julius Rosenwald Fund, and the National Conference of Christians and Jews were among the organizations that provided funding for intercultural education (DuBois, 1984; Montalto, 1982; Vickery & Cole, 1943). A number of other organizations, including the National Association for the Advancement of Colored People (NAACP), the National Urban League, the China Institute, and the Japan Institute also provided funding, but on an intermittent basis (Montalto, 1982). The membership of the civic and civil rights groups that funded intercultural programs were primarily made up of ethnic and racial minorities.

The specific goals for funding organizations varied, but overall they were dedicated to social justice and civil rights. Intercultural education provided a means for the organizations to promote social justice in U.S. society through schools. Even though individual members of groups such as the American Jewish Committee and the National Conference of Christians and Jews were financially successful, they were members of ethnic groups that were on the margins of U.S. society. Their ability to be included and fully participate in American society depended, in large part, on the acceptance of their ethnic groups. Intergroup education was a way to influence school knowledge and consequently reduce the stigma associated with their ethnic and religious groups.

As ethnic and religious groups moved closer to the mainstream, they were less interested in the issues of people on the margins of society. Over time, for example, Jewish groups became less supportive of intergroup educators who promoted ethnic affirmation more strongly than religious tolerance and prejudice reduction. Intercultural programs that emphasized ethnic groups and cultural contributions were seen by some Jewish organizations as highlighting differences rather than similarities and from the perspective of people in those organizations, intercultural educators ran the risk of eliciting old animosities and anti-Semitic feelings (Montalto, 1982).

SEGREGATION IN NEW YORK CITY SCHOOLS

Segregation, which existed in schools throughout the United States during the time of the intercultural education movement, was another visible and powerful illustration of cultural borders. African American children were required to attend "colored schools" in New York City well into the 1880s. African American leaders fought to overturn school segregation, but lost when the U.S. Supreme Court ruled in 1896 that states could set up "separate but equal" facilities. The schools, however, were never equal. The quality of schools and the resources available to them varied depending on the neighborhood. Over time, the New York City Board of Education slowly began to open schools to African American children, and by 1900 the last New York City school that officially excluded African American students had closed.

Even though African American students could attend schools with Whites, African American teachers were only allowed to teach Black students. The first African American teacher hired to teach in a mixed school in New York City was Miss Susan Elizabeth Frazier. Frazier was born in New York City on May 29, 1864, and attended public schools there. In 1888, she graduated from Hunter College. Layle Lane, another early African American teacher in the New York City schools, taught in the social studies department at Benjamin Franklin High School in the late 1930s and early 1940s. She worked closely with Leonard Covello to link BFHS to East Harlem.

Segregation in New York City schools, like schools in most northern cities, was not sanctioned by law. It was, however, sanctioned by custom. Segregated housing and discriminatory mortgage practices resulted in racial segregation in the public schools. The expansion of the Black community in New York City after the great migration, along with restrictive covenants excluding Blacks from buying or renting houses in White communities, resulted in overcrowded Black residential communities. Consequently, a number of schools were all Black. Some schools in New York City, like Clinton High School, which was named for the city's former mayor DeWitt Clinton, were integrated. Countee P. Coullen, the renowned African American poet, graduated from Clinton in 1922. Clinton teachers were actively involved in union activities and engaged in demonstrations and strikes for teacher rights and social causes.

Between 1920 and 1930, the Black population in Harlem more than doubled, growing from 83,807 in 1920 to 204,313 in 1930 (*Amsterdam News*, 1936). By the 1930s, segregation in the New York City schools was firmly established. By the end of the 1940s, segregation was so firmly accepted that Blacks were generally not welcome at predominantly White schools. During the 1940s and 1950s, segregation was effectively maintained through zoning, the location of building sites for new schools, student assignment policies, and teacher assignments.

Blacks were actively engaged in advocating for better schools during the 1930s and were successful in bringing information about the conditions in Harlem schools to the school board. In September 1935, teachers in Harlem formed the Harlem Committee of the Teachers Union. A major goal of the committee was to support the nascent grassroots movement of concerned parents and community members. The committee worked closely with parents and community activists to improve Harlem schools. Committee members made presentations in community meetings, churches, and at rallies. They also compiled information on the condition of schools in Harlem and accompanied parents when they presented the information to district administrators. When parents needed to visit the principal or a district administrator, a member of the committee was available to go with them. However, unlike teachers at BFHS who linked the school to the community and worked with community members, the Harlem committee was not an example of the school reaching out to the community. It was an example of the community making demands on the school and a small group of teachers responding. Teachers in Harlem schools frequently saw their assignment there as a form of punishment (Zitron, 1968). Members of the Harlem committee were the exception. They worked with members of the community to improve schools in Harlem. They demanded that more Black teachers be hired and insisted that Black history be included in the curriculum. Committee members led study groups on Negro history and culture and distributed skits, plays, radio scripts, and other classroom materials to interested teachers.

Blacks continued to demand that schools be integrated, but they also did not let up on their demand for schools in the African American community to be improved. They called attention to the limited curriculum that was available in Black schools. Vocational training courses and programs that could lead to "good jobs" were typically not available in Black schools. Blacks were discouraged from seeking training for jobs in the skilled trades. Otherwise well-meaning principals and teachers felt that "if we can't place the boy in the job for which we are to train him, then it is futile to give him the training" (Zitron, 1968). Blacks were in a no-win situation. They weren't able to get jobs in the skilled trades because they had not taken the courses that were required for the jobs. However, the required courses were not offered at their schools because school administrators believed that because of prejudice and discrimination, Blacks would never be hired in the skilled trades.

From curricular issues to facilities, it was clear that predominately Black schools were not among the city's premiere schools. School buildings housing Black students were often dilapidated and did not have playgrounds. In an effort to get a new school built to relieve overcrowding in Bedford-Stuyvesant schools, parents of PS 41 students circulated a petition describing a school built in 1880 in the following way:

- There is no auditorium.
- There is no gymnasium to provide for indoor play space.
- There is no infirmary. A nurse is on duty only part time.
- Toilets and extremely poor lunchroom facilities are in the same basement.
- There is no central corridor, thus creating a serious fire hazard.
- The rolling doors between classrooms result in constant interruptions for both teachers and children.
- Desks and seats are too small for children in the upper grades.
- Second, third, and fourth grades are on part time . . . .

(Zitron, 1968, p. 91)

The borders between segregated schools for Whites and Blacks were stark and undeniable. By the 1940s, more systematic efforts were underway to improve, though not desegregate, the Harlem schools.

The Harlem Project

In September 1943, with the support of the Board of Education, the New York Foundation and the Hofheimer Foundation committed $250,000 to a 2-year project in three Harlem schools. The purpose of the project was to demonstrate "what could be accomplished when private funds and public education worked together in demonstrating ways and means of improving the total educational program in order to reduce the incidence of social and emotional maladjustment and juvenile delinquency" (Polier, 1945, p. vi). The report documented the extent to which many of the same neighborhood and family problems that were characteristic of immigrant families and neighborhoods were also present in Harlem in the 1940s. It stated that "low family income, substandard housing, lax standards of law and order, incomplete and inadequate families [were] dominating characteristics of life" in Harlem schools. The report also noted that teachers in Harlem tended to live outside of the neighborhoods where they taught, and that teacher vacancies and the use of substitute teachers were high. High levels of "truancy, delinquency, emotional maladjustment, and gang fights" took up a disproportion amount of teacher time and energy. The schools themselves also had major problems. There were "inadequate buildings, large classes, curriculum limitations, insufficient staff, [and a] paucity of materials and equipment" (p. 207). The comprehensive report included 32 recommendations for improving Harlem schools. The recommendations are listed in Figure 5.1. Noting that while Harlem schools must make some significant changes, the report concluded that the problems that students faced could not be completely solved by the schools alone. Changes also had to be made within the broader community. The project staff stated that "The school can play a significant role in the educational and emotional adjustment of children in underprivileged areas, but it cannot correct such pervasive economic and social evils as result from segregation and prejudice" (p. 209). The report challenged the broader community to live up to its claim of democracy by not allowing Harlem to continue in "its isolation from the rest of the city because its members are denied the opportunity to live where they pleased, to make friends on the basis of mutual interests, and to work at jobs of their own choosing according to their ability" (p. 209).

The report specifically pointed to the importance of intercultural education and the key role the social studies could play in improving Harlem schools. Insights similar to those cited in the report had been identified previously by intercultural educators and implemented in Benjamin Franklin High School and other schools in New York City. They had not, however, been implemented in Harlem schools with predominately Black student bodies. After the Harlem race riot of 1935, efforts were made to increase the number of certified teachers in Harlem schools, implement after-school clubs and programs, and to develop community programming. Educators turned to the approach that had been used to respond to immigrant children to respond to Black students in Harlem. They did not

Figure 5.1. Recommendations from the Harlem Project Report

1. With adequate resources the school can effectively attack and diminish delinquency.
2. In disprivileged areas, the role of the school must be extended.
3. The philosophy of the "new program" must be wholeheartedly supported.
4. The adjustment of problem behavior must be started early and must continue until satisfactory adjustment is reached.
5. Mental hygiene standards should be applied in the training and selection of teachers.
6. Teachers should be trained in the meaning of gross social pathology.
7. The new program must be implemented.

A MORE STABLE SCHOOL LIFE

8. The whole scheme of the 6-3-3 division of the first twelve years of school should be reconsidered.
9. Transfer procedure, when a child's family moves out of the district but within a short radius of the school, should be made more flexible. Such transfers should be based on the interest of the child.

MORE ASSISTANCE FOR CHILDREN WITH ACADEMIC PROBLEMS

10. Remedial instruction, a revised curriculum, and work-school programs rather than earlier discharge from school are substitutes for "marking time."
11. New and better textbooks should be supplied, not only written at a vocabulary level in keeping with pupils' capacity to comprehend but also with content aimed at their interest level.

TRUANCY ONLY A SYMPTOM OF MALADJUSTMENT

12. Social treatment rather than law enforcement is needed in handling problems of truancy.
13. Community registration of juvenile delinquents should be instituted. An adequate method for measuring juvenile delinquency is needed.

MORE SPECIAL PERSONNEL FOR THE SCHOOLS

14. Teachers need help in understanding the meaning of a child's behavior in order to provide the necessary help.
15. Better ways are needed than those now in use to measure the intellectual and academic achievements of children in the various schools.
16. Additional school services are essential in underprivileged areas.
17. The school needs added services from psychologists.
18. A social worker should be assigned to each school.
19. The bureau of child guidance should be expanded.
20. More health services are needed.
21. Additional teacher positions should be allotted to the schools for special services.
22. After-school activities in the afternoon, evening, and summers should be extended for children, young adults, and parents.

Figure 5.1. (continued)

IMPROVED METHODS IN THE SELECTION AND TRAINING OF TEACHERS

23. The experience in the project schools showed how important understanding of children as well as academic competence is in a teacher.
24. Teachers should be selected as people as well as pedagogues.
25. Outmoded procedures of board of examiners should be changed for tests that will measure candidates' usefulness in modern education.
26. Supervisors should be selected for their ability to provide "creative supervision."
27. The emotional qualities of applicants for teaching and administrative positions should be tested along with intellectual capacity.
28. Teacher appraisal and transfer should be improved.
29. Good selection of teachers should be followed by placement where abilities are fully used.
30. A single-salary schedule is essential.
31. The overhauling should start at the very beginning—at the teacher training institution when students apply for entrance.
32. Training centers should provide training under conditions like those in which the teacher will later work.

consider, however, the extent to which race made intergroup tensions more complex and difficult to resolve.

People of Color in the Intergroup Education Movement: A Reflection of the Times

The segregation that existed in U.S. society during the 1920s into the 1950s was reflected in the intergroup education movement. When people of color participated in the movement, they were generally on its periphery. On a limited basis they participated in intergroup workshops, wrote for intergroup publications, and served as staff members on intergroup projects. For example, Allison Davis (1945), an African American anthropologist at the University of Chicago, wrote a chapter in the 16th yearbook of the National Council for the Social Studies about intergroup education. Alain Locke (Locke & Stern, 1942), another African scholar, coedited a path-breaking book in intergroup education entitled *When Peoples Meet*. Harriet Rice, an African American educator, coauthored, with Rachel Davis DuBois, a pamphlet describing the Woodbury Assembly Programs (DuBois with Okoroduru, 1984). Mew Soong Chock Li, a Chinese American from Hawaii, was one of the most visible persons of color in the movement. She presented at intercultural education workshops and coauthored several publications with Rachel Davis DuBois. She was also active in the Workshop for Cultural Democracy (DuBois & Li, 1971).

Few people of color, however, held high administrative posts in intergroup education organizations. Charles Johnson, an African American sociologist who went on to become the president of Fisk University in Nashville, Tennessee, was one of a handful of people of color who directed intergroup education projects. Staff at the Service Bureau for Intercultural Education worked with Johnson to implement a 3-week summer workshop sponsored by the Swarthmore Institute of Race Relations in 1938 (DuBois, 1984). Johnson's focus in the workshop on racial relations reflected the importance that Blacks placed on race as a critical issue in intergroup relations.

While people of color were not generally involved at the decision-making level in the intergroup education movement, they maintained liaisons and friendly relationships with intergroup educators. Rachel Davis DuBois used her contacts in the ethnic minority community to secure funding for publications and intercultural activities. In 1937 when she was unable to get the Progressive Education Association (PEA) to fund a Black teacher to attend a PEA intercultural education workshop at Ohio State University, she went to her friend Walter White of the NAACP. He authorized funds from the NAACP that enabled Irene Hypps, an African American teacher and former assistant editor of *Crisis* magazine, to attend the workshop (DuBois, 1984).

Unlike intergroup education, multicultural education is a multiethnic movement. It includes men and women who are African American, American Indian, Asian American, European American, and Latino (Banks & Banks, 2004). The insights and perspectives that are generated from a synergy of groups, including feminist scholars like Sandra Harding and Lorraine Code, provide occasions for learning in multicultural education circles that would not have typically occurred among intercultural educators. In addition, the National Association for Multicultural Education (NAME) provides opportunities for practitioners and scholars from a wide range of disciples and groups to come together and to learn from one another at annual conferences.

Black Scholarship and the Intergroup Education Movement

With few exceptions, Black scholarship was not influential in intergroup education. For the most part, White scholars had little contact with people of color. Whites for the most part did not attend meetings of Black scholarly associations such as the Association for the Study of Negro Life and History or publish in Black scholarly journals such as the *Quarterly Journal of Negro History* (Goggin, 1993). Blacks, likewise, did not generally attend the meetings of White scholarly associations. Those meetings were often held in cities were Blacks where barred from convention hotels. Also, with few exceptions, Blacks were not published in the *American Historical Review* or other White scholarly journals (Goggin, 1993). As a result, the transformational scholarship of scholars like Carter G. Woodson and Charles H. Wesley were not widely known to practitioners who worked in the intergroup education movement. This scholarship did, however, influence scholarship in the field of multicultural education (Banks, C.A.M., 1996). The liberatory scholarship of Woodson, W.E.B. DuBois, and others provided the foundations of multicultural education (Banks, C.A.M., 1996).

The barriers to Black scholars and Black scholarship in intergroup education is significant for at least two reasons. The recognition of Black scholars by leaders in the intergroup education movement would have acknowledged that Blacks were capable of significant scholarship. That recognition could have helped counter commonly held beliefs about the limits of Black intellectual capabilities. Second, Black scholars could have added an important authentic voice to intergroup education discourse and contributed important transformative perspectives to it.

CONCERNS ABOUT NATIONAL UNITY EXACERBATE BORDERS IN INTERCULTURAL EDUCATION

By the late 1930s, a number of teachers in the New York City schools were members of the second generation. A high proportion of the teachers were the children of Jewish immigrants who had come to the United States at the turn of the 20th century. These teachers frequently had personal knowledge of and experience with prejudice and discrimination. Consequently, many supported school programs that taught students to be more tolerant. They were also inclined to support progressive political causes. During the 1930s, both of the teachers' unions in New York City had ties to radical politics. Shaffer (1996) states that communists dominated the New York City Teachers Union and the Socialist Party dominated the New York Teachers Guild. Intercultural educators along with members of the Teachers Union, intellectuals, workers, and other groups were drawn to radical politics. Radical politics provided a language for critiquing American capitalism and it held out the promise that there would be an end to intolerance and systematic discrimination. In the early 1930s, the Communist Party was one of the few political groups that publicly condemned Hitler and Fascism (Fried, 1997).

Intercultural educators' affinity for radical politics resulted in personal and professional associations with individuals such as Vito Marcantonio. Marcantonio and Covello both lived in East Harlem where Marcantonio was born in 1902. Marcantonio became a politician and served East Harlem in the U.S. Congress from 1935 to 1950. As a radical politician he was vilified by the press during the McCarthy era. Unlike other politicians, however, he stood up to McCarthy. He insisted that the Communist Party was a legitimate American political party. While the people of East Harlem and intergroup educators may not have completely agreed with his point of view on communism, they respected him, appreciated his leadership, and remained loyal to him until he died on August 9, 1954. Covello was one of his honorary pallbearers.

By the mid-1940s there was growing concern among government officials about the Soviet Union's influence among labor leaders, intellectuals, workers, and other U.S. citizens. Government officials believed that members of those groups would succumb to communist propaganda or be used by communists to promote their agenda. The House of Representatives' Committee on Un-American Activities, under the leadership of Martin Dies, became a focal point in the fight against communist power in the United States. The House of Representatives created the Special Committee on Un-American Activities in 1938. The committee initially focused on communists in places such as government, trade unions, and Hollywood. By 1940, the U.S. Congress passed the Alien Registration Act, which allowed the government to investigate and jail subversives. Within months, over 4.5 million aliens were registered. As World War II started to slow down, Representative John E. Ranking of Mississippi reinvigorated the committee with a mandate from the House authorizing the committee to investigate

> the extent, character, and objects of un-American propaganda activities in the United States [and] the diffusion within the United States of subversive and un-American propaganda that is instigated from foreign countries or domestic origin and attacks the principles of the form of government as guaranteed by our Constitution" (Fried, 1997, p. 16).

Fears of the nation fracturing into competing ethnic and religious groups raised concerns with some Americans that communists would target racial and ethnic groups and exploit their anger about the prejudice and discrimination they faced. Segregation was commonplace and even existed in the armed forces and Red Cross blood banks. This was ironic because African American soldiers who were fighting to protect and defend the world against Hitler were targets of prejudice and discrimination at home. The Ku Klux Klan was active throughout the United States, in northern as well as southern communities. When asked why the Committee on Un-American Activities didn't investigate the Ku Klux Klan, Ranking, who was a chief sponsor of the committee, replied that, "the Klan wasn't un-American, it was American" (As cited in Commager, 1947, p. 198). With this kind of attitude reflected by high-ranking government officials, it isn't surprising that the leadership of radical groups thought racial and ethnic minorities would be receptive to organizations that offered an alternative to the intolerance they were experiencing in American society.

Although intercultural education was not a radical movement, it was viewed as such by some conservative groups because of its message of racial and ethnic equality. Individuals such as Rachel Davis DuBois, who encouraged the maintenance of ethnic heritage and provided opportunities for students to learn about the history, contributions, and cultural characteristics of racial and ethnic groups, were viewed with suspicion and considered un-American by some groups. In the mid-1920s, when Americanization was at its height, DuBois began instituting assembly programs designed to promote ethnic pride and cross-cultural understanding at Woodbury High School. As her work became known in the community, she was approached by members of the Woodbury American Legion and asked to resign her teaching position at Woodbury High School (DuBois & Okorodudu, 1984). As concerns about immigration became more widespread and Americanizing immigrants became more of a focus for schools, DuBois was viewed as a radical and her work was described as "Bolshevik." During her tenure at Woodbury High School, she was the subject of false rumors that implied that she refused to salute the U.S. flag, believed in the cult of nakedness, and supported intermarriage among the races (DuBois, 1984). In addition to her ideas on ethnic maintenance, as a Quaker and a pacifist DuBois advocated for peace. Her ideas about peace as well as her ideas about race and ethnicity made her suspect to conservatives who wanted to stop immigration and assimilate the immigrants who remained in the United States as fast as possible.

Things turned around by the early 1940s, and intercultural education was viewed by many educational and political leaders as a means to maintain a united America. In 1942, as director of the Intercultural Education Workshop, DuBois prepared a pamphlet for the U.S. Office of Education entitled *National Unity through Intercultural Education*. The pamphlet provided teachers with specific ideas for integrating intercultural education into primary, intermediate, and secondary classrooms as well as resources, activities, annotated readings, and references for materials that could be used in language arts, social studies, art, music, foreign languages, home economics, and sports classes.

DuBois's pamphlet was one of 24 that were published in the Education and National Defense Series. Other pamphlets in the series included *Population Adrift* and *Helping the Foreign-Born Achieve Citizenship*. According to

U.S. Commissioner of Education John W. Studebaker, the pamphlets were designed to "assist educational institutions and organizations in making the greatest possible contributions toward the promotion of understanding and the encouragement of effective citizenship in our democracy." (DuBois, 1942, back cover). The pamphlets were available from the U.S. Government Printing office for 15 cents. With a U.S. flag and photographs of Asian, Mexican, Canadian, and Czechoslovakians on the cover, the pamphlets presented a very attractive, though somewhat misleading image of national unity.

After World War II, conservative perspectives on intercultural education resurfaced. In 1953, Senator Joseph McCarthy called DuBois before the Senate Subcommittee on Government Operations for questioning. She ultimately received an apology from McCarthy for requiring her to come before the subcommittee. Nevertheless, she felt victimized. She noted that after she was called before the subcommittee, requests for her work decreased and projects that had been in the making failed to materialize (DuBois, 1984). People she thought were her friends began to avoid her (DuBois, 1984). By the early 1950s McCarthyism had spread fear throughout the United States. The threat of being accused of being un-American made a focus on ethnicity and ancestral homelands a dangerous memory for many U.S. citizens. Moreover, it repositioned intercultural education as irrelevant and unnecessary.

Part III

THE STRUGGLE TO INCLUDE
TRANSFORMATIVE VOICES
IN SCHOOL KNOWLEDGE

P ART III includes two chapters that highlight the challenges that arise when efforts are made to include transformative voices in school knowledge. They will also provide insights drawn from the experiences of intergroup educators that multicultural educators can consider as they continue to reform schools.

Chapter 6, "The Demise of a Movement," describes intergroup education as a movement that was caught in a time warp. It failed to change with the times. As the thrust for social justice moved in the 1960s from personal to structural discrimination and racial minorities demanded full inclusion in U.S. society, intergroup educators seemed out of step with the times. Intergroup educators focused their attention on prejudice and discrimination at the personal level and did not give much attention to the structures in American society that supported those perspectives. Focusing on prejudice and discrimination at the personal level was an approach that worked with European immigrants. By the 1960s, the children and grandchildren of immigrants from southern and eastern Europe were able to benefit from society's acceptance of ideas, such as tolerance and brotherhood. These were ideas that intergroup educators championed. By the 1960s many of the leaders in intergroup education had left the movement and were working on other curricular issues and problems.

Chapter 6 also includes a glimpse into the lives of African Americans, Chinese immigrants, and Puerto Ricans on the mainland. This information provides a basis for understanding the sociopolitical context in which the intergroup education movement found itself in the 1950s and 1960s. The overviews reveal the hopes and dreams of people of color and highlight the real-life challenges they confronted in trying to achieve them. Most importantly they reveal the extent to which intergroup educators were out of touch with the concerns of people of color.

The McCarran Act, which was part of the sociopolitical context that surrounded the demise of intergroup education, is also discussed in Chapter 6. The McCarran Act reified earlier limits on immigration and served as a sign that people of color were seen as a problem in the United States.

The legacy of intergroup education to multicultural education is discussed in Chapter 7. The chapter is framed around four lingering questions. Each of the questions is tied to an issue that was confronted but not resolved by intergroup educators. The inability of intergroup educators to resolve these issues was implicated in their ultimate demise. Today key aspects of these same questions confront multicultural educators and must be resolved if multicultural education is to become, unlike intergroup education, fully institutionalized in schools. Chapter 7 allows multicultural educators to look back at the work of intergroup educators and draw insights and lessons that they can use as they work to narrow the gap between real and ideal American Creed values.

6

Cycles of Change: The Waning Influence of Intercultural Education

THE SOCIOPOLITICAL context that surrounded and sustained the intergroup education movement had begun to change by the 1950s. White ethnics, who to a great extent were moving into mainstream U.S. society, had less need for and interest in intercultural education. Intercultural education was a movement that had seemingly lost its raison d'être. World War II was over, and instead of a time of upheaval it was a time of prosperity. White ethnics, aided by Veterans Administration and Federal Housing authority loans, began leaving urban areas for suburbia. Even though they were still targets of prejudice and discrimination, cultural assimilation, an economy that provided access to good paying jobs, and a new national enemy—communism—allowed White ethnics to move toward the center of U.S. society.

The power of intergroup educators' networks to synergize and keep their message alive for over 2 decades is testimony to their resilience and persistence through difficult and challenging times. However, as White ethnics moved out of the margins, intercultural educators were not able to refocus their energy and attention and directly confront the societal structures that prevented racial and ethnic minorities from moving from the margins of U.S. society to its center. They continued to focus their attention on creating the conditions for tolerance and brotherhood, but did not adequately address segregation, institutional racism, and other barriers that prevented racial minorities from gaining access to good schools and meaningful curricula—all of which were necessary for upward social mobility. Consequently, unlike White ethnics, racial minorities did not realize the full benefits of intergroup education.

As White ethnics moved into the mainstream of U.S. society, people of color were left behind in schools that were becoming increasingly segregated and less equal. African Americans, for example, were trapped in inner-city neighborhoods by "red-lining" mortgage-lending practices and e covenants. Red-lining occurs when banks draw a redline around where they do not make loans. The cultural geography of urban urban school districts reflected these practices with suburban school distric₅ becoming overwhelming White and urban districts increasingly becoming populated by minority students (Rury, 2002).

INTERGROUP EDUCATORS TURN THEIR FOCUS
TO HUMAN RELATIONS

As intergroup tensions related to minorities increased and European ethnic groups began moving into the mainstream, intergroup educators began working with teachers and school administrators to help them focus more directly on ethnic and racial minorities. William Heard Kilpatrick captured this effort when speaking on behalf of the Bureau for Intercultural Education:

> The Bureau exists to serve the cause of democracy and justice, for neither democracy nor justice can be satisfied short of the rule of mutual respect and kindly dealings among all our people. At present, such respect and kindliness for certain minority groups are too often lacking; actual discriminations, in fact, abounds. This is a situation that public education, to be true to itself, can neither overlook nor disregard. The obligation is positive: definite educational steps must be undertaken to help make the needed respect and kindliness prevail. To help the schools discharge this particular duty is the precise aim and effect of the Bureau for Intercultural Education. (quoted in VanTil, 1945, p. 3)

Dangerous Business: Teaching Students
to Think, Doubt, and Question

Intergroup educators used democratic education to focus attention on Kilpatrick's call for "mutual respect and kindly dealings" for minority groups. However, even with its emphasis on democratic education, conservatives who wanted schools to promote unquestioning patriotism viewed intergroup educators with suspicion. The kind of democratic classrooms that intergroup education sought to create, characterized by free and open discussion, were seen as dangerous. During World War II, however, the overarching concern that prejudice and discrimination could fracture the United States resulted in a broad range of support for the intergroup message of toleration and brotherhood. There was also support for in-service programs that would help teachers develop the skills and attitudes needed to implement programs for intergroup and interracial understanding.

In-service intercultural training for teachers increased during the 1940s. However, intergroup education never fully permeated schools and teacher resistance to diversity was frequently tolerated. In 1942, when Miss Quinn, a junior high school civics teacher in New York City, used anti-Semitic materials in her class and was accused of saying that all communists were Jews and that Italian children were "greasy foreigners," school officials did not take immediate action (Zitron, 1968). It was only after 3 years of pressure from community groups, teachers, and parents that charges were brought against Miss Quinn. The school board found her guilty of neglect of duty and poor judgment but acquitted her of most of the other charges. Miss Quinn continued to teach in New York City and in 1949 came to the public's attention again when she "made anti-Negro statements during a current events lesson" (Zitron, 1968, p. 96). Miss Quinn was informed of superintendent Jason's dissatisfaction with her behavior, but no further action was taken.

The pressure to implement prejudice reduction programs began to subside after World War II. As the nation moved into the Cold War, right-wing groups began to challenge the content of intergroup education programs and the people teaching in them. On October 13, 1947, *The Tablet*, a publication of the Catholic diocese of Brooklyn, joined the attack on intercultural education and ran an article stating that "The word 'intercultural' has now come to be associated with propaganda of the Communist Party line" (Zitron, 1968, p. 97). The article stated that 6 out of the 20 lectures at an intercultural workshop focused on prejudice. It noted that

> one lecture on the means of combating prejudice might be expected—but six? The overemphasis on prejudice is part of the party-line technique which seeks to divide and conquer by stirring up hate among minority groups by making them feel more discriminated against than they actually are. (Zitron, 1968, p. 97)

In-service courses in New York City schools continued to be reduced until by 1954 there were only two courses left.

INTERGROUP EDUCATORS AND THE CONTRADICTIONS OF RACE AND EQUITY

Intergroup educators, for the most part, used the same strategies that they used for European immigrants in their work with racial and ethnic minorities. There were, however, several important differences between European immigrants and racial and ethnic minorities. Responding to segregated schools and communities, textbooks and materials that misrepresented racial minorities, as well as school administrators who used discriminatory hiring and student placement practices, required more than a verbal commitment to tolerance and brotherhood. It required broad-based action predicated on an understanding of the deep structure of prejudice and discrimination that had built up over generations in the United States. The racialized thinking that supported that structure was not only embraced by mainstream Americans; it was also accepted by the new immigrants. Soon after their arrival in the United States immigrants from southern and eastern Europe quickly learned the meaning of the various social categories that existed in U.S. society and the stigma associated with minorities (Jacobson, 1998). Most intercultural educators did not seem to recognize or were not prepared to address the enormity of the multilayered problem of prejudice and discrimination with respect to racial and ethnic minorities.

In what follows, readers are given a glimpse into the lives of African Americans, Chinese immigrants, and Puerto Ricans on the mainland. The overviews of these groups reveal their hopes and dreams and highlight the real-life challenges they confronted in trying to achieve them. Most importantly they reveal the extent to which intergroup educators were out of touch with the concerns of people of color.

African Americans

African Americans who had fought to secure the freedom of Europeans during World War II returned to the United States hoping that their lives and those of their children would be better. New York, Detroit, Cleveland, Chicago, Pittsburgh, and other northern industrial cities, where large numbers of African Americans had settled during the 1930s and 1940s, were not only sites of struggle; they were sites of hope and possibility. The Harlem Renaissance had sparked the growth of a new African American intellectual elite who were writing, creating art, and engaging in political activities. Things seemed to be changing for the better.

The activist and politician Adam Clayton Powell, Jr., was elected to the U.S. Congress from Harlem in 1945. In 1948, President Truman signed Executive Order 9981 ending segregation in the U.S. Armed Forces. Even though A. Philip Randolph, who threatened to encourage Blacks not to enlist in the armed forces or refuse to serve if drafted, pressured Truman into signing the Executive Order, it was a welcomed act and an encouraging sign of change. In 1950, Gwendolyn Brooks became the first Black person to receive a Pulitzer Prize for *Annie Allen*. Later, Ralph J. Bunche became the first Black person awarded the Nobel Peace Prize for his work as a mediator in the Palestine crisis. The Tuskegee Institute's Department of Records and Research reported that 1952 was the first year in the 71 years since it had begun a systematic tabulation of statistics on lynching that there were no reported lynchings in the United States (Tuskegee Institute, 1952). For many years, Ida B. Wells-Barnett (2002) an African American woman, called attention to lynching and other forms of violence directed against African Americans. The Tuskegee data suggested that Wells's ardent voice, along with those of many others in the campaign to end lynching, had finally been heard. These kinds of accomplishments, though intermittent and riddled with challenges and contradictions, were a source of pride and inspiration for a people who had been ignored and dismissed throughout much of U.S. history.

Keeping the Faith in Difficult Times. George Theophilus Walker's life reflects the ways in which hope mediated reality for African Americans during the postwar years. Walker's father was a West Indian who had emigrated to the United States and eventually settled in Washington, D.C., after he graduated from Temple University Medical School. George was born on June 17, 1922 in Washington, D.C., which was a segregated city from 1881 to 1967.

Congress never adopted official segregation laws, but a form of de facto segregation was reinforced and supported by community norms and sanctions. Throughout the early years of the 20th century, Blacks who wanted to visit the U.S. Congress were required to sit in the "colored gallery" in the Senate chamber. Black cooks and waiters could work in cafeterias and restaurants in the U.S. Capitol and in surrounding office buildings, but they were barred from eating in the Capitol and nearby establishments. Segregation in Washington, D.C., did not begin to break down until the Civil Rights Movement during the 1960s. Unlike intergroup educators, civil rights workers directly confronted structural barriers like segregation that blocked racial minorities from full inclusion in U.S. society.

Walker's mother taught him to play the piano and to appreciate classical music. His hard work and perseverance paid off when, in 1996, Walker became the first African American to receive the Pulitzer Prize in music. His biographical journey is an example of the complexity of the American experience with respect to race, prejudice, and discrimination. Walker was the first African American concert artist to graduate from the renowned Curtis Institute of Music in Philadelphia. He became the first African American instrumentalist to perform at Town Hall when he made his debut on piano in 1945. Walker noted that these accomplishments did not erase the prejudice he had to face. He said,

> It took me longer than my other white friends to get a management contract. I realized early that it was clearly a racial thing. I had obstacles they didn't

have even though I may have had a more exemplary background and always did exceptional auditions. (Edmonds, 1999, p. 5)

Walker eventually made his debut concert tour in Europe. However, like many African Americans of his day, he had to navigate through difficult times and circumstances to experience success. Undaunted by prejudice and discrimination, Walker went on to earn his doctorate in 1955 from the prestigious Eastman School of Music. Unable to earn a living as a concert performer, he spent most of his career as a university professor. Like so many African Americans before him, Walker had made a way out of no way. His resilience and determination not only served him well; it served as a beacon of hope for others.

The prejudice and discrimination that Walker and literally thousands of African Americans of his generation faced were not a major focus for intergroup educators. They were, however, the focus of transformative scholars and activists such as W.E.B. DuBois (1899/1973), Carter G. Woodson (Woodson & Wesley, 1922/1962), and Anna Julia Cooper (1892/1988). Building on their legacy, African Americans worked with other racial and ethnic groups during the Civil Rights Movement to directly confront segregation and other structural barriers to inclusion.

Chinese Immigrants

Chinese immigrants also had reason to hope for a better life in the United States after World War II. The Chinese experience in the United States up to that point had not indicated that American Creed values of freedom, justice, and equality applied to them. Throughout their history in the United States, the Chinese had been limited to menial jobs and had their rights restricted. Moreover, mainstream Americans generally regarded the Chinese as racially inferior and inassimilable (McClain, 1994).

The Chinese began arriving in the United States as sailors and merchants in the late 1700s. According to the 1855 New York State census, some immigrants like William Brown, who was Chinese, took English names, married European women, and remained in the United States. Chinese immigrants, primarily laborers, continued immigrating to the United States until 1882, when the U.S. Congress passed the Chinese Exclusion Act. The first act, which prohibited Chinese laborers from coming into the United States for 10 years, was followed with a series of extensions, the last of which was approved in 1904.

The Chinese Exclusion Acts essentially stopped new Chinese immigrants from coming to the United States. However, by 1870 about 65,000 Chinese were already living in the United States (Hing, 2001). They faced unrelenting discrimination, a fact illustrated by courts in cases like *U.S. v. Fong Yue Ting* and legislation such as the Geary Act, which threatened their ability to stay in United States. The Chinese also used the courts to fight for their rights. For example, in 1898 the Supreme Court in *United States v. Wong Kim Ark* found that Chinese children born in the United States were legally American citizens. This ruling provided a ray of hope in a long history of anti-Asian legislation. Eventually, laws that limited the ability of people of Chinese descent from fully participating in American society began to change. China was a U.S. ally during World War II and the exclusion laws became somewhat of an embarrassment to U.S. political leaders. The Chinese Exclusion Act was repealed in 1943. While the repeal did not result in a significant increase in Chinese immigrants, it did result in large numbers of Chinese who were already in the United States becoming naturalized citizens and being drafted into the military.

As racial antipathies toward the Chinese waned, the Japanese became the new target for prejudice and discrimination directed against Asians. To distinguish themselves from Japanese Americans and to signal their patriotism during World War II, some Chinese Americans wore buttons stating "I am Chinese" (Takaki, 1989). After the war, Chinese veterans were able to use the G.I. Bill to advance their education. The *War Brides Act*, which was passed in 1945, enabled Chinese women to join their husbands. That act, along with the G.I. Fiancées Act passed in 1946, helped stabilize the Chinese community even though it remained primarily a male community into the early 1960s (Jackson, 1995).

Chinatowns. During the 1940s and 1950s, the Chinese in New York City, like those in cities throughout the United States, located their homes, organizations, and businesses in communities called Chinatowns. The Chinese gathered together in ethnic communities as a result of discrimination and limited access to housing outside of Chinatown. With the repeal of the exclusionary laws in the 1940s, Chinatowns were no longer simply places of refuge offering protection to the Chinese. The communities were transformed into sites where the Chinese could have their social, economic, and political needs addressed.

Chinatown in New York City is located in lower Manhattan. The *New York Times* estimated that by 1859, 150 Chinese men lived there. That number grew to over 2,000 by the early 1870s. In 1949 there was a dramatic increase in the number of people living in New York's Chinatown when thousands of Chinese nationals who were studying in the United States were stranded when the People's Republic of China was established. Chinatown remained the primary home community for native-born Chinese Americans as well as Chinese nationals into the 1960s. As the number of

Chinese in New York City grew, the community expanded into parts of Little Italy and the Lower East Side.

Chinese language schools, which were established in Chinatowns, gave Chinese children an opportunity to learn to read and write characters. Even though the schools were often associated with religious organizations that were seeking converts, they were viewed positively by parents who wanted their children to be culturally literate and to be able to communicate with their relatives in China and with older Chinese relatives in the United States. The Chinese Public School in New York City (Niuyue Huaqiao Gongli Xuexiao) opened in 1908. The primary purpose of the school, which was supported by tuition and donations, was to teach students Chinese language and culture.

Intergroup educators worked with the Chinese community and received some funding from Chinese organizations. They did not, however, locate any of their major programs or services in New York's Chinatown, where the majority of Chinese in New York city lived and went to school. Intergroup educators' primary support for Chinese Americans was through publications and materials on successful Chinese Americans like Lue Gim Gong. His biography and the contributions and cultural characteristics of Chinese Americans were described in a bureau publication entitled *Lue Gim Gong: A Chinese American Horticulturist*. Substantive efforts such as those that supported incorporating Italian and German into the foreign language curriculum in New York City public schools were not forthcoming. Intercultural educators did not work with the Chinese American community to gain support for Chinese language instruction in public schools. Chinese Americans were on the margins of U.S. society as well as on the margins of the intercultural education movement.

Puerto Ricans in New York City

Puerto Rican merchants began arriving in New York City in the early 17th century to sell sugar, rum, tobacco, and other products from Puerto Rico (Fitzpatrick, 1971). From the 17th century to the early part of the 20th century, the small but varied Puerto Rican population in New York City included professionals, intellectuals, political exiles, contract laborers, and social activists. Even though they were a diverse population, as a group they struggled with prejudice and discrimination and limited access to jobs, health care, and housing. During the early years of the 20th century, the Puerto Rican community in New York City had more men than women and more people who identified themselves as White than as Black (Jackson, 1995). Some Puerto Ricans who looked as if they were African Americans lived in segregated neighborhoods. However, activities within the

Puerto Rican community and within their organizations were frequently integrated.

The number of Puerto Ricans in the United States increased during the 1940s as people left Puerto Rico in search of economic opportunity. Strikes, unemployment, and a sugar and coffee industry that had been severely damaged by natural disasters hit the Puerto Rican economy hard and caused many people to migrate to the mainland. By the 1950s, Puerto Rican migration to New York City had begun to have an impact on educational services. Enrollment of Puerto Ricans in public schools grew from 14% of the city's population in 1951 to 32% in 1953 (Watkins, 1957). Public School 108 in East Harlem was opened in 1951 to accommodate the growing Puerto Rican population. By 1953, due to the large number of students in the first and second grades, students at P.S. 108 were put on a split schedule.

Poor educational planning for the rapidly increasing number of students put pressure on school facilities and teacher turnover. Schools with large numbers of Puerto Rican students tended to have younger and less experienced teachers than other schools in the district. Of the 52 teachers at Public School 108 in 1953 only three had 10 years experience, 23 were on probation, 12 were substitute teachers who had been given a full-time assignment, and eight had recently completed their probationary period (Watkins, 1957).

Many Puerto Rican newcomers were Roman Catholic and, consequently, had access to parochial schools in addition to public schools. The Catholic Church established Commander Shea School in East Harlem for Puerto Rican students in 1943. The school instituted orientation classes for newcomers and hired a teacher who graduated from the University of Puerto Rico and understood the students' cultural background. One of the major differences between the public and parochial schools was that the parochial schools were able to select their students. Unlike the public schools, they did not have to take new students in the middle of the term. This was a decided advantage because enrolling new students throughout the term was very disruptive. This simple rule afforded the parochial schools a level of stability that was absent in the public schools. Since the parochial schools did not require that their students provide a baptismal certificate or other evidence of church membership, Catholic and non-Catholic parents who were looking for quality schools frequently turned to parochial schools.

Intercultural Educators and the Puerto Rican Community. After retiring from BFHS, Leonard Covello served as an educational consultant to the Education Section of the New York City Office of the Migration Division of the Department of Labor. He was appointed to the position by the

Secretary of Labor of the Commonwealth of Puerto Rico. Covello had worked closely with the Puerto Rican community during his tenure as principal at BFHS. Under his leadership, BFHS developed a special orientation course for Puerto Rican students. The course was designed to orient Puerto Rican students to the school community, city, state, and to the nation as a whole. The course also included information on the duties and responsibilities of good citizens and the educational and vocational opportunities available to BFHS students. In a fashion that paralleled his work with European immigrants, Covello linked BFHS to the Puerto Rican community by setting up neighborhood clubs, instituting Puerto Rican annual Festivals, organizing a Puerto Rican Parent–Teachers Association, and holding receptions for Puerto Rican leaders. Covello's efforts were well received within the Puerto Rican community. As a result of his contacts in the community, he was able to document authentic concerns of the Puerto Rican community in his 1951 report *Puerto Rican Pupils in New York City Public Schools.*

These overviews of the experiences of African Americans, Chinese Americans, and Puerto Rican Americans highlight the structural nature of the issues they confronted and the extent to which the problems they confronted were multigenerational. Subsequent generations of ethnic and racial minorities faced problems that were not dissimilar from those their ancestors faced at the beginning of the 20th century.

THE MCCARRAN ACT: A RESPONSE TO RACIAL AND ETHNIC MINORITIES

By the middle of the 20th century, large numbers of African Americans, Puerto Ricans, and immigrants from the Caribbean, Latin America, and East Asia had joined European immigrants in New York City and other northern cities. Concerns about these newcomers reflected fears that were similar to those raised about the Italians, Jews, and other southern and eastern European immigrants who had arrived in large northern cities at the beginning of the century. The U.S. Senate responded to the concerns by appointing a committee under Senator Pat McCarran's leadership to study U.S. immigration laws, concerns, and needs. The committee issued a report that was over 300 pages long. The report formed the basis for the 1952 McCarran–Walter Immigration Bill. The bill ostensibly removed racial barriers to immigration, but in some significant ways it reified the restrictive immigration policies that were established by the Immigration Act of 1924. For example, strict immigration quotas were assigned to people from "undesirable" parts of the world, such as Asia. The bill's discriminatory intent was captured in the following poem, entitled "McCarran Act," which was published in July 1952 (cited in Wittke, 1964, p. 5).

> *The blood that made this nation great*
> *Will now be tested at the gate*
> *To see if it deserves to be*
> *Admitted to democracy,*
> *Or rather to that small elite*
> *Whose hemoglobin counts can meet*
> *Requirements of purity*
> *Consistent with security*
> *And with that small and rabid mind*
> *That thinks itself above mankind.*

President Truman vetoed the McCarran–Walter Immigration Bill on June 25, 1952, stating, "Our immigration policy is equally, if not more, important to the conduct of our foreign relations and to our responsibilities of moral leadership in the struggle for world peace" (Cited in Wittke, 1964, p. 5). The bill, however, was passed over Truman's veto.

The McCarran Act reflected the view that racial and ethnic minorities were a problem and the best way to address the problem was to limit immigration. This response to minorities was particularly problematic for indigenous minority groups, the population growth of which were not affected by immigration. The McCarran act, along with a history of prejudice and discrimination, sent a strong message that minorities were not welcome in the United States.

AN EGALITARIAN MOVEMENT DIES

During the 1930s and 1940s, intercultural educators were consistent in voicing concerns about tolerance and brotherhood. They established networks of academic, financial, and educational leaders who helped disseminate their message and promote their ideas. From its East Coast office in New York City and its West Coast office in Los Angeles, the Bureau for Intercultural Education sponsored workshops for teachers and community leaders at Stanford University, the University of Minnesota, Goddard College, Columbia University, Montclair College, and the University of California at Berkeley. These workshops, which were held during the summers of 1944 and 1945, illustrated the bureau's commitment to teacher education as a way to improve the educational experiences of students.

Under the leadership of H. H. Giles, who also served as a curriculum consultant to the Progressive Education Association's Commission on the Relation of School and College, the Bureau for Intercultural Education brought university faculty and school staff together to develop curricula and materials and to design and implement community studies. The bureau also began to make a more direct and focused effort to ground its work in research and social science literature. Partnering with highly respected scholars such as Robert Havighurst, Louis Raths, and Gordon W. Allport, the bureau worked with researchers to better understand intergroup tensions and to make research findings accessible to young people and to the community at large.

However, by the close of the 1950s an overall effort to consciously promote an organized intercultural educational program had ceased. There had been a slow decline in the amount of publicity and national interest in intergroup education throughout the 1950s. Efforts to reinvigorate the movement failed. Moreover, the field had lost several of its most ardent leaders. Covello retired as principal of Benjamin Franklin High School in September 1956. Granrud had also retired. Taba had begun to move away from intergroup education and refocus her work on social studies and curriculum theory. Rachel Davis DuBois remained committed to the ideals of intergroup education but shifted her focus to the Civil Rights Movement. Friends like Leonard Covello, who served on the board of directors of her organization, the Workshop for Cultural Democracy, continued to support her work. By the 1960s, support for intergroup education had been weakened by the sense that all was well. There didn't seem to be a need for intergroup education. The civil unrest that occurred throughout the 1960s was a shock to a nation that believed it had largely solved its intergroup problems.

7

The Legacy of Intercultural Education to Multicultural Education

INTERCULTURAL EDUCATION has been identified by scholars as a historical antecedent of multicultural education (Banks, J. A., 2004; Montalto, 1982). It is linked to multicultural education by several egalitarian characteristics that were identified and laid claim to in the early 1930s by intercultural educators. In subsequent years, those characteristics, which include a deep commitment to social justice and citizen action, have, over time, also become closely associated with multicultural education. As intercultural educators did in the past, multicultural educators today center their work in schools and take seriously their responsibility to help prepare students to live in a pluralistic democratic society (Banks, J. A., 1997; Clinchy, 1942). Leaders in each of the movements understood that prejudice and discrimination were antithetical to democracy and they worked to ensure that students develop the skills, attitudes, and knowledge needed to recognize and respond to them. However, while there are similarities between intergroup education and multicultural education, there are also important and significant differences (Banks, C. A. M., 1995). Two of those differences, the social context in which they were developed and the scope of the movements, are discussed below.

COMPARISON OF THE SOCIAL CONTEXT
IN WHICH INTERGROUP EDUCATION AND MULTICULTURAL
EDUCATION DEVELOPED

Intercultural education and multicultural education began at different times in U.S. history and are a reflection of the social issues that were paramount at those times. Intercultural education developed in the early part of the 20th century in response to inequities suffered by immigrants from southern and eastern Europe. However by the 1950s, as members of those groups became assimilated and moved into the mainstream, the movement began to fade. Yet there was still a need for a movement that could mount a response to the social inequities faced by groups who remained on the margins of society. As intergroup education was fading, African Americans, who were still second-class citizens, continued to push for equal rights. Two important markers in their efforts were the Supreme Court decision in *Brown v. Board of Education, Topeka, Kansas*, and the Civil Rights Movement of the 1960s. Individuals such as Thurgood Marshall and Kenneth Clark, as well as groups such as the National Association for the Advancement of Colored People (NAACP), helped pave the way for the historic 1954 Supreme Court decision striking down segregation in U.S. public schools. This major civil rights victory sparked a renewed effort in the quest for full inclusion in American society. By the 1960s, the Civil Rights Movement was well underway. The momentum of the Civil Rights Movement, with its focus on the political, economic, and social structures supporting prejudice and discrimination, provided new opportunities to address inequities in education. One of the many areas that became a focus in education was the paucity of information on African Americans in school curricula. As African Americans began to demand that educators include information about them in school curricula, many educators were unaware of the curriculum materials and projects that had been developed by intergroup educators or of the efforts of European immigrant groups in earlier decades to force educators to include information about *their* histories and heroes in school curricula. Intergroup education had not become institutionalized in U.S. schools and was only a dim memory to a few educators.

African American scholars, drawing on the liberatory scholarship of individuals like W.E.B. DuBois (1899/1973) and Carter G. Woodson (Woodson & Wesley, 1922/1962), established a new discipline called Black studies to respond to the call for Black perspectives on American society and information on the role and experiences of African Americans in American society (Banks, J. A., 1996). Multicultural education evolved out of the Black studies movement of the 1960s, as did subsequent egalitarian movements, including women's studies, ethnic studies, and multiethnic education (Grant & Ladson-Billings, 1997).

In a pluralistic society, problems involving intergroup tensions are perennial and present challenges to every generation. Both intercultural educators and multicultural educators responded to the challenges of diversity in their generation: intergroup education in the first half of the 20th century and multicultural education in the second half. Drawing on the work of a diverse group of scholars and disciplines, including Carlos Cortés (1973) in Mexican American Studies, Jack Forbes (1973) in American Indian

Studies, Lowell Chun-Hoon (1973) in Asian American Studies, and Hilda Taba and her colleagues (1949) in intergroup education, multicultural educators continued the quest intercultural educators had begun in the 1930s to expand the reach of the American dream to groups on the margins of U.S. society.

THE SCOPES OF INTERGROUP EDUCATION
AND MULTICULTURAL EDUCATION COMPARED

Multicultural education differs from intercultural education in that it is more broadly conceptualized. Multicultural education not only focuses on race, ethnicity, and religion—issues that were centered in intercultural education—it addresses issues related to gender, social class, exceptionally, and language, and their interaction (Banks & Banks, 2004; Grant & Sleeter, 1986). The broad scope of multicultural education has led some scholars to call it a meta-discipline (Banks & Banks, 2004).

In addition, curricular content in multicultural education programs is broader than that in intercultural education programs. Intergroup education programs, for the most part, embodied what J. A. Banks (2004) calls contributions and additive approaches. Heroes, holidays, and cultural contributions were incorporated into Irish Day, Italian Day, and Chinese Day celebrations and curriculum units (DuBois, 1942). Prejudice and discrimination were examined on an individual level (Taba, Brady, Robinson, & Vickery, 1951). Intergroup educators did not directly address structural and institutional racism, empowerment, poverty, and societal inequities. Multicultural theorists argue that these issues should be incorporated into the content integration, knowledge construction, and social action components of multicultural education programs (Banks & Banks, 2004). It is important to note, however, that even though the major theorists in multicultural education argue that these transformative elements should be included in effective multicultural programs, some multicultural education programs are organized around contribution and additive approaches that are similar to those embraced by intercultural educators.

The scope and the social context in which multicultural education and intercultural education developed are just two of the many differences between them. Those differences, however, should not be interpreted as an indication that the fields are unrelated. Multicultural education and intercultural education are connected through a complex pattern of issues and characteristics that at times intersect and at other times diverge. Immigration is an example of one of those issues.

Immigration: A Connection Between Multicultural and Intercultural Education

The number of U.S. immigrants from 1991 to 1999 was almost identical to the number of immigrants who arrived in the U.S. from 1901 to 1910 (U.S. Census Bureau, 1975, 2000). A major difference between the two groups of immigrants is that almost 92% of the immigrants who settled in the United States during the first decade of the 20th century came from Europe, while only 14.8% came from Europe during the last decade of that century (Gibson & Lennon, 1999). See Tables 7.1 and 7.2 for a historical overview of the countries of origin of U.S. immigration.

At the beginning of the 20th century, U.S. immigrants were primarily from Italy, Russia, and other European nations. However, by the end of the century they came primarily from the Caribbean, Central America, South America, Mexico, and Asian nations such as China, India, and the Philippines (Gibson & Lennon, 1999). Another important difference between immigrants at the beginning and the end of the 20th century is the percentage of the U.S. population that they represented. In the early 1900s, immigrants accounted for about 15% of the total U.S. population compared to about 9% of the U.S. population in 2000 (U.S. Census Bureau, 2000).

While anti-immigrant attitudes are not as virulent today as they were in the past, negative attitudes toward newcomers persist. A Harris poll (Spain, 1999) conducted in 1992 suggests that there was a tendency to extol

Table 7.1. Historical Overview of the Countries of Origin of U. S. Immigrants

Top Ten Countries in 1900	*Top Ten Countries in 2000*
1. Italy	1. Mexico
2. Russia	2. Former Soviet Union
3. Germany	3. China
4. Ireland	4. Philippines
5. United Kingdom	5. India
6. Austria	6. Vietnam
7. Sweden	7. El Salvador
8. Hungary	8. Haiti
9. Poland	9. Cuba
10. Norway	10. Dominican Republic

Source: U. S. Department of Homeland Security, *Yearbook of immigration statistics, 2002.* Washington, DC: U. S. Government Printing Office, 2003.

Table 7.2. Country of Birth of Illegal
Aliens in the United States as
of January 2000

		Total
1.	Mexico	4,808,000
2.	El Salvador	189,000
3.	Guatemala	144,000
4.	Colombia	141,000
5.	Honduras	138,000
6.	China	115,000
7.	Ecuador	108,000
8.	Dominican Republic	91,000
9.	Philippines	85,000
10.	Brazil	77,000
11.	Haiti	76,000
12.	India	70,000
13.	Peru	61,000
14.	Korea	55,000
15.	Canada	47,000

Source: U. S. Department of Homeland Security,
Yearbook of immigration statistics, 2002. Washington, DC:
U. S. Government Printing Office, 2003.

the virtues of immigrants who came to the United States in the past while raising concerns about present-day immigration. Fifty-nine percent of the people surveyed in the Harris poll indicated that immigration has historically been good for the United States. However, 69% of the non-Black respondents believed that present-day immigration is not good for the nation. Findings from a survey conducted by the National Opinion Research Center in 1994 (cited in Spain, 1999) indicate that Americans are uncertain about the extent to which immigration is beneficial. About 62% of the people surveyed believe immigration is too high and should be reduced. The survey also found that approximately 68% of the respondents believe that "additional immigration would make it harder to keep the country united" (Spain, 1999, p. 5). Moreover, "about 62 percent of the respondents thought immigration was unlikely to contribute to higher economic growth, and 85 percent thought that higher immigration would create higher unemployment" (Spain, 1999, p. 5). As the economy improved from the early 1990s, attitudes toward immigration became more positive. A March 2001 Gallup poll found that 45% of Americans believe that immigration improves U.S. culture by increasing its diversity. However, 38% believe that U.S. culture is threatened by immigration (Gallup Poll, 2001).

Although there have always been strong voices against immigration, it continues. Historically immigration has been associated with military or economic concerns in the immigrant's nation of origin. The Irish, for example, left their homeland in the mid-1800s to escape a potato famine. In the late 1800s, Chinese immigrants came to the United States to fill a labor gap. In recent years, immigrants from Vietnam and other Southeast Asian nations, as well as immigrants from Central and Latin American countries, fled from their nations after U.S. military involvement in their homelands. Immigrants from Mexico and other parts of the world are currently coming to the United States in search of greater economic opportunities. The nation's military presence in the Middle East and other parts of the world and its global trade relationships with other nations, reflected in treaties such as NAFTA, will likely fuel continued immigration. The nation is reacting to its newest immigrants in ways that are similar to its response to immigrants at the turn of the 20th century. Lessons drawn from the work of intercultural educators who initiated programs in schools and communities to challenge negative perspectives on immigrants can help contemporary educators today better respond to the challenges of pluralism in a democracy. Those lessons are a legacy from intercultural education to multicultural education.

THE MORE THINGS CHANGE, THE MORE THEY STAY THE SAME

One might assume that individuals who had suffered prejudice and discrimination and were now members of the mainstream would be strong allies for others who were trying to move from the margins of society to its center. The history of the intercultural education movement, however, tells a different story. By the beginning of the 21st century White ethnics, whose ancestors were on the margins of U.S. society in the early 20th century, had largely moved into the mainstream. The margins, however, didn't disappear. They continued to be vibrant and well populated with indigenous groups and new waves of immigrants.

One of the characteristics of movement from the margins to the center is the adoption of mainstream rhetoric. When an immigrant group experiences structural assimilation (Gordon, 1964), it is not uncommon for members of the group to become gatekeepers and defenders of the status quo who try to limit access for other groups. These individuals frequently use the same arguments against other groups that were used to discriminate against their ancestors only a few generations earlier (Ignatiev, 1995). Consequently, it is not surprising that many White ethnics, whose ancestors were on the margins of U.S. society in the early 20th century, don't sympathize with present-day immigrants. Moreover, they often do not recognize that the issues and concerns that are raised about present-day immigrants mirror the attitudes mainstream Americans had about their relatives when they first arrived in the United States (Jacobson, 1998).

Nativism Returns

Nativism has had a long history in U.S. society. It frequently surfaces when large numbers of immigrants enter the country. In 2002, Patrick Buchanan voiced anti-immigrant sentiments similar to those used by nativists in the early 1900s. Buchanan has said, in part,

> America and the West face four clear and present dangers. The first is a dying population. Second is the mass immigration of peoples of different colors, creeds, and cultures, changing the charter of the West forever. The third is the rise to dominance of an anti-Western culture in the West, deeply hostile to its religions, traditions, and morality, which have already sundered the West. The fourth is the breakup of nations and the defection of ruling elites to a world government whose rise entails the end of nations. . . . Of the four clear and present dangers, the population crisis of the West is the most immediate, and most dangerous. . . . Legal immigration should be rolled back to 250,000 each year. Welfare benefits should be restricted to Americans. Immigration laws should be rewritten to end "chain immigration," where new immigrants are entitled to bring in their extended families. In short, immigration laws should be rewritten, with the emphasis on what is best for America. (Buchanan, 2002, pp. 228, 231, 234)

Buchanan argues that immigrants are responsible for a wide range of ills that are afflicting the U.S., including the high cost of welfare, health care, and education, as well as the rising crime rate and unemployment. While Buchanan's views do not represent mainstream America, there was enough interest in them for his book, *The Death of the West: How Dying Populations and Immigrant Invasions Imperil Our Country and Civilization*, to stay on the *New York Times* best-seller list for several weeks. It is ironic that Buchanan, a person whose Catholic religion may have placed him in the margins of society at the beginning of the 20th century, was able to use rhetoric similar to that used by nativists in the early 1900s to raise concerns about new immigrants.

As in earlier years, anti-immigrant groups are outspoken and are raising fears and concerns about immigration (Bennett, 1988; Higham, 1972). Data from the 2000 census, which shows an increase in the immigration of Hispanic Americans, is frequently used by anti-immigrant groups to support their argument that immigrants (Hampson, 2001) are invading the United States. While the demographic profile of the United States is changing, the meaning of the changes isn't entirely clear. Nevertheless there is a sense among many Americans that something is wrong and they are afraid (Ungar, 1995).

FOUR LINGERING QUESTIONS

Four questions that were first raised in the intercultural education movement and continue to confront multicultural educators today are used to frame this discussion about the legacy of intercultural education to multicultural education. Intercultural educators grappled with these questions, but were unable to develop and mount adequate responses to them. The questions have lingered over time and in different forms, and they now confront multicultural educators. If multicultural education is to stand the test of time, become fully institutionalized in schools and universities, and continue to challenge the nation to live up to its democratic ideals, it will need to deal effectively with these questions. These are:

1. What and where is the center of the field?
2. If multicultural education is to maintain its integrity, what can change and what must remain the same?
3. Who is training the next generation of leaders?
4. How do you maintain a focus and sustain interest in issues that are not on the national agenda or may even be viewed as being antithetical to national interests?

What and Where Is the Center of Multicultural Education?

This first question challenges multicultural educators to identify its basic tenets. Tremendous progress has been made toward answering this question with the publication of the first and second editions of the *Handbook of Research on Multicultural Education* (Banks & Banks, 1995, 2004). However, much work remains to be done. Multicultural education is defined in the *Handbook* as

> a field of study designed to increase educational equity for all students that incorporates, for this purpose, content, concepts, principles, theories, and paradigms from history, the social and behavioral sciences, and particularly from ethnic studies and women's studies. (Banks & Banks, 1995, p. xii)

The *Handbook* goes on to distinguish multicultural education from in[...] tional and global education, noting that multicultural education "focuses on ethnic, racial, cultural, and gender groups within the boundaries of a nation-state, such as the United States, the United Kingdom, and Canada" (xii).

The center of intercultural education moved with its leadership and its funding sources from one focus to another. The changes reflected multiple voices within intercultural education as well as powerful external voices. Consequently, the goals, the audience for its work, and other key elements of the movement were always in flux. Like intercultural education there are multiple voices in multicultural education. Those voices range from critical multicultural education (Sleeter & McLaren, 1995) to activity-oriented multicultural education (Tiedt & Tiedt, 1999). The multiple voices in multicultural education are reflected in the broad range of perspectives that are presented in texts, materials, and workshops; definitions of key concepts; as well as the identification of groups and issues that are considered appropriate areas of study. Expertise in the field also varies. Individuals who are considered expert authorities in multicultural education range from scholars who work in academic institutions to consultants who work in the private sector. The preparation and backgrounds of individuals who work in multicultural education also varies widely. It includes individuals who have completed academic multicultural and social science programs as well as individuals whose expertise lies in their life experiences and self-study. Even though these diverse perspectives are sometimes in conflict, each is presented as the legitimate voice of multicultural education. This is particularly problematic for practitioners who are charged with designing and implementing multicultural education programs and adding multicultural perspectives to their curricula.

Looking back to the work of intercultural educators can provide some insight on how they acknowledged and tried to respond to practitioners' need for help in implementing intercultural education programs, resolving the problem of who could speak with authority about the field, and deciding on the focus of their programs.

In October of 1944, the Bureau for Intercultural Education, with financial support from the Julius Rosenwald Fund, sponsored a conference for school administrators. The conference was designed to help the participants center their work in intercultural education, reduce the isolation of administrators who were trying to improve human relations in their schools, and help the administrators establish a network of like-minded individuals. Most importantly, the conference provided a forum for the attendees to learn from each other. While their specific circumstances and intergroup problems varied, the participants agreed that certain tenets were important for educators to keep in mind as they conceptualized and implemented intercultural education programs. The tenets that were identified at that and other bureau conferences can provide important insights for educators today. Two of those tenets are discussed below.

1. Effective Multicultural Education Programs Should Be Home-grown. The school administrators who attended the 1944 bureau conference came from different localities and had different responses to the challenge of implementing human relations programs in their schools. The student and community populations that they served, as well as their specific concerns, issues, and sources of support, were different. Consequently, the variety of programs represented at the conference provided an opportunity for the administrators to compare and contrast their programs with those of others. That process laid the groundwork for an important lesson. While the administrators had much to learn from each other, their programs were by necessity different.

Identifying and imposing a master multicultural education program that is universally applicable and can be rapidly implemented in p-12 schools is a recipe for failure. Yet when test scores indicate that academic disproportionality exists in a school or when intergroup tensions occur in a school or community, educators face tremendous pressure to quickly find and implement "the perfect multicultural education program." Achievement, however, can actually be a casualty of such a program. Educators who search for a "model program" they can adopt and implement in their schools will very likely find after they've implemented it that the model is lacking in some important ways. Intergroup educators came to this conclusion over half a century ago. Nothing substitutes for the hard work of local program development lead by experts who are committed to social justice.

Resources such as the *Handbook of Research on Multicultural Education* (Banks & Banks, 2004) can help educators ground their programs in transformative academic knowledge and serve as a departure point for sound program development at the local level. It is important for educators to ground their work in transformative academic knowledge because it provides a strong foundation for educators to thoughtfully explore and consider the issues confronting their school or district. For example, the question of whether to highlight similarities among groups or focus on their differences frequently comes up when educators plan units for elementary and middle school students. Schools may respond differently to this question depending on the particular issues they are grappling with, the background and training of the teachers, and the broader community in which the school is located.

As a field, intergroup educators focused on the similarities of groups in the hope that they would be able to bridge differences and that the differences would eventually disappear. While this approach helped some groups move from the margins of society to the center, it was not completely successful. It may have been more fruitful for intergroup educators, in some cases, to focus on differences. Race, ethnicity, gender, and social class continue to be important factors in human identity. While acknowledging the importance of recognizing similarities, multicultural theorists encourage educators to give students opportunities to focus on differences as well as similarities. It is important to remember, however, that focusing on superficial cultural differences can leave students with the impression that cultural characteristics are static and unique to a particular group. The issues that divide our nation are not primarily cultural. There are economic, educational, and other differences that block the full inclusion and participation of diverse groups in U.S. society. Those differences are embedded in institutional structures and are implicated in more visible cultural differences. In an effective multicultural education program, students would learn how these kinds of substantial differences have been continued and sustained. Decisions about the particular mix and focus of similarities and differences should be made on the ground where educators are able to respond to the specifics of their classrooms and their local context.

Ultimately educators who want to implement effective multicultural education programs must allow time for: building their own and their colleagues' multicultural skills and knowledge, involving parents and community members in the planning process, uncovering the information that will allow them to identify and specifically address the concerns and issues that are important in their schools and communities, and garnering the necessary resources. Lessons from the intergroup education movement suggest that while it is important to learn from other programs and build on them, nothing will substitute for taking the unique elements and concerns of a specific school and community into account when developing an effective multicultural education program.

2. Students Should Not Be the Sole Focus of Multicultural Education Programs. In addition to students, teachers, administrators, parents, and community members should be involved in multicultural education programs. Covello's work at Benjamin Franklin High School highlighted the importance of involving parents and community members in schools. He argued that because adults in East Harlem influenced students' attitudes about race, ethnicity, and other forms of diversity, programs designed to help reduce prejudice were doomed to failure if they didn't reach out to parents and community members. Covello and the teachers at BFHS were able to blur the line between school and community by going outside the walls of the school and working cooperatively with parents, organizations, and community groups. Their community links provided an opportunity for BFHS teachers and staff members to make the schools' commitment to American Creed values of freedom, justice, and equality clear to parents and community members. Parents and community members were invited to serve on school committees where they could learn about academic perspectives on prejudice and discrimination and participate in projects to reduce prejudice. Garnering the support of parents and community members can help synergize and amplify the school's message.

A similar perspective was reflected by intercultural educators at the Bureau for Intercultural Education in their summer workshops. In the summer of 1941, the Bureau for Intercultural Education sponsored a workshop on intercultural education at the Colorado State College of Education. The teachers who participated in the workshop concluded that if intercultural education simply "prevented teachers from passing their misinformation, prejudice, and ignorance on to their students" it would be an important addition to teacher training (Clinchy, 1942, p. 61). These intercultural educators saw teacher training as an important component of their work. As discussed in Chapter 4, one of the goals of intercultural educators was to help teachers confront their prejudices. They understood that teachers would not be able to develop curricula that could help students uncover and respond to their prejudices until they confronted their own prejudices. This is particularly important today because teachers frequently teach students who speak languages, come from communities, and are members of racial or ethnic groups that are unfamiliar to them.

Many of the leaders in intercultural education were immigrants themselves or were members of the second generation. In addition, intercultural educators frequently taught students from their own ethnic groups or from other immigrant groups. Intercultural educators were able to establish links between the school and community because they understood ethnic communities and the people who lived there. Many of them had grown up in ethnic communities and had continuing contact with members of the communities.

Unlike ethnic students in the past, students of color today are primarily taught by teachers who do not have a personal connection to the students and communities in which they teach. The number of students of color is increasing as the number of teachers of color is decreasing (Branch 2001; Council of the Great City Schools, 1993, Lewis, 1996). Encouraging and supporting teachers to reach out to communities less well known to them will require teacher training and a commitment to building stronger community–school relations. As the ethnic and racial texture of our society continues to deepen and as social class, language, and other forms of diversity become more salient, linking schools to communities can help teachers better understand their students and increase their ability to draw on the community as a rich resource.

In addition to involving parents in schools and helping teachers grapple with the psychodynamics of their own attitudes toward diverse groups, students need to be involved in their communities. Several approaches that were used at Benjamin Franklin High School to involve students in their community were discussed in Chapter 3. Although the term *service learning* wasn't used by BFHS educators, it captures the spirit of many of their community-based projects. Service-learning programs provide rich opportunities for students today to be involved in their communities. Many service-learning programs, however, are only available to students at the secondary or university level. Providing more opportunities for students at the elementary and middle school levels to work in the community can enrich the curriculum as well as provide opportunities for students to be engaged in meaningful work. Most importantly, it gives the teachers an opportunity to see students working in more authentic settings (Moll, 1992). Multicultural education programs that incorporate service-learning components not only hold out the opportunity for increasing student learning; they can help educators broaden the scope of their programs to include teachers, parents, and community members (Boyle-Baise, 2002).

Every teacher knows that students are influenced by their home and community environments. When students are surrounded by individuals who don't understand or appreciate social justice and diversity, it is difficult for them to embrace those values. The unfortunate thing is that too often the powerful negative influences outside of school that are at work on students' values, worldviews, and appreciation of equity aren't that different from those they encounter at school. Intergroup educators showed that it is possible to intervene on the side of democratic values. While this is not easy and intergroup educators were not always successful, it is an important lesson.

If Multicultural Education Is to Maintain Its Integrity, What Can Change and What Must Remain the Same?

Intercultural educators have grappled with this question about what can change and what must remain the same throughout their existence, and now multicultural educators are grappling with it. There was a lack of unanimity on the part of intergroup educators in the past, and there is a lack of unanimity among multicultural educators leaders today, about what ideas, theories, perspectives, and groups should be at the center of their movements, as well as how information about them should be presented. Without a clear understanding of what is at the center of a movement, it is difficult to determine what ideas and perspectives can and should be dropped or modified. Both multicultural education and intergroup education have leaders who express different perspectives on what should be included in curricula. Intergroup educators, for example, were split on the role schools should play in helping to reduce intergroup tensions. Some intergroup educators, such as Leonard Covello (1941), believed that intergroup education in schools should help students engage in a gradual and voluntary process of assimilation that would enable them to be proud of their cultural heritage. He believed that an overemphasis on "Americanism" could have negative consequences that could lead to separatist influences. Other individuals who commented on this issue, such as Ruth Benedict, believed that focusing on cultural characteristics of immigrants and minorities reinforced cultural borders and should not be included in intercultural education curricula. She urged intergroup educators to focus their efforts on helping mainstream Americans to understand the negative impact that prejudice and discrimination have in a democracy.

Similar debates are occurring in multicultural education circles today. For example, the appropriate location in the school curriculum for information and discussion on sexual orientation is currently being discussed. Some multicultural educators argue that sexual orientation is an appropriate topic for multicultural education texts, materials, courses, and programs (Gollnick, & Chinn, 2002). Others focus their work more narrowly on race and ethnicity. Debates also surround the appropriate focus in texts and materials on topics related to social action, celebratory aspects of ethnic history, and examples of oppression (Sleeter, 1995). While it would be unlikely that a multicultural leader would take an extreme position arguing for a narrow position on what should or should not be at the center of the field, it isn't clear to what extent the perspectives on issues that are being debated can or should be changed. Moreover, it isn't clear if dropping or significantly changing the issues or perspectives on them would affect the integrity of the field.

Multicultural education has entered into a period of critical self-examination similar to that of intercultural education during the 1940s. Spurred by external challenges to its legitimacy, intercultural educators began a period of introspection, reflection, and evaluation. Intercultural educators critically analyzed their materials to determine their accuracy and the extent to which their work reflected sound social science knowledge. In addition, internal struggles within the movement resulted in some intercultural educators responding to external challenges to the movement by trying to hold their ground and resist change. They ignored the concerns and questions that were being raised about their work and instead raised questions about the commitment, values, and concerns of people who challenged them.

Multicultural education has developed an academic presence gaining recognition as an important area of study for educators. He as the field becomes more integrated into the basic school curriculum, standards may need to be developed. Using a process similar to that used by W.E.B. DuBois (1968) when he developed the Atlanta Conference Studies, scholars in multicultural education will have to engage in research that will refine our "tools of investigation and perfect our methods of work" (p. 217) so that we can more clearly identify and respond to the factors that prevent students from diverse racial, ethnic, social class, and gender groups from succeeding in school. More studies that investigate the effect of university-level multicultural education classes as well as the attitudes, behaviors, and the ability of students to work effectively with diverse populations will also need to be undertaken. University programs designed to provide practitioners with multicultural skills and knowledge will need to be reviewed and revised so that they reflect a clear understanding of what it means to be an expert in multicultural education. The field currently has one national organization specifically devoted to multicultural education, the National Association for Multicultural Education (NAME). *Multicultural Perspectives*, the official newsletter of NAME, provides information on multicultural programs, publications, and activities. However, more organizations and scholarly journals may need to be instituted so that multicultural scholars will have formal structures in which they can critically analyze the work of colleagues and engage in ongoing conversations about their ideas.

Who Is Training the Next Generation of Leaders?

When we reflect on the question of who is training the next generation of multicultural leaders, we shouldn't limit our thoughts to baccalaureate- and graduate-level training. Future multicultural leaders are in elementary, middle schools, and high schools today. We need to consider who is teaching the next generation, how they were trained, and what is their connection to the students they are teaching.

Intergroup education died out, in part, because there was no one left to move into leadership positions when the old guard either retired or began to pursue other interests. Intercultural education was not seen by young scholars and educators as a field on the cutting edge. Moreover, it is difficult to recruit young scholars into a field when the field has a negative image and is under attack. Such was the case for intercultural education by the mid-1950s. The patriotism and loyalty of intercultural educators was openingly being questioned by conservative groups (Zitron, 1968). In addition, intercultural education was seen by many as an anachronism. By

the late 1950s it was all but forgotten. It was no longer a field where excit-
ing new scholarship and ideas were being discussed and formulated. Consequently, there was little interest on the part of the best and the brightest
young scholars, intellectual leaders, and social activists to enter the field.

The failure to attract new leaders had dire consequences for intercultural education. Multicultural leaders can learn about the importance of
training the next generation from the experiences of intercultural educators. It is particularly important for multicultural educators to continually
attract new leaders because they bring fresh ideas and are more likely to
be in touch with the changing nature of the sociopolitical context in which
issues related to diversity are identified and solutions to address them are
formulated. Individuals who were born after the Civil Rights Movement
need to be brought into multicultural education to work with senior scholars in the field and mentored for leadership positions. Young teachers
working in schools today went through schools of education at a time when
nativism, Americanization, and other negative aspects of immigration for
European Americans were very likely not discussed in their history, social studies, or multicultural education classes. Consequently they view the
current response to immigrants from Latin America and Asia as a new
phenomena, not one related to the nation's ongoing cycles of intergroup
tensions. Moreover, discrimination based on race and gender has, within
their lifetime, always been illegal. For many, overt discrimination based
on race, ethnicity, and gender is something they read about in textbooks,
not something they have recognized in their daily lives. Consequently, their
personal understanding of concepts such as immigration, race, class, and
gender is different from those of senior scholars in multicultural education who were born and grew up during a time when prejudice toward
outgroup members was understood and discrimination based on race,
gender, and ethnicity was legally sanctioned. Senior leaders in multicultural
education helped define and operationalize key concepts in the field in a
sociopolitical context that is different from that of today. While discrimination and racism continue to exist in U.S. society, they are reflected in
different ways than they were when multicultural education was established. For example, in the 1960s discrimination and prejudice were generally viewed as a Black–White issue. Today prejudice and discrimination
are viewed within a much more complex and dynamic environment: one
that includes cross-ethnic and racial forms and variations of prejudice and
discrimination. Modern-day interethnic relations range from ethnic conflicts between groups, such as those involving Koreans and African Americans (Chang, 1993), to those involving students whose multiple identities
present them with conflicting messages about cultural ways of being (Yeh
& Drost, 2002).

The lines between racial groups are becoming blurred. A growing number of students and parents are members of more than one racial group. Even though marriage between people of different races is still an exception to the rule, more and more people are marrying interracially. As a result, the number of students with parents or grandparents of different races is increasing. In 2000, about 2.4% of the U.S. population, or about 6.8 million people, identified with two or more races. While this is a relatively small percentage of the U.S. population, the percentage of people who are multiracial is more salient when geographic regions and subgroups within the poplation are examined. For example, children are more likely to be multiracial than adults. In 2000, about 1.9% of U.S. adults identified themselves as multiracial compared to 4% of children. Also, racial groups that have small populations tend to have higher perecentages of multiracial people.

Among all the racial groups, American Indians were the most likely to marry someone outside their racial group (Pollard & O'Hare, 1999). Data from the 2000 census indicate that approximately 40% of American Indians are multiracial. Asians also tend to marry at a high rate outside their racial group. The 2000 census indicates that about 14% of Asians report that they are multiracial, compared to 5% of Blacks and 3% percent of Whites (Lee, 2001). About 52% of the total number of the multiracial Asians are Asian and White. Historically this population has been referred to as "Amerasians" and has been associated with the interracial marriages of service personnel stationed in Asian countries after World War II and the Vietnam War. Today the term *Hapa*—a Hawaiian term meaning half White and half Hawaiian—is frequently used to refer to Asians of mixed-race ancestry (Lee, 2001). Also adding to the increasing number of interracial families are the growing numnber of children adopted from other countries. Foreign-born children, usually Asian, are being adopted by Whites. In 2000, immigration visas were issued to 5,053 orphans from China, 4,269 orphans from Russia, and 1,794 orphans from South Korea. The vast majority of the adoptees are girls (Lee, 2001). Drawing leaders from the ranks of young people who have grown up in this new and changing sociopolitical context can help provide new insights, research questions, and perspectives that can help multicultural education remain a viable and relevant field.

How Do You Maintain a Focus and Sustain Interest in Issues that Are Not on the National Agenda or May Even Be Viewed as Being Antithetical to National Interest?

This is a particularly important question for multicultural education because of its commitment to social justice. Issues related to social justice are never fully resolved. The national response to them is cyclic and temporary. In the years since the 1964 Civil Rights Act, support for social justice issues such as school desegregation and affirmative action come and go. For example, in 2003 a divided Supreme Court supported affirmative action. But the court also said that race cannot be the determining factor in school admission decisions. Writing for the majority in the 5–4 ruling, Justice Sandra Day O'Connor quoted from the landmark *Brown v. Board of Education* ruling,

> This court has long recognized that education is the very foundation of good citizenship. Effective participation by members of all racial and ethnic groups in the civic life of our nation is essential if the dream of one nation, indivisible, is to be realized. (*Grutter v. Bollinger et al.*, 2003, p. 19–20)

At the same time, the Supreme Court voted 6–3 to strike down a point system used by the University of Michigan in undergraduate admissions. Moreover, in 2002 the U.S. Supreme Court officially ended busing for integration in Charlotte, North Carolina when it decided not to revisit the Charlotte–Mecklenburg's school desegregation case. Without identifying an alternative approach, public school systems throughout the United States continued to abandon bussing as a means to integrate schools systems. While there was never universal support for bussing as a means to achieve school desegregation or for affirmative action as a way to balance the scale in a society graping with historic and contemporary forms of prejudice and discrimination, these approaches carried a certain moral imperative that suggested they should not be dismissed out of hand.

Today, however, many social justice issues are viewed as special-interest issues. Being able to sustain a movement through times when interest in social justice is high is relatively easy. Intercultural educators found that there was renewed interest in their message and perspectives during World War II when there was concern about the nation fracturing into competing ethnic groups. Political, civic, and educational leaders who recognized that something had to be done to improve the social climate in schools and the community welcomed their efforts. However, as external pressures eased and intergroup tensions seemed less salient, their support subsided. The cycle of interest and disinterest in intergroup education suggests that in times when national interest and commitment to diversity is low, a movement that pushes for equity is vulnerable and is at great risk of being attacked and having its message distorted. Multicultural educators will need to think deeply about how to sustain the movement during times when diversity isn't viewed as an asset.

ONE ERA ENDS AND A NEW ONE BEGINS

Multicultural educators have much to learn from the experiences of inter-cultural educators. The issues and questions that concerned them continue to concern educators today. The shortcomings, struggles, and victories of intercultural educators can provide important insights for educators today, who, like intergroup educators in the past, are being called on to help students develop the skills, attitudes, and values necessary to become active participants in a pluralistic democratic society.

More than 70 years ago intercultural educators envisioned a more just and humane society. They had a powerful dream and the courage, perse-verance, and fortitude to work to make it a reality. Even though they fell short of their dream, gains were made in creating equity, and our schools and society are better for their efforts. Their mantle has now passed to multicultural educators who are, in their own way, continuing the struggle for a just and humane society.

Notes

Introduction

1. Gunnar Myrdal used the term American Creed in his classic study of race relations in the United States entitled *An American Dilemma*. The term refers to a pattern of values and ideals that serve as a standard by which the nation's accomplishments can be judged. Freedom, justice, and equality are examples of American Creed values. These values, according to Myrdal, are widely understood and appreciated in the United States and set a high standard for human interrelations. American Creed values and ideals are written into the Declaration of Independence, the Preamble to the Constitution, the Bill of Rights, and the constitutions of several states. As such, American Creed values serve as the foundation of America's national morale.

Chapter 1

1. The Irish began arriving in the United States in 1816, but their numbers did not dramatically increase until after 1846 when an estimated 350,000 people in Ireland died of starvation as a result of the potato blight. Between 1860 and 1914 approximately 2.4 million Irish arrived in the United States and primarily settled in New York, Boston, and, in later years, Chicago. During their early years in the United States, the Irish were commonly described as dirty, stupid, intemperate, corrupt, and immoral. Discrimination reflected in signs that read "Irish Need Not Apply" revealed the extent to which they were a stigmatized group. Prejudice along with a lack of education limited the Irish to unskilled manual labor jobs (Allen & Turner, 1988; Wittke, 1958).

Germans began arriving in the United States around 1710 and settled in Pennsylvania where they were known as the Pennsylvania Dutch. By 1860 they had established thriving communities in New York and Chicago with German-language newspapers, schools, bookstores, and churches. Their numbers increased dramatically between 1830 and 1930 when 6,000,000 Germans entered the United States. Early German immigrants, like the Irish, also faced discrimination. They were commonly referred to as infidels, radicals, socialists, and beer loafers. Their image was especially damaged after World War I when they were associated with labor unrest and unemployment (Jones, 1992; Wittke, 1949). However, by the 1920s the Germans and Irish had begun to establish themselves as bankers, professionals, and clerks and took their place in mainstream American society. Russians, Italians, and other new immigrants took jobs in personal and domestic services that were no longer being filled by German and Irish workers (Lieberson, 1980).

2. D. W. Griffin's *Birth of a Nation*, which was released in 1915, glorified White supremacy and the close of Reconstruction in 1877. The movie gave form to stereotypes of African Americans as a menace and represented the Ku Klux Klan as a group organized to protect the White community from Blacks. *Birth of a Nation* was so popular, even among immigrants who were not considered White, that it became a cultural icon.

The Jazz Singer was Hollywood's first talkie and as such was widely viewed and discussed. The movie starred Al Jolson as Jack Robin a Jewish American who changed his name from Jakie Rabinowitz. In the movie Jack becomes rich and famous by appropriating jazz songs from African Americans and singing them in blackface. According to Jacobson (1998), Jolson's blackface routine created a complex racial triangulation among Hebrews, African-Americans, and White Americans. That triangulation positioned African Americans as an important point of reference for the definition of Whiteness with Whiteness ultimately being anything other than Black.

Chapter 4

1. While far from perfect, the access that minorities had to schools in Seattle was much better than that which they had historically been given. Throughout the nation during the early 20th century, racial minorities had limited access to high-quality schools. Blacks, for example, not only experienced segregation in the South; they attended segregated schools in northern cities such as Chicago and Detroit. In 1863, the Irish community pressured the Chicago school board to pass the "Black School Law." This law restricted Black children to segregated schools. The law was repealed in 1865, but was followed by restrictive covenants that resulted in segregated neighborhoods and de facto segregation in schools (Peterson, 1985). In California during the 1800s and the early 1900s Asians attended segregated schools. In the late 1800s, at the urging of Andrew Moulder, superintendent of schools in San Francisco, the California State legislature passed a bill that permitted school districts to establish segregated schools for "Mongolians." However, after the Japanese government applied political pressure, Japanese students weren't required to attend the segregated Oriental school in San Francisco.

Chapter 5

1. An overview of the ideological foundations for the positions discussed in this section are covered in Chapter 1.

References

Adamic, L. (1940). *From many lands*. New York: Harper.

Adamic, L. (1944). *A nation of nations*. New York: Harper.

Adamic, L. (1934, November). Thirty million new Americans. *Harper's Magazine, 169*, 684–694.

Adler, A. (1929). *The science of living*. Garden City, NY: Garden City Publishing.

Adorno, T. W., Frenkel-Brunswick, E., Levinson, D., & Sanford, R. (1950). *The authoritarian personality*. New York: Harper Press.

Alland, A., & Wise, J. W. (1945). *The Springfield plan*. New York: The Viking Press.

Allen, J. P., & Turner, E. J. (1988). *We the people: An atlas of America's ethnic diversity*. New York: Macmillan.

Allport, G. W. (1944). The bigot in our midst. *The commonweal*. (found in Covello's files MSS40; Covello; 53/21.)

Allport, G. W. (1954). *The nature of prejudice*. Reading, MA: Addison-Wesley.

Apple, M. W., & Christian-Smith, L. K. (Eds.). (1991). *The politics of the textbook*. New York: Routledge.

Banks, C. A. M. (1995). Intellectual leadership and the influence of early African American scholars on multicultural education. *Education Policy, 9*(3), 260–280.

Banks, C. A. M. (1996). The intergroup education movement. In J. A. Banks (Ed.) *Multicultural education, transformative knowledge and action: Historical and contemporary perspectives*. (pp. 251–277). New York: Teachers College Press.

Banks, C. A. M. (2003). Parents and teachers: Partners in school reform. In J. A. Banks and C. A. M. Banks (Eds.), *Multicultural education: Issues and perspectives* (4th ed., pp. 402–420). New York: John Wiley & Sons.

Banks, J. A. (1993). The canon debate, knowledge construction, and multicultural education. *Educational Researcher 22*(5), 4–14.

Banks, J.A. (1995). The historical reconstruction of knowledge about race: Implications for transformative teaching. *Educational Researcher 24*(2), pp. 15–25.

Banks, J. A. (1996). Black studies. In J. Salzman, D. L. Smith, & C. West (Eds.). *Encyclopedia of African-American culture and history* (pp. 364–369). New York: Macmillan.

Banks, J. A. (1997). *Educating citizens in a multicultural society*. New York: Teachers College Press.

Banks, J. A. (2004). *Multicultural education: Historical development, dimensions, and practice*. In J. A. Banks & C.A.M. Banks, *Handbook on research on multicultural education*. San Francisco: Jossey-Bass.

Banks, J. A., & Banks, C. A. M. (Eds.). (1995). *Handbook on research on multicultural education*. New York: Macmillan.

Banks, J. A., & Banks, C. A. M. (Eds.). (2004). *Handbook on research on multicultural education*. San Francisco: Jossey-Bass.

Bass, B. M. (1981). *Stogdill's handbook of leadership*. New York: The Free Press.

Beineke, J. A. (1998). *And there were giants in the land: The life of William Heard Kilpatrick*. New York: Peter Lang.

Benedict, R. (1934). *Patterns of culture*. Boston: Houghton Mifflin.

Benedict, R. (1942). American melting pot, 1942 model. In the Department of Supervisors and Directors of Instructors of the National Education Association, The National Council of Teachers of English, and The Society for Curriculum Study. *Americans all: Studies in Intercultural education*. Washington, DC: The Department of Supervisors and Directors of Instruction.

Benedict, R., & Wetfish, G. (1943). *The races of mankind*. Public Affairs Pamphlet No. 85. New York: Public Affairs Committee.

Benedict, R., & Wetfish, G. (1948). *In Henry's backyard: The races of mankind*. New York: Henry Schuman.

Bennett, D. H. (1988). *The party of fear: From nativist movements to the new right in American history*. Chapel Hill: University of North Carolina Press.

Bernard, F. (1976, July 5). Springfield: A melting pot for many ethnic backgrounds. *State Register*.

Bernard-Powers, J. (1999). Composing her life: Hilda Taba and social studies history. In Margaret Smith Crocco and O. L. Davis, Jr. (Eds.), *Bending the future to their will: Civic women, social education, and democracy* (pp. 185–206). Lanham, MD: Rowman & Littlefield.

Bianco, E. (1992, June). Class of '92 honors Japanese-American. *Skagit Valley Herald*, pp. 1, 8.

Biddick, M. (1945). *Schools are organizing to improve human relations*. New York: Bureau for Intercultural Education.

Bismarck, North Dakota Curriculum Team. (1931). *Problems of American democracy*. Bismarck, ND: Department of Public Instruction. (Special Collections, Milbank Memorial Library, Teachers College Columbia, f375.3, So1–ND, 1931.)

Bleifeld, M. (1939). A biology unit dealing with racial attitudes. *The American Biology Teacher, 2*(1), 7–9.

Bleifeld, M., Goldstein, H., Nestler, H. A., Robinson, R., Rock, J. G., Sygoda, D., Weinberg, S., & Nagler, H. (1939). Outline of a Teaching Unit on Mankind. *The Teaching Biologist, 9*, 27–44.

Boas, F. (1915). *Race and nationality. International conciliation Special Bulletin*. New York: American Association for International Conciliation.

Boas, F. (1928). *Anthropology and modern life*. New York: W. W. Norton.

Bogardus, E. S. (1925a). Social distance and its origins. *Journal of Applied Sociology, 9*, 216–225.

Bogardus, E. S. (1925b). Measuring social distances. *Journal of Applied Sociology, 9*, 299–308.

Bogardus, E. S. (1933, January-February). A social distance scale. *Sociology and Social Research*, 265–271.

Bourne, R. S. (Ed.). (1920). *History of a literary radical and other essays*. New York: B. W. Huebsch.

Boyle-Baise, M. (2002). *Multicultural service learning: Educating teachers in diverse communities*. New York: Teachers College Press.

Brady, E. H. (1992). Intergroup education in public schools, 1945–51. In *Jubilee conference: Hilda Taba—90* (pp. 15–29). Tartu, Estonia: Tartu University.

Brameld, T. (1947). Intercultural democracy-education's new frontier. *The Educational Forum, 12*(1), 67–73.

Branch, A. (2001). Increasing the numbers of teachers of color in K–12 Public Schools. *Educational Forum, 65*(3), 254–261.

Bresnahan, D. (1971). *The Springfield plan in retrospect*. Unpublished doctoral dissertation, Teachers College, Columbia University, New York.

Buchanan, P. J. (2002). *The death of the West: How dying populations and immigrant invasions imperil our country and civilization*. New York: Thomas Dunne Books.

Burns, J. M. (1978). *Leadership*. New York: Harper & Row.

Cahnman, W. J. (1978). Robert E. Park at Fisk. *Journal of the History of the Behavioral Sciences, 14*, 328–336.

Carlson, R. (1987). *The Americanization syndrome: A quest for conformity*. New York: St. Martin's Press.

Chang, E. T. (1993). Jewish and Korean merchants in African American neighborhoods: A comparative perspective. *Amerasia Journal, 19*(2) 5–21.

Chase, G. (1940). *Report of the committee for evaluation of the work of the Service Bureau for Intercultural Education*. New York: New York City School Board.

Chatto, C. I. (1944). Education for democratic living. *Journal of Education, 127*, 189–191.

Chatto, C. I., & Halligan, A. L. (1945). *The story of the Springfield plan*. New York: Barnes & Noble.

Cheney, B. A., Bottomley, H., Carrier, F. W., Durfee, M. K., Green, R. A., Kelly, W. F., & Shipman, W. M. (1935). A syllabus in American history and problems of American democracy for secondary schools. New York: D. C. Heath & Company. (Special collections, Milbank Library, Teachers College, Columbia University, f375.3, So1-NE, 1935.)

Chin, F. (1978, October 11). How shall injustice be served? *The Weekly*, pp. 9–15.

Chun-Hoon, L. K. Y. (1973). Teaching the Asian-American experience. In J. A. Banks (Ed.), *Teaching ethnic studies: Concepts and strategies* (pp. 118–147). Washington, DC: National Council for the Social Studies.

Clinchy, E. R. (Ed.). (1942). *The world we want to live in*. New York: Doubleday.

Cohen, J. (Ed.). (1996). *For love of country: Debating the limits of patriotism*. Boston: Beacon Press.

Cole, S. G. (1941). *Intercultural education*. New York: American Jewish Committee.

Cole, S. G. (1946). What is intercultural education? In G. B. De Huszar (Ed.), *Anatomy of racial intolerance*. New York: H. W. Wilson.

Collins, P. H. (1990). *Black feminist thought: Knowledge, consciousness, and the politics of empowerment*. New York: Routledge.

Commager, H. S. (1947, September). Who is loyal to America. *Harper's Magazine, 195*(1168), 193–199.

Committee on the Study of Teaching Materials in Intergroup Relations. (1949). *Intergroup relations in teaching materials: A survey and appraisal*. Washington, DC: American Council on Education.

Congressional Record. (1924). *Congressional Record*, 65, 68th Congress, 1st Session, Washington, DC: Government Printing Office. 5965–5969.

Cook, L. A. (1938). *Community backgrounds of education*. New York: McGraw-Hill.

Cook, L. A. (Ed.). (1950). *College programs in intergroup relations: A report by twenty-four colleges participating in the college study in intergroup relations, 1945–49*. Washington, DC: The American Council on Education.

Cook, L. A. (1951). *Intergroup relations in teacher education*. Washington, DC: American Council on Education.

Cook, L. A., & Cook, E. (1954). *Intergroup education*. New York: McGraw-Hill.

Cook, L. A., & Cook, E. (1957). *School problems in human relations*. New York: McGraw-Hill.

Cooper, A. J. (1988). *A voice from the South by a Black woman of the South*. New York: Oxford University Press. (Original work published 1892)

Cortés, C. E. (1973). Teaching the Chicano experience. In J. A. Banks (Ed.), *Teaching ethnic studies: Concepts and strategies* (pp. 180–199). Washington, DC: National Council for the Social Studies.

Council of the Great City Schools. (1993). Diversifying our great city school teachers: Twenty year trends. *Urban Indicator*, 1(2), 1–3.

Covello, L. (1936). A high school and its immigrant community: A challenge and an opportunity. *Journal of Educational Sociology* 9(2), 331–346.

Covello, L. (1937, October). *Trends and purposes in our school*. Address delivered to the faculty at Benjamin Franklin High School. New York, NY.

Covello, L. (1939a). Language as a factor in integration and assimilation. *The Modern Language Journal*, 23(5), 323–333.

Covello, L. (1939b). Inter-racial and inter-cultural relationships. Paper presented at Intercultural conference. New York, NY.

Covello, L. (1941). *Reconciliation of heritages in our American life*. Address delivered at the annual dinner of the Service Bureau for Intercultural Education. New York, NY.

Covello, L. (1942). Unpublished report on Benjamin Franklin High School. (MSS 40, Covello 34/11).

Covello L. (1943). BFHS Papers. Unpublished materials. (MSS 40, Covello 50/4;60/13).

Covello, L. (1945). Letter to BFHS Parents. Unpublished material. (MSS 40, Covello 54/8).

Covello Archives (1938). MSS 40, 5/4. Advertisement on American All-Immigrants All.

Covello Archives (1939). MSS 40, 34/15; 51/22, 24; 52/5, 7; 57/23, 27 Course material.

Covello Archives. (1943). MSS 24/16. Speech given at New York Public Schools, Fall In-service Day.

Covello Archives. (1945). MSS 40, 42/8. Course material.

Covello Archives. (October 9, 1945). MSS 40, 54/8. Memo to school faculty.

Covello Archives. (November 20, 1946). Report filed by Mary Riley.

Covello, L., with D'Agostino, G. (1958). *The heart is the teacher*. New York: McGraw-Hill.

Cremin, L. (1988). *American Education: The metropolitan experience 1876–1980*. New York: Harper & Row.

Crew, S. R. (1987). *Field to factory: Afro-American migration 1915–1940*. Washington, DC: Smithsonian Institution.

Crocco, M. S. & Davis, O. L. Jr. *Bending the future to their will: civic women, social education, and democracy* (pp. 185–206). New York: Rowman & Littlefield.

Cuban, L. (1984). *How teachers taught: Constancy and change in American classrooms, 1890–1980*. New York: Longman.

Dabney, T. L. (1934). The study of the Negro. *Journal of Negro History*, *19*, 266–307.

Davis, A. (1945). In Taba, H. & VanTil, W. (Eds.). *Democratic human relations: Promising practices in intergroup and intercultural education in the social studies*. (pp. 263–279). Washington, DC: National Council for the Social Studies.

Davis, A. (1948). *Social-class influences upon learning*. Cambridge, MA: Harvard University Press.

Davis, O. L., Jr. (1999). Rachel Davis DuBois: Intercultural education pioneer. In M. S. Crocco & O. L. Davis, Jr. *Bending the future to their will: civic women, social education, and democracy* (pp. 169–184). New York: Rowman & Littlefield.

Department of Supervisors and Directors of Instructors of the National Education Association, the National Council of Teachers of English, and the Society for Curriculum Study. (Eds.). (1942). *Americans all: Studies in intercultural education*. Washington, DC: Department of Supervisors and Directors of Instruction, National Education Association.

Directors of Instructors of the National Education Association, the National Council of Teachers of English, and the Society for Curriculum Study. *Americans all: Studies in intercultural education* (pp. 14–24), Washington, DC: Department of Supervisors and Directors of Instruction, National Education Association.

Donovan, M. S., Bransford, J. D., Pellegrino, J. W. (Eds.). (1999). *How people learn: Bridging research and practice*. Washington, DC: National Academy of Sciences—National Research Council, Department of Education.

Douglas, S. J. (1999). Listening in: Radio and the American imagination from Amos'n'Andy and Edward R. Murrow to Wolfman Jack and Howard Stern. New York: Times Books.

Douglass, H. P. (1926). *The Springfield church survey: A study of organized religion with its social background*. New York: George H. Doran Company.

Drachsler, J. (1920). *Democracy and assimilation: The blending of immigrant heritages in America*. New York: Macmillan.

DuBois, R. D. (1928). *Education in world mindedness: A series of assembly programs given by students at Woodbury High School, Woodbury, New Jersey, 1927–1928*. [Publisher not given]. Philadelphia.

DuBois, R. D. (1930). *The contributions of racial elements to American life* (2nd ed.). Philadelphia: Women's International League for Peace and Freedom.

DuBois, R. D. (1936). Exploring sympathetic attitudes towards peoples. *Journal of Educational Sociology 9*, 391–394.

DuBois, R. D. (1937). Intercultural education at Benjamin Franklin High School. *High Points 19*, 23–29.

DuBois, R. D. (1939). *Adventures in intercultural education: A manual for secondary school teachers*. New York: Intercultural Education Workshop.

DuBois, R. D. (1942). Conserving cultural resources. In the Department of Supervisors and Directors of Instructors of the National Education Association, the National Council of Teachers of English, and the Society for Curriculum Study. *Americans all: Studies in intercultural education* (pp. 148–159). Washington, DC: Department of Supervisors and Directors of Instruction.

DuBois, R. D. (1943). *Get together Americans: Friendly approaches to racial and cultural conflicts through the neighborhood-home festival*. New York: Harper & Brothers.

DuBois, R. D. (1945). *Build together Americans*. Philadelphia: Hinds, Hayden & Hildredge.

DuBois, R. D., & Li, M. (1963). *The art of group conversation: A new breakthrough in social communication*. New York: Association Press.

DuBois, R. D., & Li, M. (1971). *Reducing social tension and conflict through the group conversation method*. New York: Association Press.

DuBois, R. D., with Okorodudu, C. (1984). *All this and something more: Pioneering in intercultural education*. Bryn Mawr, PA: Dorrance & Company.

DuBois, W. E. B. (1968). *The autobiography of W. E. B. DuBois: A soliloquy on viewing my life from the last decade of its first century*. New York: International Publishers.

DuBois, W. E. B. (1973). *The Philadelphia negro: A social study*. Millwood, NY: Kraus-Thompson. (Original work published 1899).

Edmonds, A. (1999). Making our mark: George Walker Pulitzer Prize winning composer. *Sojourner, 3*(10), 5, 38.

Erickson, E. (2004). Culture in society and in education practice. In J. A. Banks & C. A. M. Banks (Eds.), *Multicultural education: Issues & perspectives* (5th Ed.). New York: John Wiley.

Evans, R. W. (2003). *The social studies wars: What should we teach our children?* New York: Teachers College Press.

Fairchild, H. P. (1913). *Immigration: A world movement and its American significance*. New York: Macmillan.

Fairchild, H. P. (1926). *The melting-pot mistake*. Boston: Little, Brown.

Fairchild, H. P. (1953). Conditions in America as affected by immigration. In B. M. Ziegler (Ed.), *Immigration: An American Dilemma* (pp. 34–49). Boston: D. C. Heath.

Fields, H. (1938, February). A social studies record. *Frontline* 5–7. (MSS 40 Covello, 34/23)

Fitzpatrick, J. P. (1971). *Puerto Rican Americans; the meaning of migration to the mainland*. Englewood Cliffs, NJ: Prentice-Hall.

Fleming, T. J. (1970). *The golden door*. New York: Grosett, Dunlap.

Forbes, J. (1973). Teaching Native American values and cultures. In J. A. Banks (Ed.), *Teaching ethnic studies: Concepts and strategies* (pp. 200–225). Washington, DC: National Council for the Social Studies.

Fried, A. (1997). (Ed.). *McCarthyism the great American red scare: A documentary history*. New York: Oxford University Press.

Gallup Poll. (March, 2001). *American ambivalent about immigrants*. www.gallup.com.

Gibson, C. & Lennon, E. (1999). *Region of birth of the foreign-born population*. Washington, DC: U.S. Census Bureau, Population Division.

Giles, H. H. (1945). Organizations in the field of intercultural relations. *Harvard Educational Review, 15*(2), 87–92.

Goggin, J. (1993). *Carter G. Woodson: A life in Black history*. Baton Rouge: Louisiana State University Press.

Gollnick, D. M., & Chinn, P. C. (2002). *Multicultural education in a pluralistic society*. (6th ed.) Upper Saddle River, NJ: Merrill.

Goodman, M. E. (1952). *Race awareness in young children*. New York: Macmillan.

Gordon, M. (1964). *Assimilation in American life: The role of race, religion, and national origins*. New York: Oxford University Press.

Gould, S. J. (1981). *The mismeasure of man*. New York: Norton.

Graham, P. A. (1967). *Progressive education: From arcady to academe: A history of the progressive education association, 1919–1955*. New York: Teachers College Press.

Grant, C. A., & Ladson-Billings, G. (1997). *Dictionary of multicultural education*. Phoenix: Oryx Press.

Grant, C. A., & Sleeter, C. E. (1986). Race, class, and gender in educational research: An argument for integrative analysis. *Review of Educational Research. 56*, 195–211.

Grant, M. (1918). *The passing of the great race*. New York: Charles Scribner's Sons.

Green, M. A. (1886). *Springfield 1636–1886: History of town and city*. Boston: Rockwell & Churchill.

Grutter v. Bollinger et al., 539 U.S. (2003). No. 02-241.

Gwinn, M. A. (1989, March 19). Unlocking the past. *The Seattle Times/Seattle Post-Intelligencer*, pp. 12–19, 32–35.

Hampson, R. (April, 2001). 1990s boom reminiscent of 1890s immigration fuels growth, just as it did a century ago. *USA Today* [Final edition], p. A3.

Hartstone, J. (1992). Honored five decades later. *The Sun*, pp. A1, A3.

Henderson, A. (1987). *The evidence continues to grow: Parent involvement improves student achievement*. Columbia, MD: National Committee for citizens in education.

Herskovits, M. J. (1938). *Acculturation: The study of culture contact*. New York: J.J. Augustin.

Herskovits, M. J. (1958). *The myth of the Negro past*. Boston: Beacon Press.

Higham, J. (1972). *Strangers in the land: Patterns of American nativism 1860–1925*. New York: Atheneum.

Hing, B. O. (2001). *Our numbers past and present*. Asian Week Archives. Available: http://www.asianweek.com/2001_04_06/news14_blast_numbers.html

Houston Curriculum Guide, (1931). *Life on the American frontier, a study of the westward movement in American history*. Unit III. Houston: Houston Public Schools.

Hutchinson, E. P. (1949). *Immigration policy since World War 1. The Annuals, 262*, 15–21.

Ignatiev, N. (1995). *How the Irish became White*. New York: Routledge.

Jackson, K. T. (Ed.). (1995). *The encyclopedia of New York City.* New Haven, CT: Yale University Press.

Jacobson, M. F. (1998). *Whiteness of a different color: European immigrants and the alchemy of race.* Cambridge, MA: Harvard University Press.

Johanek, M. C. (1995). *The public purposes of public education: The evolution of community-centered schooling at Benjamin Franklin High School, 1934–1944.* Unpublished doctoral dissertation, Teachers College, Columbia University, New York.

Jones, J. M. (1938). *Americans all . . . immigrants all: A manual.* Washington, DC: The Federal Radio Education Committee in cooperation with the United States Office of Education.

Jones, M. A. (1992). *American immigration.* Chicago: University of Chicago Press.

Kaestle, C. F. (1978). Social reform and the urban school: An essay review. In D. R. Warren (Ed.), *History, education, and public policy.* (pp. 127–147). Berkeley, CA: McCutchan.

Kallen, H. M. (1924). *Culture and democracy in the United States.* New York: Boni & Liveright.

Kessner, T. (1977). *The golden door: Italian and Jewish immigrant mobility in New York City, 1880–1915.* New York: Oxford University Press.

Kilpatrick, W. H., & Cole, S. G. (1943). Cultural democracy in war and peace. *Intercultural Education News, 4*(2), 1–2.

Kilpatrick, W. H., & VanTil, W. (Eds.). (1947). *Intercultural attitudes in the making, ninth yearbook of the John Dewey Society.* New York: Harper & Brothers.

Kitamoto, F. (2002, March 30). *Speech given on the occasion of the Nikkei Internment and exclusion memorial and dedication ceremony.* Bainbridge Island, WA: Archival papers of Carol Kubota.

Kliebard, H. M. (1995). *The struggle for the American curriculum: 1893–1958.* (2nd ed.). New York: Routledge.

Klineberg, O. (1955). *Race differences.* New York: Harper & Brothers.

Krull, E. (1992) Preface. In *Jubilee conference: Hilda Taba—90* (pp. 5–6). Tartu, Estonia: Tartu University.

Krull, E., & Marits, A. (1992). Hilda Taba and Estonian educational science. Taba's childhood, schooling, and the acceptance of her educational ideas in Estonia. In *Jubilee conference: Hilda Taba—90* (pp. 51–59). Tartu, Estonia: Tartu University.

Lacey, K. (2002). Radio in the Great Depression. Promotional Culture, Public Service, and Propaganda. In M. Hilmes & J. Loviglio (Eds.), *Radio reader: Essays in the cultural history of radio.* (pp. 21–40). New York: Routledge.

Lasker, G. (1929). *Race attitudes in children.* New York: Henry Holt.

Laurie, H. (1940a, January). The congress on education for democracy. *Seattle Principals Exchange, 4*(4), not paginated.

Laurie, H. (1940b, February). The congress on education for democracy. *Seattle Principals Exchange, 9*(5), 4–5.

Laurie, H. (1940c, April). Importance of evaluation. *Seattle Principals Exchange, 4*(7), not paginated.

Lee, S. M. (2001). *Using the new racial categories in the 2000 census.* Washington, DC: The Annie E. Casey Foundation and Population Reference Bureau.

Lewin, K. (1997). *Resolving social conflicts: Field theory in social science.* Washington, DC: American Psychological Association.

Lewis, D. L. (2000). *W. E. B. DuBois: The fight for equality and the American century, 1919–1963.* New York: Henry Holt and Company.

Lewis, Mark S. (1996). Supply and Demand of Teachers of Color. *ERIC Digest.* [ED390875]

Lieberson, S. (1980). *Ethnic patterns in American cities.* New York: Free Press.

Locke, A., & Stern, B. J. (Eds.). (1942). *When peoples meet: A study in race and culture contacts.* New York: Progressive Education Association.

Luch, M. (1940, May). Folk dancing develops poise and understanding. *Seattle Principals Exchange* 4(5), not paginated.

MacDonald, C. (1940, October). Pecan, pickaninnies, spirituals. *The Seattle Educational Bulletin,* 17(1), 2.

Marks, C. (1989). *Farewell—we're good and gone: The Great Black migration.* Bloomington: Indiana University Press.

McClain, C. J. (1994). *In search of equality: The Chinese struggle against discrimination in nineteenth-century America.* Berkeley: University of California Press.

McMahon, P. (April 9, 2002). Census data stir up White supremacists. *U.S.A. Today,* p. A3.

Merrick, J. B. (1940, April). Spring festivals. *Seattle Principals Exchange,* 4(7), not paginated.

Michael-Bandele, Mwangaza. (1993). *Who's missing from the classroom: The need for minority teachers.* Trends and Issues Paper, No. 9., Washington, DC: ERIC Clearinghouse on Teacher Education [ED352361].

Miller, C. (1944). Country wages total war on prejudice. *Nation's Schools,* 33, 16–18.

Milner, D. (1983). *Children and race.* Beverly Hills, CA: Sage.

Minard, R. D. (1931). *Race attitudes of Iowa children.* Iowa City: The University of Iowa.

Moll, Luis, et al. (1992). Funds of knowledge for teaching: Using a qualitative approach to connect homes and classrooms. *Theory into practice,* 31 (1) 132–41.

Montalto, N. V. (1982). *A history of the intercultural education movement 1924–1941.* New York: Garland Publishing.

Mortenson, M. C. (1942, March). War and the children. *Seattle Principals Exchange,* 6(7), 7.

Myrdal, G. (1944). *An American dilemma.* New York: MacGraw-Hill.

National Education Association of the United States. (1943). *What the schools should teach in wartime.* Covello Papers MSS40, Covello, 50/4.

Negro History Week. (1940, December). *Seattle Principals Exchange,* 5(3), 9.

Nelli, H. S. (1983). *From immigrants to ethnics: The Italian Americans.* New York: Oxford.

Nelson, B. E. (1988). *Good schools: The Seattle public school system, 1901–1930.* Seattle: University of Washington Press. New York State Census. (1855). Available: http://freepages.genealogy.rootsweb.com/~nyirish/1855%20NYS%20 census%209–6 . . . 1–210.html

Nussbaum, M. C. (1996). Patriotism and cosmopolitanism. In J. Cohen (Ed.), *For love of country: Debating the limits of patriotism* (pp. 2–17). Boston: Beacon Press.

Olneck, M. R. (1990). The reoccurring dream: Symbolism and ideology in Intercultural education and multicultural education. *American Journal of Education, 98*, 147–174.

Olneck, M. R. (1995). Immigrants and education. In J. A. Banks & C. A. M. Banks (Eds.), *Handbook of research on multicultural education* (pp. 3–24). New York: Macmillan.

Omoto, S. (2001, September 1). Comments on Executive Order 9066. Carol Kubota archives.

Orsi, R. A. (1985). *The madonna of 115th Street: Faith and community in Italian Harlem, 1880 to 1950.* New Haven, CT: Yale University Press.

Park, R. E. (1928). Human migration and the marginal man. *American Journal of Sociology, 33*, 881–893.

Park, R. E. (1935). Assimilation. In *Encyclopedia of the social sciences, II* (pp. 281–283). New York: Macmillan.

Park. R. E. (1950). *Race and culture.* New York: Free Press.

Park, R. E. (1955). *Society: Collective behavior, news, and opinion, sociology and modern society.* Glencoe, IL: Free Press.

Park, R. E., & Miller, H. E. (1921). *Old world traits transplanted.* New York: Macmillan.

Parker, L., & McMahon, P. (2002, April 9). Immigrant groups fear backlash. *U.S.A. Today.*

Parrish, L. W. Y. (1992, June 4). Righting a 50-year-old wrong. *The Seattle Times,* pp. 1, 2.

Payne, E. G. (1946). The Springfield plan. *The Journal of Educational Sociology, 14,* 395–397.

Perrone, V. (1998). *Teacher with a heart.* New York: Teachers College Press.

Petersen, I. B. (1937). *An integrated nationality course in social science for grades IV and V.* Ironwood, MI: Ironwood Public Schools. Special Collections, Milbank Memorial Library, Teachers College, Columbia University.

Peterson, P. E. (1985). *The politics of school reform 1870–1940.* Chicago: University of Chicago Press.

Pettigrew, T. F. (2004). Intergroup contact: Theory, research and new perspectives. In J. A. Banks & C. A. M. Banks, *Handbook of research on multicultural education* (pp. 770–781). San Francisco: Jossey-Bass.

Polier, J. W. (1945). *The report of the Harlem Project.* Special Collections, Milbank Memorial Library, Teachers College, Columbia University. B/E. Series 240, Box 2, Folder 8.

Pollard, K. M., & O'Hare, W. P. (1999). America's racial and ethnic minorities. *Population Reference Bulletin, 54*(3), 1–48. Washington, DC: Population Reference Bureau.

Ravitch, D. (1983). *The troubled crusade: American education, 1945–1980.* New York: Basic Books.

Ravitch, D. (1990, October 24). Multiculturalism, yes, particulars. *The Chronicle of Higher Education, 37*(8), 44.

Ravitch, D., & Goodenow, R. K. (1981). *Educating an urban people: The New York City experience.* New York: Teachers College Press.

Riley, M. (1946). *Report on community conference*. In Covello Manuscript (MSS 40, 42/7).

Ross, E. A. (1914). *Immigrants in politics: The political consequences of immigration. In B. M. schooling, and the acceptance of her educational ideas in Estonia.* In *Jubilee conference: Hilda Taba—90* (pp. 51–59). Tartu, Estonia: Tartu University.

Rury, J. L. (2002). *Education and social change: Themes in history of American schooling*. Mahwah, NJ: Lawrence Erlbaum.

Santayana, G. (1905). *Life of reason*. New York: C. Scribner's Sons.

Savage, B. D. (1999). *Broadcasting freedom: Radio, war, and the politics of race, 1938–1948*. Chapel Hill: University of North Carolina Press.

Seattle, University of Washington Archives. (n. d.). Reel 2. Hiroyuki Ichihara Papers.

Seattle Principals Exchange (1942, March). Who is an alien? *Seattle Principals Exchange, 6*(5), 4.

Seller, M. (1977). *To seek America: A history of ethnic life in the United States*. New York: Jerome S. Ozer.

Shaffer, R. (1996). Multicultural education in New York City during World War II. *New York History, 77*(3), 301–332.

Shepard, W. H. (1925). *Course of study in community problems*. Minneapolis, MN: Minneapolis Public Schools.

Sleeter, C. E. (1995). An analysis of the critiques of multicultural education. In J. A. Banks & C. A. M. Banks (Eds.), *Handbook of multicultural education* (pp. 81–94). San Francisco: Jossey-Bass.

Sleeter, C. E., & Grant, C. A. (1988). *Making choices for multicultural education: Five approaches to race, class, and gender*. Columbus, OH: Merrill.

Sleeter, C. E., & McLaren, P. L. (Eds.). (1995). *Multicultural education, critical pedagogy, and the politics of difference*. Albany: State University of New York Press.

Smedley, A. (1993). *Race in North America: Origin and evolution of a worldview*. Boulder, CO: Westview Press.

Smith, E. D. (1924, April 9). *Congressional Record*, 65, 68th Congress, 1st Session. Washington, DC: Government Printing Office. pp. 5961–5962.

Spain, D. (1999). *American's diversity: On the edge of two centuries*. Washington, DC: Population Reference Bureau.

Special Collections, Milbank Memorial Library, Teachers College. Series 562, Folder 3, Board of Education, New York Public Schools.

Stendler, C. B., & Martin, W. E. (1953). *Intergroup education in kindergarten-primary grades*. New York: Macmillan.

Stephan, W., & Stephan, C. (2004). Intergroup Relations in Multicultural Education Programs. In J. A. Banks & C. A. M. Banks, *Handbook of research on multicultural education* (pp. 782–798). San Francisco: Jossey-Bass.

Summer Teaching. (1941, June). Many Seattle teachers join summer faculties. *The Seattle Educational Bulletin, 17*(8), 4.

Taba, H. (1945). The contributions of workshops to intercultural education. *Harvard Educational Review, 15*(2), 122–128.

Taba, H. (1953). *Leadership training in intergroup education*. Washington, DC: American Council on Education.

Taba, H., Brady, E. H., Jennings, H. H., Robinson, J. T., & Dolton, F. (1949). *Curriculum in intergroup relations: Case studies in instruction for secondary schools.* Washington, DC: American Council on Education.

Taba, H., Brady, E., & Robinson, J. (1952). *Intergroup education in public schools.* Washington, DC: American Council on Education.

Taba, H., Brady, E., Robinson, J., & Vickery, W. R. (1951). *Diagnosing human relations needs.* Washington, DC: American Council on Education.

Taba, H., & Elkins, D. (1950). *With focus on human relations.* Washington, DC: American Council on Education.

Taba, H., & VanTil, W. (Eds.). (1945). *Democratic human relations: Promising practices in intergroup and intercultural education in the social studies.* Washington, DC: National Council for the Social Studies.

Taba, H., & Wilson, H. (1946). Intergroup education through the school curriculum. *Annals of the American Academy of Political and Social Science, 244,* 19–25.

Takaki, R. (1989). *Strangers from a different shore: History of Asian Americans.* Boston: Little Brown.

Thorndike, E. L. (1939). American cities and states: Correlation in institutions, activities, and the personal qualities of residents. *Annuals of the New York Academy of Sciences, 39,* 213–298.

Tiedt, P. L., & Tiedt, I. M. (1995). *Multicultural teaching: A handbook of activities, information, and resources.* Boston: Allyn & Bacon.

Tiedt, P. L., & Tiedt, I. M. (1999). *Multicultural teaching: A handbook of activities, information, and resources.* Boston: Allyn and Bacon.

Trager, H. G., & Yarrow, M. R. (1952). *They learn what they live: Prejudice in young children.* New York: Harper & Brothers.

Troen, S. K. (1975). *The public and the schools: Shaping the St. Louis schools system, 1838–1920.* Columbia, MO: University of Missouri Press.

Tuskegee Institute (1952). *Race relations in the south.* Tuskegee, AL: Tuskegee Insitute.

Tyack, D. B. (1974). *The one best system: A history of American urban education.* Cambridge, MA: Harvard University Press.

Tyack, D. (1995). Schooling and social diversity: Historical reflections. In W. D. Hawley & A. W. Jackson (Eds.), *Toward a common destiny: Improving race and ethnic relations in America.* San Francisco: Jossey-Bass.

Ungar, S. J. (1995). *Fresh blood: The new American immigrants.* New York: Simon & Schuster.

Uno, E. (1974). Racism, greed, and hysteria led to concentration camps. *The Pacific Citizen. Special Holiday Edition,* 1–2.

U.S. Census Bureau (1975). *Historical statistics of the United States, colonial times to 1970, bicentennial edition, Part 2.* Washington, DC: U.S. Government Printing Office.

U.S. Census Bureau (2000). *Statistical abstract of the United States: 2000* (120th ed.). Washington, DC: U.S. Government Printing Office.

U.S. Department of Justice. (1984). Freedom of Information Act (FOIA) request for documents on Otohiko Koiura. (File number 100-21237). Federal Bureau of Investigation.

VanTil, W. (1945). The work of the bureau for intercultural education. In W. VanTil (Ed.), *Bureau for Intercultural Education: Work in Progress*. New York: Bureau for Intercultural Education.

Vickery, W. E., & Cole, S. G. (1943). *Intercultural education in American schools: Proposed objectives and methods*. New York: Harper & Brothers.

Waller, J. F. (1932). *Outside demands and pressures on the public schools*. New York: Teachers College, Columbia University.

Watkins, S. C. (1957). *After Ellis Island: Newcomers and natives in the 1910 census*. New York: New York University Press.

Wells-Barnett, I. B. (2002). *On lynchings*. Amherst, NY: Humanity Books.

Williams, J. E. & Morland, J. K. (1976). *Race, color and the young child*. Chapel Hill: University of North Carolina Press.

Wittke, C. F. (1949). Immigration policy prior to World War I. *The Annuals, 262*, 5–14.

Wittke, C. F. (1958). *The Irish in America*. Baton Rouge: Louisiana State University Press.

Wittke, C. F. (1964). *We who built America; The saga of the immigrant*. Cleveland: Western Reserve University Press.

Woodson, C. G., & Wesley, C. H. (1962). *The Negro in our history*. Washington, DC: The Associated Publishers. (Original work published 1922)

The World Book Encyclopedia. (1998). *The world book encyclopedia* (Vol. 10). Chicago: World Book.

Worlton, J. T. (1940). *Secondary school program of studies*. Salt Lake City: Salt Lake Public Schools. (Special Collections, Milbank Memorial Library, Teachers College, Columbia University, f375.3, So1–SLC.)

Yavner, L. E. (1945). *Administration of human relations programs in New York City schools. Yearbook of the John Dewey Society*. New York: Harper & Brothers.

Yeh, C. J. & Drost, C. (2002). Bridging Identities among Ethnic Minority Youth in Schools. *ERIC Digest*. [ED462511].

Yu, H. (1996). Constructing the "Oriental Problem" in American thought, 1920–1960. In J. A. Banks, *Multicultural Education, Transformative Knowledge and Action* (pp. 156–175). New York: Teachers College Press.

Ziegler, B. M. (Ed.). (1953). *Immigration: An American dilemma* (pp. 71–77). Boston: D. C. Heath & Co.

Zimmerman, J. (1999). Storm over the schoolhouse: Exploring popular influences upon the American curriculum, 1890–1941. *Teachers College Record, 100*(3), 602–626.

Zimmerman, J. (2002). *Whose America? Culture wars in the public schools*. Cambridge: Harvard University Press.

Zitron, C. L. (1968). *The New York City teachers union 1916–1964: A story of educational and social commitment*. New York: Humanities Press.

Index

Transformative knowledge, 29–30
Turner, E. J., 23, 53, 163

Ungar, S. J., 148, 174
Uno, E., 96, 103, 174

VanTil, W., 1, 4, 17, 38, 175
Vickery, W. E., 4, 88–90, 94, 115, 143, 175

Wade, John E., 84, 99
Walker, George Theophilus, 133–134
Washington, Booker T., 25
Washington Elementary School, during the internment, 102–103
Watkins, S. C., 137, 175
Wells-Barnett, Ida B., 133, 175
Wesley, Charles H., 123, 142
Wetfish, G., 32, 59, 81, 94, 164
Williams, J. E., 60, 175
Williamstown Institute, 5–6
Wilson, H., 81–82, 86, 90, 93, 174
Wilson, Woodrow, 12–13

Wirth, Louis, 25
Wise, A. L., 17, 39, 41, 165
Wittke, C. F., 139, 175
Woodson, C. G., 24, 123, 134, 142, 175
Workshop for Cultural Democracy, 38, 140. *See also* Intercultural Education Workshop
Workshops, intercultural, 5–6, 56–58, 131–132, 139, 149, 152
Worlton, J. T., 85, 175

Yarrow, M. R., 3, 18, 94, 173–174
Yavner, Louis E., 110, 175
Yeh, C. J., 156, 175
Young, Donald, 37
Young, Pauline, 25
Yu, H., 25, 175

Ziegler, B. M., 13, 175
Zimmerman, J., 2, 17, 20, 114, 175
Zito, Nancy D., 91
Zitron, C. L., 19, 27–28, 113, 117–118, 131, 155, 175

About the Author

CHERRY A. MCGEE BANKS is a professor of education at the University of Washington–Bothell. In 1997, she received the Distinguished Teaching Award from the University of Washington–Bothell and in 2000 she was named a Worthington Distinguished Professor. Her current research focuses on intergroup education and the role that public school educators play in linking schools to communities and, consequently, helping students and parents appreciate diversity, reject prejudice and discrimination and embrace democratic ideals. Professor Banks has contributed to such journals as the *Phi Delta Kappan, Social Studies and the Young Learner, Educational Policy, Theory Into Practice*, and *Social Education*. Professor Banks is associate editor of the *Handbook of Research on Multicultural Education*, coeditor of *Multicultural Education: Issues and Perspectives* and coauthor of *Teaching Strategies for the Social Studies*. She has also served on several national committees and boards, including the American Educational Research Journal's editorial board and the Board of Examiners for the National Council for the Accreditation of Teacher Education.